Lacanian Theory of Discour

Lacanian Theory of Discourse

Subject, Structure, and Society

Edited by Mark Bracher,
Marshall W. Alcorn, Jr.,
Ronald J. Corthell, and
Françoise Massardier-Kenney

NEW YORK UNIVERSITY PRESS
New York and London

NEW YORK UNIVERSITY PRESS
New York and London

Library of Congress Cataloging-in-Publication Data
Lacanian theory of discourse : subject, structure, and society /
edited by Mark Bracher . . . [et al.].
p. cm.
Includes bibliographical references and index.
ISBN 0-8147-1191-X
1. Discourse analysis. 2. Lacan, Jacques, 1901– —Contributions
in discourse analysis. 3. Psychoanalysis. I. Bracher, Mark, 1950–.
P302.L26 1994
401'.41—dc20   94-14079
                         CIP

New York University Press books are printed on acid-free paper,
and their binding materials are chosen for strength and durability.

Manufactured in the United States of America

10   9   8   7   6   5   4   3   2   1

Contents

Acknowledgments

The editors would like to thank Robert Bamberg, Director of the Center for Literature and Psychoanalysis, and Eugene Wenninger, Vice Provost and Dean for Research and Graduate Studies, both of Kent State University, for their support in this project. We also thank *Prose Studies* and the *Fondation du champ freudien* for permission to reprint previously published material. Chapters 3, 5, and 10 originally appeared in *Prose Studies* 11 (1988). Chapters 6, 7, 8, 9, 11, and 12 originally appeared in *Hystérie et obsession* (Paris: Navarin, 1986); and Chapter 4 in *Que veut une femme?* (Paris: Navarin, 1986).

Lacanian Theory of Discourse

Introduction

Mark Bracher

The Real and the Subject of Discourse

The purpose of this collection is to provide an exposition of a theory of discourse that, we believe, offers unique possibilities for understanding both the constitutive and the transformative functions of discourse in human affairs. One major advantage that Lacan's theorizing about discourse has over other contemporary theories (particularly Marxism and poststructuralism) lies in its articulation of the relation between language and what is not language, an articulation that avoids both the Scylla of (Marxist) reflectionism, where language and culture are hurled against the rock of the real, and the Charybdis of (poststructuralist) idealism, where all that passes is sucked in and devoured by language. Lacan's formulation of what might be termed a circular causality between the Symbolic and the Real also makes it possible to account for the fact that individual subjects are produced by discourse and yet manage to retain some capacity for resistance.

This point is developed in depth by Marshall Alcorn in "The Subject of Discourse: Reading Lacan through (and beyond) Poststructuralist Contexts," in which Alcorn draws important distinctions between Lacan's formulation and that of poststructuralism concerning the relation between systems of discourse and individual human subjects. As Alcorn demonstrates, Lacan's formulation (which is still seen by many critics as essentially poststructuralist) has important consequences for understanding the political significance of discourse, since it is able to explain how resistance (in both the political and psychoanalytic senses) against interpellation by discourse can be produced within discourse itself, and how the subject, in addition to being produced by ideology, is also capable of producing ideology.

In "*Extimité*," Jacques-Alain Miller pursues further the paradoxical relationship between the subject and what is other, which includes the relation of language to what is not language, that is, of the Symbolic to

1

the Real. This relationship to the most intimate part of oneself, which is paradoxically something extremely foreign and other, plays a decisive role, Miller indicates, in phenomena such as religious belief and racism. While religion functions to cover that most profound *jouissance* that constitutes one's extimacy, racism results from what one imagines about the *jouissance* of the Other, for it is the Other's *jouissance* that is the ground of the alterity of the Other. Thus, Miller argues, "If no decision, no will, no amount of reasoning is sufficient to wipe out racism, it is indeed because it is founded on the point of extimacy of the Other." Race as a factor in human affairs is thus a phenomenon of discourse rather than of biology.

Miller goes on to show that what founds the Other's alterity, the object *a*, also founds what is Real in the Symbolic Other. The extimate relationship between the Real and the Symbolic is illustrated through the example of a bomb threat experienced by the members of Miller's seminar, in which the effect of the exclamation "Bomb!" demonstrates the double manner in which a real object, the bomb, is an effect of the discourse of the Other: first, insofar as bombs in general are products of the discourse of science rather than phenomena of nature; and second, insofar as the bomb referred to in the exclamation later proved not to have existed, without this fact diminishing the very real effects that it had on the seminar. Miller concludes his essay by demonstrating additional ramifications that the extimacy of the object *a* in relation to the Other has for the efficacy of discourse.

Slavoj Žižek's contribution, "A Hair of the Dog That Bit You," pursues the significance of the extimate object in the areas of ethics, aesthetics, and art—particularly film. In the realm of ethics, extimacy manifests itself as the radical evil that logically precedes good and makes good possible. This extimacy is evident in the Kantian subject's experience of moral law as an unbearable traumatic pressure, which points to something in the self that resists the law. It is also evident in those evil acts that meet the Kantian criteria for an ethical act, such as Don Giovanni's refusal to repent and his consequent eternal damnation. Such experiences, which indicate the subject's fixation on some Thing that derails the customary (Symbolically ordered) course of life, connect evil with the death drive and manifest the subject itself as essentially evil.

Žižek finds this dialectic of good and evil clarified by the relation of the Kantian Beautiful and Sublime. The fact that the beautiful is for

Kant a symbol of the good and the sublime is a manifestation of the moral law in us is another indication of the chasm in the moral law, Žižek argues: the Kantian ethical stance, insofar as it eludes the domain of the good, is allied with radical evil.

Žižek also identifies various instances of extimacy in film. One of the most striking is the mad cannibalistic psychiatrist, Hannibal Lecter, in *The Silence of the Lambs,* who, Žižek argues, represents the collective imagination's failed attempt to represent what we can identify as the Lacanian analyst. Similar to Lecter, who literally eats his victim's entrails and figuratively does the same with Clarice Specter when he coerces her to confide the kernel of her being or fundamental fantasy (the crying of the lambs), the Lacanian analyst steals the kernel of the analysand's being, denouncing the object *a* as a mere semblance and thus confronting the analysand with the Lacanian injunction, "Eat your *Dasein.*"

Numerous other instances of the extimate object are observable in film, fiction, and art, according to Žižek. It is present in *Madame Bovary* and other works of realism in the breakdown of representation that occurs in the encounter with the traumatic Thing behind the curtain. In Flaubert's novel, this traumatic Thing is sexuality itself, the representation of which is omitted. In the paintings of Magritte, extimacy is indicated in the split between symbolized reality and the surplus of the Real, which sometimes appears as a void gaping in the heart of reality, inhabited by monstrous apparitions. In films this extimacy is often present in the form of the monster or object of horror (e.g., the Alien, vampires, etc.), as well as in the form of the gaze that enthralls a subject by seeing what in the subject is more than the subject. The subject's extimacy can also be seen to emerge at the end of some films, when the subject is reduced to being an object in his or her own picture. This moment reveals the distance between desire, which remains within the narcissistic economy of the Imaginary and Symbolic orders, and drive, which is tied to the economy of the extimate Real object that lies at the heart of these orders but nonetheless remains fundamentally unassimilated by them.

Serge André, in "Otherness of the Body," examines a particularly crucial instance of extimacy, the otherness of the body—one's own body as well as the body of the other person. André begins by considering the relationship between the *jouissance* of the body, or the Other, and the *jouissance* of speech, which Lacan terms phallic *jouissance,* and pursues the role of this relationship in the problematic nature of the relation between the sexes. While the typically masculine or phallic approach to the sexual relation involves fantasy and the Symbolic aspect of the Other, the typically feminine approach traverses the Real aspect of the Other, which exceeds the Symbolic order and thus has a particularly close relationship with the position accorded to God. The connection derives from the fact that the Symbolic aspect of the Other contains signifiers such as "unutterable" and "unnameable," which point to a lack in the Symbolic Other's capacity. "Does this imply that there may actually be something else?" André asks. "That is the question." And femininity is a prime candidate, André explains, for what is "Other than what can be named by the signifying chain organized in [the Other]. . . . If 'God' is involved, according to Lacan, it is because the ambiguous status of femininity carries the weight of an appeal to being—to a being that would find its foundation elsewhere than in the place of speech." Thus "femininity inescapably leads to the question of the Other. . . . In that part of her *jouissance* that transcends the phallic reference, a woman can only want as a partner a being who is himself placed beyond the law of the phallus." Thus, while a man responds with a fantasy to the incapacity of the Symbolic to totally assimilate the Real, a woman tends to respond by dreaming of a supreme Being that would make her all Woman.

The tension between Woman and the body, André suggests, is homologous with the relation of the subject to the body, where the intervention of language constitutes simultaneously an access and a barrier: it provides access to the body as symbolized, and a barrier to the body as Real, the body being "on the one hand a web of signifiers, and on the other, an unsymbolizable Real being, unnameable." The relation between these two aspects of the body, André maintains, is homologous with the dialectic between the two *jouissances*. There are thus parallels between three pairs of terms: man and woman, subject and Other, and subject and body, and the relations between them are illustrated by the paradox of Zeno, in which Achilles can never come to coincide precisely with the tortoise, always remaining either behind or ahead of it. This dialectic repeats itself within language, in the relation between signifiers of the unnameable—$S(A)$—and signifiers of oneness, which suggest that subjects could in fact unite with what is outside language and which thus motivate men's pursuit of Woman, as well as the attempts by subjects to rejoin their own bodies. "Why does a man relentlessly seek the Woman, why does the subject drive himself crazy to rejoin his body? Because the *signifiance,* on which they depend, offers the signifier 'One,' ... [which] suggests to the subject that it could unite with this outside-language, that it could, or even should (the commanding effect of the master signifier) become one with women or with the body." Hence the paradox: "One should make One with the Other, ... but in the case of success, there would be no Other, and in the case of failure, it is unity that falls apart." And "this principle of irreducible heterogeneity leads to the fundamental failure of the sexual act": one sex can never truly meet the other. André concludes with an account of perversion as an attempt to experience the otherness of the Other and an analysis of religion as a symptom that contains (i.e., both enacts and defends against) psychosis for a woman.

Discourse Structures and Subject Structures

A second major advantage that Lacan's theory of discourse holds over other theories is its synthesis of categories of discourse with categories of psychological structure in a single model. This built-in connection between linguistic and discursive phenomena on the one hand and (both collective and individual) psychological structures on the other provides Lacanian theory with an unparalleled power to explain how a given discourse or text affects (both temporarily and consciously, and also more or less permanently, or structurally) the human subjects who either produce or receive it. It is this aspect of Lacan's thought that I attempt to sketch out in my essay, "On the Psychological and Social Functions of Language: Lacan's Theory of the Four Discourses," by providing a brief exposition of Lacan's formalization of discourse structure. In his general formula for the structure of interaction between the sender and receiver of a message, Lacan provides a basic paradigm that we can use to gauge the psychological significance of a given message for both parties, which can be made more precise through attending to the four major modes of discourse produced by the various permutations of this basic paradigm. Lacan's schema of discourse offers a means not only of gauging the psychological and social effects of particular texts and discourse but also of calculating how to intervene in these discourses in order to produce psychological and social change.

The next four essays explain various aspects of the connections between specific discourse structures and certain general structures of subjectivity that, in extreme form, constitute hysterical and obsessional neuroses. In "Hysterical Discourse: Between the Belief in Man and the Cult of Woman," Julien Quackelbeen and his coauthors explain that all neurotics can be characterized by their refusal to assume the humility that is called for by the fact that the Symbolic order cannot adequately cover the Real. Hysterics try to avoid this fact through a double refusal. First, they deny the subject's powerlessness to generalize on the basis of its own unique, particular being, and second, they deny the impossibility of adequately characterizing their own particular being by means of universal categories of the Symbolic order. The first denial takes the form of an insistence that somewhere there exist humans who are not subject to the castration produced by the Symbolic order—that is, subjects whose *jouissance* is not partially evacuated from their bodies by their accession to language. The hysteric manifests this insistence by her requirement that every man demonstrate his transcendence of Symbolic castration and in her belief that there exists somewhere a totalizing knowledge (S_2) that can capture the truth of her object a, the Real that is currently unaccounted for by the Symbolic. The second denial appears as the conviction that the Other possesses the unifying signifier for Woman. The hysteric thus madly devotes herself to the Cult of Woman in the hope that she will be able to discover the essence of Womanhood. The first denial, belief in Man, posits an Other without flaw; the second, the cult of Woman, posits a signifier of the essence of Womanhood. These two tacit assumptions about the nature of the Symbolic order in its relation to the Real produce a number of ramifications, one of which is the hysteric's adamant refusal of any semblance or masquerade and another of which is her rather contrary limitless devotion to a master who sustains her illusion that there is an essence of Womanhood. The authors conclude with some considerations about how the discourse of the analyst intervenes in such a way as to change the hysteric's ossified discourse structure.

In "Discourse Structure and Subject Structure in Neurosis," Alexandre Stevens and Christian Vereecken and their coauthors summarize the basic features of hysterical and obsessional neurosis formulated by Freud and then translate Freud's discoveries into discourse structures. Both the hysteric and the obsessional have a particular relation to the discourse of the master: the hysteric searches for a master in order to dominate him, while the obsessional has found the master and waits for him to die in order to take his place. But while the hysteric occupies the position of S, agent in the discourse of the hysteric, demanding that the other provide the master signifier (S_1) for her, the obsessional has returned to the discourse of the master, where he attempts to embody, although without running the risk thus entailed, the master signifier (S_1), which will give him complete unity and control. As Lacan observed, the hysteric "experiences herself in homage addressed to another, and offers the woman in whom she adores her own mystery to the man of which she takes the role without being able to enjoy it," whereas the obsessional transfers the *jouissance* of which he is supposedly deprived to an imaginary other that assumes it as *jouissance* of a spectacle.

"The Other in Hysteria and Obsession," by Alicia Arenas and others, elaborates yet other dimensions of the discordance between Symbolic and Real in the structures of hysteria and obsession. Since in the Real there is no essential, universal relation between the sexes, every instance of *jouissance* (the Real of one's body) is potentially destructive of the formulas of identity that the Symbolic order provides for all men and women, which include (implicitly at least) certain prescriptions and prohibitions concerning how the body (one's own and the other's) is to be enjoyed. The hysteric experiences this division between the Real and the Symbolic quite openly and painfully and, as noted above, searches constantly for a signifier that will do justice to the Real, thus opening a gap between knowledge and *jouissance* that is impossible to close. The hysteric "places herself as subject of the signifier and suffers in her own flesh the structure of language that scissors her body and mortifies it." The traumatic experience endured passively by the hysteric is thus the essential experience of the subject as such:

$$\frac{S_1}{S} \rightarrow \underline{S_2}$$

The obsessional, in contrast, "declares himself agent of the mortifying action of the signifier, in redoubling it." That is, the obsessional thinks himself the master of language, and attempts "to resorb the S_2 into the S_1, to make the signifier sign, abolish the parasitism of the signifier in the subject." All the defining characteristics of obsession, such as the compulsion to concentrate and the erotization of thought, derive from the obsessional's attempt to calculate *jouissance,* that is, to make it pass into the signifier. All of the obsessional's energy is devoted to filling everything with the phallic, master signifier and avoiding the Real. But ultimately the Real in the form of the object *a* appears in the failure of knowledge.

Like the previous pieces in this section, the essay concludes with brief considerations of the way in which the analyst's discourse intervenes in the discourse of the hysteric and in its obsessional dialect. Psychoanalysis, the authors observe, is a social link that is based on the object *a.* And the hysteric is already oriented to the object *a,* which occupies the place of truth in her discourse and thus positions her already in the position of the analysand. The obsessional, in contrast, is attempting to flee the object *a* and *jouissance,* and the analyst must lead him to the place of his subjective division by introducing the Real of his *jouissance.*

It is the discourse of the analyst and the manner in which it operates in relation to the subjective structure of the analysand that is the focus of Nestor Braunstein's "Con-jugating and Playing-With the Fantasy: The Utterances of the Analyst." It is possible to offer interpretations from the position of agent in each of the four discourses, but the interpretation offered by the discourse of the analyst is unique. Interpretations offered from the other three discourses share the feature of being propositions that claim to be true. An interpretation offered by the discourse of the master—for example, the pronouncements of a hypnotist—imposes words of order (S_1) with the assumption that when they are followed they will close up the division within the subject. Interpretations offered from the discourse of the university speak in the name of a preexisting truth—for example, truth about the unconscious that Freud or the science of psychoanalysis has discovered—and function like an ideology, suppressing the subject. Interpretations from hysterical discourse, characteristic of Kleinian analysis, ask the analysand to validate the analyst's characterization of the analysand's unconscious. All of these forms of interpretation, Braunstein observes, follow the formula: "I will tell you what your speaking means" ("Je te dirai ce que ton dire veut dire"). Such interpretations, substituting one saying for a previous saying, are essentially metaphoric and thus have the structure of a symptom.

True analytic interpretation, in contrast, offers no propositions about any aspect of the analysand. Rather, it offers statements designed to expose to the analysand his or her unconscious desire and the object *a,* the piece of the Real around which unconscious signifying chains (associations) are constellated. Such exposure will pressure the analysand him- or herself to articulate and provide meaning for this element that was heretofore left out of his or her system of meaning.

But how can one construct interpretations of this sort, which reveal something to patients and pressure them to speak, without making any statements that assert or imply any particular state of affairs? Braunstein finds a paradigm for such nonpropositional statements in utterances in which the verb remains unconjugated, in the form of infinitive, gerund, or participle. Not conjugating the verb permits a certain free play; the verb functions as a sort of joker, leaving the statement open to various permutations. For example, the verb "see" could be taken by the analysand to mean seeing someone else, being seen, making oneself seen, etc. In contrast, a conjugated verb would modalize the statement and thus entail a demand for acquiescence from the analysand. Other forms of nonpropositional statements include citing the analysand's own statements and uttering proverbs, which say nothing in themselves but rather pressure the listener to make sense out of them.

Braunstein compares the two structures of statements—propositional and nonpropositional—with the structure of fantasy. The structure of the propositional statement is subject, verb, complement, with the verb functioning to close the gap in the subject by suturing it to the complement. In the basic structure of fantasy, in contrast—$\$ \Diamond a$—the lozenge between the subject and the object represents the cut, the impossibility of suture or encounter between the two. It is this structure that propositions employing nonconjugated verbs (or analogous techniques) can mirror and evoke for analysands, bringing them face to face with the object *a* without proposing (and hence implicitly demanding) what their relationship with it is or means. In this respect the discourse of the analyst, is, as Lacan put it, a discourse without words: it establishes a subject position and social link for others not by articulating it and establishing its meaning, but by enabling others to do so themselves.

Discourse and Society

While various social and cultural phenomena are dealt with by each of the essays of the first sections, the final four essays of the collection make such phenomena the focus of their analyses, using Lacanian theory to illuminate the role of discourse in the force exerted by four major social phenomena: totalitarian terrorism, religious belief, education, and gangs. The first two pieces share a concern with how certain discourse structures are used by individuals with certain subject structures to cope with the unspeakable of the Real. In "I Don't Know What Happened: Political Oppression and Psychological Structure," Luz Casenave demonstrates how the amnesia of Milena, an Argentine literature professor who witnessed the assassination of her husband, is imbricated with the signifiers of terror and death in the discourse of the master. A week after the assassination, Milena resumed her teaching at the university, and at the moment when she began to discuss the basic ideas of Kafka's *The Trial* and *Metamorphosis,* she was struck by an amnesia that wiped out her literary knowledge and forced her to give up both her course and her position at the university.

This amnesia, Casenave argues, was a response to several psychological requirements with which Milena was faced. First, the political terror reigning at the time required that she keep quiet, obeying the demand of the master that she not know anything. In addition, the violence of the assassination of her husband apparently resurrected old images—such as her father's threat (and her own desire) to kill her mother—which made her panic. The total abandonment that she felt when confronted with her husband's assassination also apparently made her regress to originary situations of submission, impotence, and speechlessness.

Her statement, "I don't know what happened," repeated in the analysis, thus referred both to the amnesia and also to the difficulties she had in understanding her own life, serving as a metaphor condensing various scenes in her life in which she couldn't find her place. The statement testifies that when confronted with lack, she couldn't find a signifier to represent it. But in speaking of her failure in this manner, she nonetheless managed to attach herself to a Symbolic element that allowed her to speak of the void that she was confronted with in the event.

That the amnesia arose when she was lecturing on Kafka suggests a connection at the level of signifier between the titles, *The Trial (Le Proces)* and *Metamorphosis,* and the imagined and possible trial of her husband or his assassins, or the Kafkaesque military process that terrorized her, as well as the metamorphosis she witnessed in her husband as she watched him lie bleeding, changing from life into death, prevented from offering him any aid. Thus Milena's symptom was as much a phenomenon of discourse as of totalitarian power, and it demonstrates how an individual is inscribed in a transsubjective order, beyond the family novel, articulating the individual's Imaginary to the Imaginary of the social order.

In "On Blasphemy: Religion and Psychological Structure," Miguel Bassols and Germán Garcia investigate another way in which human subjects try to deal with the unspeakable through language. Blasphemy, the authors find, derives from the recognition that the Symbolic Other (in this case, the concept of God) has failed to incorporate all of the Real. More specifically, what blasphemy aims at is the *jouissance* that is not accounted for by the legal positions and linguistic categories constituting the Symbolic order. This can be seen quite clearly in the case of Schreber, who found himself in the untenable position of being attracted to a nonphallic (i.e., non-Symbolic-order) *jouissance,* which assumed the form of a fantasy that it would be wonderful to be a woman submitting to sexual penetration by a man, even God. Schreber's Symbolic order offered no provision for a man to experience such a *jouissance,* and he experienced this fact as his having been allowed by the Creator to fall: he found no support in the Other, the Symbolic order. Schreber saw only two possible responses to this conflict: either to die or to develop a *jouissance* not regulated by the phallus (i.e., outside the Symbolic order). His choice of the latter involved the reshaping of his entire cosmos, and in this light his blasphemy appears as the point of culmination of the construction of his delirium as revelation.

Blasphemy is not limited to subjects with psychotic structures, however; it is found in various other types of clinical structures as well. While in psychosis, blasphemy is situated as what can be understood when the object is not inscribed in the Symbolic, in neurosis, it responds to the limit of Imaginary coherence as constituted in the dialectic between the ego and the other. In short, blasphemy responds to that zone in discourse that lies at the very center of the psychic economy, that of extimacy. Thus, if theology substitutes the term end for that of desire, blasphemy hollows out the end in order to reintroduce desire.

The final two essays demonstrate the manner in which structures of discourse underlie two powerful but different social institutions: schools and gangs. Renata Salecl's piece, "Deference to the Great Other: The Discourse of Education," demonstrates how the Lacanian concept of the

Other can explain the ideological force of aspects of education that other analyses, including those of Marxism and speech-act theory, have been unable to account for. Many who critique education assume that its primary coercive effect derives from teachers' occupying the position of master. Salecl demonstrates that this assumption is incorrect, however. Whereas a true master simply lays down the law and insists that it be obeyed because he has so ordered, the teacher is expected always to give reasons for his or her demands. The teacher, that is, must always act in deference to an external system of knowledge, meanings, rules, laws—that is, to the Great Other. The teacher thus speaks from the position of agency in the university discourse, that of knowledge (S_2), and this structure explains two important phenomena concerning education that other analyses have not been able adequately to account for. First, it explains the power of the indirect nature of the teacher's speech acts. Writers such as Bourdieu have attributed the teacher's power to the power of the political institutions that stand behind the teacher. But if this were really the source of the teacher's power, it wouldn't make sense for the teacher to use indirect forms of request (e.g., "Could you please stop talking and do your work now?") instead of direct commands. Searle's explanation that indirect speech acts are used in order to be polite is not convincing in this case, since schools are not one of the more polite institutions. The real reason for the teacher's use of such forms of speech is to indicate deference to the Great Other, the Symbolic Order. Occupying the position of knowledge (S_2) rather than that of the master (S_1), teachers can't simply say, "Do it because I say so." Teachers must always give reasons for every request they make, and these reasons embody the implicit statement, "Do it because the Great Other wants it." Thus both Marxists and speech-act theorists misunderstand the true force of educational discourse because they both fail, in different ways, to grasp the nature and function of the Other—the former by reducing it to external institutions in society, and the latter by reducing it to a mere internal psychological data bank where laws and meanings are registered.

The second educational phenomenon that Salecl explains as a function of deference to the Great Other is the fact that education can achieve its aim of forming a certain kind of personality, a certain kind of subject necessary for the smooth functioning of society, only by aiming to produce a different result. That is, forming a certain kind of subject—

just like falling in love, or being spontaneous or generous—is a phenomenon that cannot be produced if one aims directly at producing such a result. As the experience of various Communist educational systems has shown, aiming directly at producing responsible, enthusiastic, socially productive citizens more often than not produces subjects who are cynical, resentful, and disengaged. In failing to produce their ostensibly desired result, however, such systems, Salecl observes, wind up achieving their true goal anyway: the preservation of power and avoidance of revolution, which is served quite well by the cynicism and disengagement produced in the subjects. Education is thus an instance of a more general ideological phenomenon, in which the impossibility of realizing a set of ideological goals is already assumed and incorporated into the functioning of this same ideology. Such a system functions, Salecl argues, because of deference to the Great Other: all the subjects feel that it is necessary to maintain the appearance of taking the ruling ideology seriously—that is, they believe that they must conceal from the Great Other the fact that the emperor is naked. Thus, behind education and other ideological formations lies the same Other that we find at the heart of all states of affairs that are essentially by-products rather than direct, intended results of an action: the Other is the agency that decides things for us (such as whom to love) that are impossible for us to decide directly. Like Hegel's notion of the cunning of Reason, Lacan's notion of the Great Other thus accounts for the way in which the Symbolic order regulates our fates behind our backs, pulling the strings in the theater called History.

Willy Apollon's "The Discourse of Gangs in the Stake of Male Repression and Narcissism" focuses on a quite different social institution, which seems to function precisely as an attempt to escape the Great Other. Apollon distinguishes between groups and institutions and locates the gang among the latter. Whereas groups offer identity to their members through a structure of equivalent positions related to each other by a set of rules (a Symbolic order), institutions provide identity to their participants by instituting a more local sociohistoric identification in place of the abstract and general Symbolic-order positions offered by groups. The manner in which a gang provides a sense of identity for its members can be grasped most clearly through its primary mode of denying that identity, or invalidating one's being: the insult. The insults of gangs center on one primary issue, masculinity (gangs being, even today, predominantly a male phenomenon). The most common insults, expressed by epithets like "fag," "coward," and "cuckold," all aim to invalidate a man's being by labeling him as sexually deficient. But these charges of deficient masculinity, spoken to a man by other men, are merely metaphors of the absolute but unspoken insult, sexual impotence pure and simple, which can only be based on the word of a woman.

From this structure of insults—

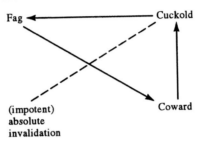

—one can draw two inferences: first, that this structure also has a positive form, which stipulates what a man must do to be a man; and second, that woman, as the other sex, must be in a position of logical exclusion in the discourse of gangs. While the positive form of the discourse of gangs is nowhere fully explicit, Apollon argues that it can be inferred from various demands that pose as a code of honor and thus set the limits of masculinity. Apollon formulates the basic injunction as, "You must have at least one son." Being a man, that is, requires that one (re)produce another man. Underlying this requirement is "the demand of the transmission of social and historical identification, through the names of the father, as ground of a sense to male existence." Apollon elaborates on the various dimensions of masculinity, identifying four basic positions a man may occupy:

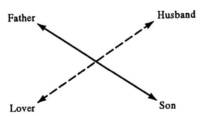

In being identified with the paternal function, however, the certainty of being a man rests once again on the word of a woman, for a man's paternal function is always open to question by the words of the mother. The tremendous vulnerability for masculinity that this logic entails explains why the structure of the gang's possibility as a discourse requires a certain silence of women. And it also explains the necessity for the censorship or denial of feminine desire, which, by exceeding the categories of the Symbolic order, threatens masculinity with "the vertigo of the unnameable." This exclusion manifests itself in the four basic positions available to women:

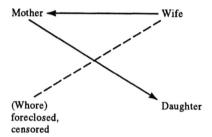

What is thus excluded by the discourse of gangs, however, is reintroduced as the object of its fantasy. Every discourse produces an object from what it excludes—an object of passion, which occupies the place of the absolute. For the gang, the fantasy is of Woman, which protects against the return of what has been excluded. It does so first by preventing gang members from seeing women as they really are and thus apprehending the true nature of feminine desire but also by coercing actual women to conform to the fantasmatic Woman of the discourse. This fantasy also serves to obscure from gang members the fact that their own desire is the desire of the desire of Woman. As an institution, then, the gang is nothing other than "the very organization of the censorship of the feminine, and the instauration of a fantasy that provides a substitute for this censored." Apollon concludes by explaining how such a discourse/institution, responding as it does to primitive narcissistic needs, is inherently averse to the introduction of the structures characteristic of group organization.

After reading Apollon's piece, we might wonder to what extent the discourse of gangs described by Apollon exceeds the locus of the gang itself and inhabits other social institutions and even some groups. Is, for example, the exclusion of the feminine that is found in other social discourses/institutions the result of the same logic as in the discourse of the gang? And can the same be said for other strategies by which men assure themselves that they are really men?

These are but two of the questions that have been raised for the editors by this essay, and we have found ourselves pondering similar questions after reading most of the other essays contained in this volume. It is our hope that other readers will be similarly stimulated by the contents of this collection. For our aim in selecting the pieces included here has not been to provide a totalizing exposition of Lacanian theory of discourse or a monolithic approach to social/discursive phenomena, but rather to demonstrate the rich potential that Lacanian psychoanalytic theory holds for understanding psychological phenomena—including collective psychological, and thus social, phenomena—in relation to language and discourse. We have found some of the essays in this volume to be quite difficult, but we have included them nonetheless because we have found that they not only provide rich insights but also repay each rereading both with further insights and with new questions and problems demanding further work from the reader. It is such work that we hope will be the ultimate result, individually and collectively, of the pieces presented here.

Part I

The Real and the Subject of Discourse

1. The Subject of Discourse: Reading Lacan through (and beyond) Poststructuralist Contexts

Marshall W. Alcorn, Jr.

Increasingly, Lacan emerges as the preeminent theorist of relationships between discourse and the subject. Lacan is unique as a discourse theorist because his thinking synthesizes ideas at the interface of two very different conceptions of the subject, the psychoanalytic and the poststructuralist. As a practicing analyst, Lacan sought to understand the human subject. As a poststructuralist, he sought to understand the subject's constitution through and by discourse. But precisely because Lacan's theoretical work derives from and ultimately moves beyond the theoretical limitations of two rather different perspectives upon the subject, his ideas about the subject require more careful attention.

Poststructuralists and Freudians hold quite different assumptions about the "subject of discourse." To understand Lacan's uniqueness as a theoretician, it is important to see where he stands in relation to Freudian and poststructuralist assumptions. A central issue dividing psychoanalytic and poststructuralist theories attends the meaning of the prepositional phrase following the noun "subject" in the phrase "subject of discourse." How *exactly* is the subject related to discourse? Structuralists and poststructuralists assert that the subject is created by, derived from, and essentially equivalent to discourse. Such an assumption puts an emphasis upon the primacy of the prepositional phrase "of discourse." The subject is a secondary derivation of discourse interaction, an illusory effect of discourse systems. Discourse contains, causes, manipulates, composes the subject, as in the phrase "the puppet of wood," where wood describes the essential nature of the puppet. If this description is correct, the relation between discourse and the subject is one-sided. Discourse operates the subject as it operates upon the subject. To study relations between discourse and the subject one must, from this perspective, study those discourse systems and mechanisms that (outside the psychoanalytically circumscribed sphere of the subject) situate, position, constitute—*contain*—the subject.

Psychoanalysts, however, assert that it is not discourse that "contains" the subject but the subject that, in some sense, "contains" discourse. In this case primacy is given to the noun "subject," and the prepositional phrase "of discourse" describes something secondary and quite different from the subject. Discourse here is something belonging to, worked upon, or contained by the subject, as in the phrase "basket of eggs," or perhaps the more problematic phrase "pool of water." Here the emphasis of the prepositional phrase directs attention to the subject's containment and manipulation of discourse. Discourse does not animate and operate the subject; instead, the subject operates discourse. A contemporary formulation of this perspective would suggest that the term "subject" defines certain subject-specific discourse functions that, because they are characteristic of what subjects are, work distinctive (we might call them "subject-driven") processes upon the field of discourse. Just as the pool of water, because it is a pool, affects what happens to the water within, the subject, because it is a subject, has certain subject-specific effects upon discourse. These subject-specific discourse functions derive from the nature of subjectivity and—rather than being mere reflections or internalized components of discourse systems external to the subject—alter, manipulate, resist, and transform those systems.

A central problem in the study of Lacan lies in the fact that the major theoretical schools that make use of Lacan tend to appropriate Lacanian thought from one pole of the subject/discourse relation and ignore the other pole. Structuralists and poststructuralists tend to ignore the specific discourse functions (described by psychoanalysts) that, lying within the subject-system, operate upon language. Psychoanalysts tend to ignore the discourse systems (described by structuralists) that, lying outside the domain of the subject, compose and situate the subject. Both Freudian and poststructuralist appropriations of Lacan are one sided in their perspective and vastly oversimplify an intellectual system promising to resolve many of the unproductive theoretical disputes attending poststructuralist and Freudian accounts of language. Lacan's position contains—and transforms—both polar formulations of the subject/discourse relationship. But just as the phrase "subject of discourse" can easily be read in terms of one meaning only, so also Lacan is frequently interpreted in terms of one figuration of the subject/discourse relation—and not the other.

Poststructuralist appropriations of Lacan frequently follow a formula described by Frederick Jameson. In *The Political Unconscious* Jameson continues his earlier support of Lacan's ideas and emphasizes the importance of Lacan's radical decentering of the ego:

> Lacan's work, with its emphasis on the "constitution of the subject," displaces the problematic of orthodox Freudianism from models of unconscious processes or blockages toward an account of the formation of the subject and its constitutive illusions which, though still genetic in Lacan himself and couched in terms of the individual biological subject, is not incompatible with a broader historical framework. Furthermore, the polemic thrust of Lacanian theory, with its decentering of the ego, the conscious subject of activity, the personality, or the "subject" of the Cartesian cogito—all grasped as something like an "effect" of subjectivity—and its repudiation of the various ideals of the unification of the personality or the mythic conquest of personal identity, poses useful new problems for any narrative analysis which still works with naive, common-sense categories of "character," "protagonist," or "hero," and with psychological "concepts" like those of identification, sympathy, or empathy.[1]

Jameson applauds Lacan's "displacement of orthodox Freudianism" because he sees Freud's displacement as leading to a suitable replacement. Instead of considering individuals, Jameson wants us to think about effects of subjectivity. Jameson's description of Lacan's subject—his attempt to characterize it as an entity "of discourse"—is an attempt to push Lacan's subject back into its "proper" poststructuralist place in the discourse systems that compose it. But we should note that Jameson is not simply describing Lacan's thought; he is appropriating it. Jameson argues that Lacan's displacement of "orthodox" Freudianism is promising; but at the same time he admits that Lacan does not *really* displace Freud, does not really overcome an archaic belief in the "individual biological subject." Lacan's rejection and displacement of Freudian ideas is to a large extent something Jameson imagines. It is something that is, in Lacan himself, Jameson points out, "still genetic."

Jameson clearly wants to make use of Lacan, to appropriate his ideas for his own purposes. For many scholars, however, Jameson's highly persuasive appropriation of Lacan is less an appropriation of Lacan and more a standardization of Lacan. Lacan, through the commentary of Jameson and others, becomes the kind of thinker Jameson imagines.

Lacan becomes another poststructuralist, a thinker for whom the subject is a subject "*of discourse.*"

Other scholars, following the lead of Jameson, show a more ardent eagerness to dismiss the clinical and psychoanalytic side of Lacan. Characteristically, this dismissal is formulated by means of a poststructuralist conceptualization of Lacan's subject. It emphasizes that Lacan's subject cannot be imagined through metaphors of containment, activity, or creativity. Eve Tavor Bannet argues:

> There is in Lacan no autonomous, self-conscious subject in whom, as in a container, knowledge, experience and emotion inhere, whose relationship to the social environment can be measured in terms of creativity and self-recognition. ... Lacan's model for man is the computer. Man is a machine whose predetermined linguistically programmed circuits are governed by binary structures: closed-open, absent-present, 01.[2]

Many things make it easy to characterize Lacan's subject in such a manner. If one reads Lacan hastily and uses quotations selectively, it is easy to find support for such claims. But anyone who reads Lacan carefully realizes that making generalizations about Lacan's teaching is a highly demanding task that requires facing—not ignoring—the contradictions in Lacan's conceptualizations.

Lacan frequently contradicts himself. Typically, these contradictions reveal Lacan in the process of thinking, in the process of finding the best metaphors or terms of comparison useful for elucidating the substance of his thought. For example, in relation to his earlier insistence that human beings are like machines (found in *Book II* of the *Seminar* and quoted by Bannet), Lacan later points out that human beings are not like machines. After considering the "originality" of human thought (a quality Bannet denies), Lacan points out:

> That is where the power revealed by the originality of the machines we have at our disposal falls short. There is a third dimension of time which they undeniably are not party to, which I'm trying to get you to picture via this element which is neither belatedness, nor being in advance, but haste, the relation to time peculiar to the human being. ... That is where speech is to be found, and where language, which has all the time in the world, is not. That is why, furthermore, one gets nowhere with language.[3]

Here Lacan insists that there is an important difference between subjects and machines. Meaning, found in speech, differs from the information found in machine language because speech is responsive to time and to desire in a way that language is not. Speech, something produced by humans, is very different from language. "The question of meaning," Lacan points out in an earlier context, "comes with speech."[4] In order to emphasize the importance of this point Lacan makes a rather dramatic and self-contradictory assertion: "One gets nowhere with language."

Lacan's repudiation of "language" (which machines have) is a privileging of speech—something possessed uniquely by humans and charged with human qualities. Speech uniquely produces meaning because speech is a "language" uniquely "configured" by subject-functions. Meaning is produced as language is driven or operated by subject-functions such as desire, temporality, repression, the Imaginary. If we consider the relationships posited here between discourse and the subject, we can see a metaphor of containment employed. Speech is something (in a sense) "contained" by subjects insofar as, though it circulates intersubjectively, it is something proper to, defined by, or "contained" by the nature of subjectivity. To understand speech, as opposed to language, one must understand what it means to be a subject. One must understand that a subject is not a machine programmed by a binary language.

In the process of arguing that speech differs from language, Lacan insists that "one gets nowhere with language." But of course Lacan is not really saying that one *always* "gets nowhere with language." Lacan is in many respects a poststructuralist; his understanding of language is central to his system. This is one of many passages that show that we must be sensitive both to the dialectical instability of Lacan's terms and to the various inflections Lacan gives to the term "language." In an earlier discussion of the importance of language Lacan, responding to a remark by Lefebvre-Pontalis, points out that he distinguishes between "language and significations." "Language is a system of signs," he says, "and as such, a complete system."[5] Emphasizing the importance of this observations, Lacan continues: "With that one can do anything."[6] Lefebvre-Pontalis responds to this emphasis upon language (which he considers misleading) by saying, "On condition that there be speaking subjects."[7] In effect, Lefebvre-Pontalis points out that you can do "anything with language," but only if there are speaking subjects. To this, Lacan partly agrees, pointing out, "Of course. The question is to know what the function of speaking subject is in all this."[8] For both Lacan and his commentators, this is indeed the key question, to know "the function of the speaking subject."

Later in the same seminar, where Lacan explores the "function of the speaking subject" "in all this," he shows, through the story of the three white disks, how human meaning, unlike machine meaning, can be produced by human temporality.[9] This leads to his later emphasis upon the distinction between speech and language and his declaration that one gets "nowhere" with language.

At the end of *Book II* Lacan comes back again to his comparison between man and the machine to say:

With a machine, whatever doesn't come on time simply falls by the wayside and makes no claims on anything. This is not true of man, the scansion is alive, and whatever doesn't come on time remains in suspense. That is what is involved in repression. No doubt something which isn't expressed doesn't exist. The repressed is always there, insisting, and demanding to be. The fundamental relation of man to this symbolic order is very precisely what founds the symbolic order itself—the relation of nonbeing to being.

What insists on being satisfied can only be satisfied in recognition. The end of the symbolic process is that nonbeing come to be, because it has spoken.[10]

Lacan's attention to repression, nonexistence, time, and recognition reveals psychoanalytic concerns that easily allow him to distinguish subjects from machines. Machines need not concern themselves with these phenomena; subjects are made subjects in being driven by these forces.

Characteristically, the Lacan of the *Seminar* is thinking and reformulating his pronouncements as he sees things in various and different relations. In *Book II,* after a lengthy and somewhat defensive discussion of whether Saint John meant speech or language in his formulation "in the beginning was the word (logos)," Lacan dismisses the increasingly complicated argument by responding,

I am not engaging you in an *ex cathedra* teaching. I don't think it would befit our object, language and speech, for me to bring something apodictic for you here, something you must just have to record and put in your pocket.[11]

Repeatedly Lacan emphasizes that he is not engaged in the formulation of dogma, but in the process of thinking. In the "Overture to the Seminar" in *Book I* he says,

The master breaks the silence with anything—with a sarcastic remark, with a kick-start.

That is how a Buddhist master conducts his search for meaning, according to the technique of Zen. It behooves the students to find out for themselves the answer to their own questions. The master does not teach *ex cathedra* a ready made science.[12]

The problem, of course, is that while the Lacan of the *Seminar* does not teach a ready-made science, interpreters of Lacan usually do. Explicators of Lacan feel that it is their job to produce stable cognitive products (convenient conceptual summaries of ideas) and to avoid initiating unstable cognitive processes of the sort that Lacan's texts not uncommonly foster. Written representations of Lacan's thought thus typically reduce its complexity as they generalize and simplify the teaching. This drive, finally, makes it is all too easy to "fix" Lacan by appropriating him along the lines of existing theoretical assumptions. Rather than becoming involved in the disruptive conceptual complexities that Lacan's thinking produces, Lacan's commentators frequently distance themselves from him in order to preserve mastery of conceptual codings. This makes it only too easy to read Lacan as one more poststructuralist thinker.

Eve Bannet quotes Lacan selectively to argue that the "consequences" of the

takeover of perception, desire, imagination, thought, experience and reality by the symbolic order are two-fold. First, it imposes conformity and abolishes individuality to the point where "the collective and the individual are the same thing." . . . Secondly it leads to a situation in which "we are spoken more than we speak."[13]

Such a situation means, Bannet points out, that "as the conscious subject is little more than a mechanism which repeats the signifiers and significations already in language, so the unconscious is a mechanism which repeats what has been repressed."[14]

This representation of the Lacanian subject is not altogether wrong. But it isn't right either. It reduces the subject to a loudspeaker system, "repeating the signifiers and significations already in language." It is quite easy to show that there is much more to Lacan's subject than this. But this description of the Lacanian subject seems plausible because it echoes concepts that poststructuralism has already established as critical dogma.

When Jameson imagines a Lacan who has fully displaced Freud, and when Bannet imagines Lacan's subject as a machine that merely "repeats the signifiers and significations already in language," both these gestures repeat a general tendency of structuralists and poststructuralists to deny Lacan's theoretical uniqueness by reading Lacan's subject as one more version of the poststructuralist subject.

There is a repeated "identity" pattern in poststructuralist thought that works to erase the human subject, to make "the subject of discourse" an entity composed, contained, derived from, and imprisoned by language (not speech). In *The Pursuit of Signs* Jonathan Culler repeats claims made earlier by Levi-Strauss and argues that as structuralism investigates the self, it erases it:

These disciplines find, as their work advances, that the self is dissolved as its various functions are ascribed to impersonal systems which operate through it. . . . As the self is broken down into component systems, deprived of its status as source and master of meaning, it comes to seem more and more like a construct: a result of systems of convention.[15]

The subject conceived by structuralism is an "effect" of discourse. It is an illusion produced by linguistic effects. The subject thus fades back, without a residue, into its constitutive element, language. The subject of discourse becomes a subject *of discourse*.

If we push Culler's position a slight step further, we can arrive at the sort of pronouncement made by Diane Macdonell in *Theories of Discourse*. Macdonell surveys the various theories of ideology and discourse that have arisen since structuralism and (giving special attention to the work of Althusser) argues that attempts to supply a theory of the subject (singular and general) for ideology or discourse will tend to idealism, to speculation about what does not exist.[16]

Such an absolute dismissal of the self has a certain plausibility. It might even be supported by certain strategic quotes from Lacan. In *Book II* of the *Seminar* Lacan insists that the subject is not an "entity," and later that the "subject is no one." But these quotations, like many others, need to be read in terms of the context and contradictions within Lacan's thought, not in terms of their agreement with existing poststructuralist ideas. Lacan is not saying that there is no subject; he is instead disputing the kinds of boundaries put upon the subject by traditional psychoanalytic theory. Lacan is disputing traditional interpretations of Freud, but he is not defining himself as a poststructuralist.

Macdonell's rejection of the self is a good example of Burke's logic of reduction: the tendency of any particular theory to purify its own language at the expense of good sense. Once something gets seen in terms of something else, Burke points out, it soon can be reduced to something that is "nothing but" that which it is seen in terms of. Because the characteristic gesture of structuralism is to see the subject in terms of language, the subject easily becomes nothing but language. These attempts to read Lacan's "subject of discourse" as a "nothing" that fades back into discourse, however, misread Lacan. Such an absolute dismissal of the self is ill considered—even for poststructuralist theory. It represents little more than an attempt to simplify discourse theory by banishing difficult concepts.

Lacan's theory of the subject offers a solution to the impasse attending the debates between Freudians and poststructuralists. For Lacan, relations between discourse and the subject are two sided. The subject operates upon discourse, and discourse operates the subject. This dialogical interaction between subject functions shaping discourse and social forces providing the original matrix of discourse is useful for understanding the particular nature of speech products. This model suggests, first, that there are specific subject functions (repression, for example) that can always deflect and give idiosyncratic shape to social discourse as self-components within the self interact to produce discourse effects. Second, Lacan forces us to recognize that we must study many *different* and *distinct* discourse functions (ideology, knowledge, narcissism, repetition) that operate upon the subject as the subject interacts in a discourse community. It is a great oversimplification to represent these discourse functions in general terms—either in terms of general "subject positions" plotted by social discourse or in terms of some autonomous ego that defines itself through discourse.

To develop a more complex picture of the subject in greater detail, we must more fully appreciate how Lacan's subject is distinct from the subject imagined by poststructuralist thought. Like the poststructuralists, Lacan "dissolves" the subject. But Lacan's insistence upon the subject's radical self-division and his description of the constitution of the subject by discourse is easily misunderstood by thinkers who approach Lacan without extensive knowledge of psychoanalysis. We can examine the differences between the Lacanian subject and the poststructuralist self by reconsidering Culler's argument. The self, he says, is "dissolved" as "its various functions are ascribed to impersonal systems that operate through it." When Culler describes the self as "dissolved," he means in part that it is "deprived of its status as source and master of meaning" as it is "broken down into component systems." Like the self Culler describes, Lacan's subject finds "its various functions" operated by "impersonal systems" that operate it. Also like the self Culler describes, Lacan's subject is deprived of its status as "master" of meaning. Unlike Culler's self, however, Lacan's subject is not simply a linguistic construct, an illusion produced by language effects.

Human subjects, unlike human bodies, are hypothetical phenomena. Detecting their presence will always be an effect of systems of belief and theory brought to bear upon the gestures and traces of an invisible origin. Lacan is very careful—and very subtle—in his account of the subject. In many ways Lacan's account of the subject is a very precise account of meaning effects produced by the "impersonal" subject-functions and subject-components alluded to by Culler. A review of this account of subject-systems, however, indicates that, while Lacan's subject disappears in one sense, it does not disappear in another sense. Lacan's subject disappears in the sense that a particular component (long idealized by psychoanalysis), the ego, can no longer aspire to control self-components and functions. Lacan's subject also disappears in the sense that human nature is not determined by a universal "inner nature" but by historical, social, and linguistic forces. Lastly, Lacan's subject disappears in the sense that the psychoanalytic cure cannot be defined by a reintegration of the fragmented self-components. Yet Lacan's understanding of the subject, as composed of components and processes essentially divided and self-alienated, neither reduces, devalues, nor eliminates either the importance or the phenomenal character of the subject.

Lacan's subject is perhaps best defined as the one who suffers. As clinician, Lacan used his analysis of the subject not as a philosophical ground for ignoring unique human beings but as a ground for understanding the therapeutic action of psychoanalysis. In this sense, in terms of Lacan's commitment to psychoanalytic training, his commitment to the practice of analysis, and his commitment to the production of scholarship, the subject is not simply "present" but is central to the whole Lacanian enterprise.

Jacques-Alain Miller, comparing Lacan to Levi-Strauss, Barthes, Foucault, and Derrida, emphasizes this important but often neglected aspect of Lacan's work:

What did Levi-Strauss, Barthes, Foucault, and Derrida do for a living? They taught and they wrote. They gave classes. They were intellectuals. They were teachers. They were university people.

What did Lacan do during his lifetime? There is one answer. He saw patients.[17]

Lacan's work shows a man constantly talking to people about the psychoanalytic drama of the subject. Because Lacan found it important to understand the subject in terms of things apparently external to it, the subject can appear to be absent from his discussion, a sort of epiphenomenon animated by discourse. Such an assumption, however, is a misreading of Lacan. Lacan's subject is "decentered," but this decentered subject is the focus for Lacan's theoretical project. Lacan's analysis of discourse indicates his interest in two things: first, the subject's position in discourse; and second, those problems attending the analyst's attempt to use discourse to *re*position the subject.

In some respects Lacan's account of the subject follows the lines of a rhetorical analysis. Lacan is interested in figures of speech and how speech, creating systems of desire and identification, moves the subject. On the one hand, this analysis is highly theoretical: Lacan is fully engaged in all the conceptual resources formulated by poststructuralist thought. But on the other hand Lacan's analysis is highly practical. As an analyst, Lacan confronted subjects who resisted, denied, and displaced linguistic effects. This forced him to formulate a description of a subject much more active and resistant than the subject imagined by poststructuralist thought.

We might best appreciate the relatively greater weight given by Lacan to the subject by considering its potential for resistance. Poststructuralist theory posits the subject as a passive entity constituted by participation in social language. The idea of resistance questions this passivity and calls attention to a subject's unique ability to deny, dismiss, or deform social directives. Resistance implies agency, an ability to counteract forces that in other contexts would successfully constitute subjects.

Paul Smith, a critic seeking to formulate a more adequate account of ideology, has critiqued the poststructuralist account of the subject in terms of its failure to explain resistance. "The stress, within current theorization, on the *subjection* of the subject," he says, "leaves little room to envisage the agent of a real and effective resistance."[18] Smith concedes that poststructuralist theory seems initially useful as a way to account for ideological operations in language. But in the final analysis such an account oversimplifies the operations of ideology. "Marx's teleological 'real individual,' and left-wing poststructuralists' 'subject in process,' " Smith says, "are both less than adequate for the task of conceiving ideology and its subjects."[19] The problem, as Smith and others see it, is that if the subject is conceived (along the lines of Althusser) as a simple effect of ideology, a unified structure "called" into place by the interpellating force of language, then the subject has no resources for resisting ideology. If the subject is to resist the force of ideology (and it must if it wants to direct political change), then it must be something other than a *simple* effect of ideology. To develop a more complex account of both ideology and the subject, Smith turns to Lacan.

In *Discerning the Subject* Smith describes the subject as an entity constructed by contradictory ideological interpellations. Subjects are formed by a disordering history, a "colligation of multifarious and multiform subject positions."[20] Describing the subject as both an entity always in process and an entity suffering conflict explains both the subject's constitution by ideology and the subject's potential for ideological resistance: the subject is formed by ideology, not in any unitary way, but through collections of differing ideological positions. The subject is thus constituted by ideology. But because no ideological position is ever absolute, the subject is always potentially able to resist (because of its inner "play" of various ideological configurations) an external univocal ideological force.

Smith's account of the subject's potential for resistance suggests a somewhat more cohesive subject than the one imagined by poststructuralism. Smith's subject is not a passive force completely animated by fluctuating currents of social discourse; it has a certain limited capacity for agency and resistance. Once agency and resistance are conceptualized as characteristics belonging to subjects, however, it is tempting to imagine the subject in traditional Freudian or "psychological" terms. The subject becomes certain "contained" characteristics. Smith, however, strongly resists this temptation. Agency, as he sees it, is only a temporary subject effect resulting from a temporary subject position, and in addition, subject structure is not stable: discourse configurations are constantly leaking in and out. The subject has no permanent "inner" material and no boundary containing stable subject-characteristics.

Smith's account of the subject reflects an impressive theoretical synthesis of Althusser and Lacan. Smith agrees with Althusser that subjects are formed through ideological forces. But Smith also promotes Lacan's ideas in insisting that social discourse does not affect the subject in an immediate way. Social discourse is always mediated through unconscious structures.

Smith's account of the subject resembles Lacan's account in many ways. Lacan's subject, like Smith's, is characterized by conflict, has no "inner" unity, and has a porous "boundary." The Lacanian Other, in part a discourse structure, is always at the conflictual core of the subject. Lacan's subject thus is always most "outside" when it is most "inside." In addition to having an alien discourse structure at the center, Lacan's subject is also porous: discourse nodules and configurations are always leaking into the subject, producing various singular effects, and thus affecting subjectivity.

Smith's account of the subject resembles Lacan's account, but it also differs in important ways. While deeply problematic, the metaphor of boundary describes Lacan's subject better than it describes Smith's. Lacan's subject, like Smith's, has a porous boundary, but Lacan's subject has more stability than the subject-in-process Smith describes. As a clinician, Lacan is very much concerned with something that used to be called individuality. Lacan discredits the term "individual" because it implies both traditional Freudian dogma and the unified self of ego-psychology. But Lacan is very much attentive to the *singular* and *particular* nature of the subject.

Lacan's account of the subject, because it describes a more "stable" subject than Smith's, better explains the particular tenacity of the subject's "resistance." Because the subject (as a discourse system) is very loosely "centered" around certain self-defining discourse patterns (Lacan, unlike Smith, emphasizes the subject's enormous capacity for repetition), it resists other discourse patterns that generate conflict: it resists political influence, just as it resists psychoanalytic influence. Both forms of resistance show the subject's active attempt to counteract the manipulating effects of discourse. The subject, thus, is not just another discourse system subjected to the effects of discourse colligation. It is a discourse system with it own particular properties; it is a discourse system driven by particular subject functions.

Just as the world's weather is determined by global and local forces, so is the world of human discourse. Global patterns of discourse reflect the shared libidinal styles of large numbers of speakers loosely united as a community by the discourse that structures their identities. Within each singular human subject, however, discourse can become uniquely configured, produced, and repetitively expressed by local conditions (the conditions of subjectivity) that are particular to each individual subject. Because of this situation, resistance and conflict between local discourse and global discourse are frequent and ongoing.

In *Book II* of the *Seminar* Lacan speaks of analysis as a project through which "the subject discovers his truth, that is to say the signification taken on in his particular destiny by those givens which are peculiar to him and which one can call his lot."[21] The subject has a "particular" destiny, in part because the subject appropriates and employs language in a "particular" way. Lacan emphasizes that the job of the analyst is to listen carefully to the "particular" language of the subject. In the *Ecrits* he speaks of this language used by the subject in psychoanalysis as a "language that seizes desire at the very moment in which it is humanized."[22] This language, he says, "is absolutely particular to the subject."[23] This emphasis upon the "absolutely particular" character of the subject's language and the "particular" character of the subject's destiny suggests that each subject has (in a loose sense anyway) properties that are somehow "proper to" or "contained by" it.

This absolute particularity of the subject's language is in part related to what rhetoricians call "style" or "voice." Each subject both appropriates discourse and expresses discourse in its own unique way. More importantly for Lacan, this particularity of speech is related to various psychoanalytic phenomena—desire, repetition, resistance, and trauma—that express the symptoms that uniquely define each particular subject. Because, in fact, human subjectivity is a particularized process constantly at work in organizing and emphasizing experience, it is the case that particular human subjects not only "contain" different speech but also create and internalize for themselves particular "editions" of social discourse. Subjectivity, thus, is itself an individualized process of subject functions that under particular conditions alter, select, and symptomatically enscript the discourse of the larger world of social interaction.

Lacan insists that the early history of the subject (in part a history of discourse) stamps upon the subject (especially in childhood) certain characteristic patterns that remain stable (though they play out their influence in various "registers") throughout later historical progression. Each subject, Lacan suggests, has unique features, constantly changing in their particularity, but nonetheless changing according to a pattern "proper to" or "contained by" the subject. The subject, Lacan says, has a "particular destiny" that is determined by "those givens which are peculiar to him." This fixed historical dimension of the subject helps explain the subject's potential for resistance because it explains the relatively fixed nature of the subject's "identity pattern" (its ideals and values).

While Lacan's subject exists in a state of self-division, it is important to recognize that this self-division is not a random and chaotic disorganization but an organized and repetitive pattern of self-division. Analysts observe that a subject's identity pattern is not easy to change; it is not easy for discourse to "intervene" in the subject in such a way as to easily redirect behavior or redefine identity. Subjects seem to have vast resources for ideological and psychoanalytic resistance. In Smith's description of the subject, resistance seems to be a kind of semiotic play, an almost random expression of disunification. Lacan's psychoanalytic account of the subject suggests that resistance is more focused, determined, and motivated. Each subject has a particular style of resistance that expresses certain predictable patterns of repression and repetition.

Lacan's account of the subject's particular nature calls attention to a certain stability within self-structure that motivates resistance. To consider the full complexity of relations between resistance and the subject, we should consider two very different forms of resistance. One can, in the first instance, resist "bad" ideology. In the second instance one can resist knowing that ideology is bad. These two instances of resistance, while closely related, are markedly different.

The first case (political resistance) seems motivated by knowledge and self-consciousness. One resists bad ideology because one knows (or believes) that the effects of such discourse cause suffering. The subject, because of knowledge and self-consciousness, is able to intervene in the production of ideological effects and to reveal and often in fact defeat those forces that hegemonically enscript human identity and produce human suffering. This "heroic" act of resistance is in fact important to idealize, and even overidealize, because it is so enormously difficult to motivate and achieve.

In another version of resistance (a version sometimes difficult to distinguish from the example of political resistance discussed above), the subject does not *use* knowledge to effect a freedom from suffering; the subject in fact *denies* knowledge in order to continue to suffer. This resistance to knowledge, motivated by both political and psychoanalytic forces, is only too common. Conservatives, for example, have trouble judging the value of ideas that they consider liberal, and liberals have trouble judging the value of ideas that seem overly radical.

In these cases subjects do not act from knowledge; they resist knowledge. Subjects do not act from a self-conscious understanding of the cause of their own suffering; they are motivated to deny an understanding of the cause of their own suffering. This resistance is motivated largely by repression, and repression is empowered by psychological forces that structure human subjectivity.

Resistance to knowledge is motivated by discourse networks that are closely linked to self-identity. It is clear that Lacan sees analytic resistance (another example of resistance to a knowledge that produces suffering) in these terms. Because of certain relatively stable but defensively dominant values and identities, subjects are unable and unwilling to entertain values and ideas that question their identity. Repeatedly Lacan describes links between resistance and subject structure. In *The Four Fundamental Concepts of Psycho-Analysis*, Lacan speaks of resistance, in rather classic Freudian terms, as related to the memory of trauma (a specific memory figuration "contained" by a specific subject). "Remembering," Lacan says in his description of resistance, "is gradually substituted for itself and approaches ever nearer to a sort of focus or centre, in which every event seems to be under an obligation to yield itself—precisely at that moment, we see manifest . . . the resistance of the subject."[24] What we see here is a glimpse of the total structure of the subject—history, trauma, repression—in terms of which resistance operates. Resistance (in this case) is not simply a blocking force directed against something the subject does not know. It is a force employed by the subject (or an essential component of the subject) preventing the subject from knowing something that it knows or suspects but wants (at some level) to repress. Because resistance is tied to self-image, repression, repetition, and trauma—essential dynamics of subjectivity—it has its own particular tenacity. In a real sense the life and death of the *subject* (as distinct from the biological individual) is at stake in its identity, at stake in its repression, and at stake in its resistance.

The resisting subject fails to see what is in front of it. Even when the missing knowledge is produced and placed in front of the subject, the consciousness of the subject seeks to deny, misinterpret, or dismiss such knowledge. One analyst in Lacan's *Seminar* describes resistance in the patient as something that

> he was on the point of discovering, he could have discovered himself, he knows it without knowing that he knows it, all he has to do is take the trouble to look up and this damn idiot . . . doesn't do it.[25]

Resistance of this sort, found in analysis, seems highly idiosyncratic and sharply linked to the particular character of each particular subject.

While we feel dismay for such analytic resistance, we admire successful political resistance. Political resistance is motivated by knowledge and self-consciousness—not by repression and fear. In effective political resistance, the subject, because of certain acknowledged and relatively stable self-interests, is able to use "knowledge" to resist ideologies that undermine its self-interest. As subjects learn "knowledge," they can be motivated to change their actions, their beliefs, and even their identities.

This plausible description of two modes of resistance, however, raises difficult questions about relationships between knowledge and subjectivity. To what extent is any discourse package we call "knowledge" a structure of subjectivity? Under what conditions can knowledge operate independently of subjectivity? Under what conditions can knowledge change subjectivity?

Some Freudians and some Marxists maintain that subjects can never use knowledge in a disinterested way because knowledge is always intertwined within the structure of subjectivity. It is fallacious to assume that there is a particular linguistic package termed "knowledge" that is in some essential way different from another linguistic package termed "the subject." Subjects and knowledge are not two completely different systems of knowledge. Because knowledge is always implicated in and in fact produced by subject functions, the discourses of knowledge and subjectivity are not different but in fact identical.

These ideas, however, suggest that any assimilation of knowledge, and any resistance to ideology, must always be prefigured in advance by a suitable subject structure. A Marxist is doomed forever to be a Marxist and a Republican is doomed forever to be a Republican. And this extrapolation from theory seems extreme—both defeatist and inaccurate. It seems a mistake to argue that knowledge is always and essentially connected to subject structure. If it were impossible to achieve some relatively objective understanding of the causes of human suffering, politics would be an impossible activity. If it were impossible to achieve some understanding of the causes of human suffering, psychoanalysis would be impossible.

While there undoubtedly are important relationships between knowledge and subjectivity, some forms of knowledge seem more independent of subjectivity than others. Many kinds of knowledge—mathematics, medicine, agriculture, metallurgy—seem relatively easy to transfer across great gaps in culture and subjectivity. Other kinds of knowledge—political, aesthetic, moral—seem especially implicated in the structures of subjectivity. I would argue that while it is difficult, it is not impossible to achieve knowledge in these fields. To pursue knowledge in these fields, however, we must be carefully attentive to the features and expressions of analytic resistance.

Neither poststructuralist nor Freudian theories of discourse, however, provide us with an adequate understanding of resistance. To pursue a better understanding of resistance we must follow the lead of Lacan in developing a more careful examination of relations between knowledge and subject structure. How is knowledge produced? What kind of "discourse element" is it? How is it "carried within" subjects? How is it related to subjectivity? How is it "passed" from one subject to another?

These questions return us to our introductory question. How exactly is discourse related to the subject of discourse? How is the particular discourse system we call the subject related to other discourse systems operating in society? What we need is not simply a better account of the relations between knowledge and the subject, but a better account of the relation between particular discourse systems and that other unique system—the subject.

Lacan offers this better account of the relations between discourse and the subject. Lacan explains both how subjects *can* resist ideology on the grounds of knowledge and how subjects are also effects of social discourse. To grasp this in detail, we must appreciate the unique nature of Lacan's subject—its status as a particular discourse structure.

Lacan teaches that the subject is a unique, though self-divided, system differing in important respects from other discourse systems that situate, constitute, and intervene in it. In this respect Lacan is not a poststructuralist. Unlike the poststructuralist subject, whose subjectivity is constantly operated by the taking of "positions" in response to social interaction, the Lacanian subject contains unique subject-driven mechanisms that both produce and feed upon social discourse in quite unique and particular ways.

Lacan describes the subject as a system whose discourse "inside" is formed from taking in material from an "outside" field of discourse. This system (the subject) has a porous boundary that "contains" (in various layers of structure) the discourse that enters it. Poststructuralist accounts of the subject offer no distinctions between the various ways discourse can be contained. The subject is often imagined as a text or site where various strands of discourse have effects. Lacan's account of the subject, however, pays special attention to the *organization* of discourse within the subject, the particular organization of discourse within the subject that produces the subject's uniqueness. This uniqueness derives from two sources. In the first instance, both chance and the biological structure of the human organism determine what particular discourse configurations enter into the subject. Different subjects, as a result of the particular concrete state of personal history, contain different discourse matter. Lacan points out that "language is completely burdened with our history."[26] Each nation, each region, each city, each suburb is the site of particular overlays of dialect and inflection. A particular subject moves about in these geographical positions according to a particular itinerary and a particular configuration of attention and response. It thus encloses a particular concrete accumulation of speech.

In the second instance, subjects are unique not simply as a result of chance encounters with the social "other" but also as a result of the way their unique subjectivity directs itself toward, works upon, and processes social interaction. As a boundary within which discourse components interact, the subject combines and modifies discourse components according to a variety of processes. These processes of discourse combination and modification are driven by various subject functions—desire, repression, the Symbolic, the Imaginary, the Real—that are particular for each subject. These subject functions produce the subject's *particularity* of discourse—a singular style of discourse that characterizes the subject.

In considering the particular discourse effects produced by a subject, we should keep in mind the important role played by the biological body. Lacan's subject is, in part, a rather unique discourse structure, because it is a discourse structure housed by a biological organism. Biology channels, and thus "operates," a variety of roles for discourse. It would take too long to discuss all the roles shaped by biological processes, but I want to emphasize one rather significant role. Because the discourse systems "contained" by Lacan's subject are "contained" by a biological body, contradictions between differing contained discourse subsystems have especially significant effects. A machine can contain contradiction as simply information about contradiction. In the human body, however, certain kinds of discourse contradiction can produce both conflict and suffering. For human subjects, suffering is not a "system" of discourse but a particularly discomforting mode of subjectivity often having biological consequences. Analysts can sometimes see the effects of discourse conflict (suffering) when certain body parts—the arm of the hysteric, for example—are unable to function. The effects of discourse conflict can also be seen in speech itself, in hesitation, denial, inflated self-assertion. In politics we see the effects of discourse conflict in other ways: when one social group wages real or metaphorical war upon another group. These conflicts exist not because discourse systems produce conflict but because discourse systems housed by biological bodies produce conflict according to a logic peculiar to the nature of subjectivity.

Resistance is a particularly important concept in this context because the subject engages in both political *and* analytic resistance in order to "contain" biological conflict and suffering. Often, in fact, political resistance is hard to distinguish from analytic resistance. When subjects are successfully engaged in political resistance, the "containment" of suffering maps out a course of thought and action that provides a real solution to human suffering. Harmful sources of power are contained by successful political action. Psychoanalysis, like political action, can of course also provide an effective containment of suffering (a real solution to human suffering). The resistance to psychoanalysis, on the other hand, is a form of negative containment. When subjects in analysis are unwilling to face the truth of their own subjectivity, containment maps out a course of thought and action that has negative effects. Containment becomes a strategy of repression and thus less a satisfactory *solution* to a problem of suffering and more a *source* of suffering resulting from the repression of conflictual knowledge.

This rather complex relationship between political resistance/containment and psychoanalytic resistance/containment has implications for understanding ideology. An ideology would be most powerful not through its ability to produce unitary meaning but through its ability to manage repression and thus "contain" conflict. Ideologies, in short, are able to make suffering seem desirable because they have strategies for generating analytic resistance to knowledge. Ideologies work precisely by generating repression, generating resistance to knowledge, and generating a form of subjectivity under which undesirable conditions seem worthwhile, pleasant, or unavoidable.

If ideologies do not exclude certain packages of knowledge and prescribe certain modes of suffering as desirable "containments" for conflict, they fail to control the ruptures within self-structure and thus fail to provide directives for social organization. Jameson, of course, insists upon the importance of political containment in his account of the political unconscious, but he fails to grasp containment in relation to those complex modes of resistance observed by analysts—unique "unconscious processes" and "blockages." Rather than seeking to understand the political implications of these modes of subjectivity, Jameson wants to dismiss them and to criticize Lacan's interest in them. In his haste to dismiss the particularity of the subject, Jameson fails to grasp the psychoanalytically complex nature of ideology. He fails to see how every political map for containment requires a psychoanalytic critique (an examination of what psychoanalytic knowledge has been repressed), just as every psychoanalytic map of containment requires a political critique (an examination of what political knowledge has been repressed).

I suggested earlier that part of Lacan's genius as a theorist lay in his ability to think beyond the limitations of both Freudian and poststructuralist conceptions of the subject. I argued that Lacan is able to explain both how subjects *can* resist ideology on the grounds of knowledge and also how subjects are socially constituted by knowledge. To understand this apparent contradiction, we must consider further what it means for Lacan's subject to "contain" discourse.

Lacan argues that a subject can take different "positions" in respect to its reception of discourse. Depending upon its mode of reception, discourse can be contained by the subject in at least two very different ways. Discourse can be present in memory as a rather free-floating and inconsequential thing. This discourse "package" does not affect other discourse contents within the self-system; it is simply a unit of memory. In this context, discourse plays no role in the constitution of the self; discourse is simply heard speech that may suffer any number of fates. It may be remembered longer, or it may be forgotten. In being forgotten, however, it is not repressed; it is simply no longer available for conscious consideration and has no apparent effect upon the subject.

When discourse has the most important effects upon the subject, it is not simply something remembered longer; it is something that works to organize or structure subject-components. The particularity of discourse, in this case, is not simply something *contained* by the self; it is something that in some sense *structures* the self. Discourse interacts with subject-components, giving them a particular form and consequence. In analysis, for example, an overly harsh superego can sometimes be made more mild by discourse that reveals its origin and operation. In this case both the experience and the general nature of the subject are changed as self-components responding to discourse begin to work in new ways. An overly critical person not only learns that it is in his or her own best interest to be less critical, but he or she also discovers inner resources for changing his or her behavior. The case here is not one in which only one self-component, the superego, changes. Instead, change is facilitated as the ego, a synthesizing agent for self-components, "processes" discourse and "learns" to respond differently to the insistence of the unconscious.

Lacan describes the ego as a system that contains "a whole organization of certainties, beliefs, of coordinates, of references." [27] The ego thus contains, in various ways and in various "packages," knowledge. This thing called knowledge, however, exists in many different states. Some knowledge "packages" that are an important part of the *subject* are prepackaged, preformed by external events, by *social* interaction. It is easy to see the particularly powerful ideological force of these components. The particular content of these components is always already determined before the birth of the subject. The subject can do nothing other than largely internalize—and thus in some manner *be*—some particular manifestation of this discourse system.

As Paul Smith cogently points out, however, Lacan's subject is structured by and upon self-division and this means that the subject can never purely be one thing. The subject is never *equivalent* to a particular organization of knowledge. The subject is a system operated by many internal agencies and structured in terms of various sublevels of organization. All of these components form a system, but the components of this system are never fully synthesized or harmonized. It is in all cases difficult to know if a "discourse component" of the self is best imagined as something like a paragraph held in memory, an emotional affect stimulated by remembered discourse, or as in fact an agency constructed by a synthesis of emotional affects.

Because knowledge can be contained in different ways and in different "layers" within the subject, it easily produces conflict. The conscious and the unconscious, for example, can contain different kinds of knowledge that can lead to conflict. While some cases of contradiction can be contained by the subject without apparent conflict, other contradictions produce significant conflict—suffering. This conflict is especially important because in certain ways this conflict rather precisely *is* the subject. Lacan describes the subject's *singularity* as an expression of the *symptom* produced by the subject's unconscious *conflict*.

The presence of conflict within the subject makes it possible for the subject to "contain" discourse material that is not a simple reflection of the social discourse systems that "position" the subject. Conflict contributes to the production of original discourse, and many specific "subject functions" can contribute to this originality. First, discourse brought into the self-system is often filtered and selectively internalized and personally organized as a result of unconscious functions of repression and desire attending to external discourse. Second, as different discourse systems within the subject compete to operate the subject, conflict is generated. This conflict plays a role in a multitude of discourse deflections noted by analysts in the speech of patients: substitution, fetishism, parapraxis, symptomatic associations. As these functions produce uniquely juxtaposed discourse structures, they produce original meaning effects that can have social and personal consequences. Additionally, Lacan's subject can generate original discourse as a result of its patterned exclusion of the Real. As this structured lack interacts with established social discourse patterns, it generates conflict—and thus also discourse. We should acknowledge, as well, that subjects do not simply take in knowledge; they produce it. In rare moments subjects construct knowledge about the cause of their conflict and suffering. This knowledge, always deeply implicated in the experience of conflict, can be both political and psychoanalytic. All these patterns of conflict and many others can not only produce unique discourse but also lead to the formation within the subject of discourse components that do not mirror existing social and ideological structures. These new discourse structures that can help define the subject are new structures unique to the subject. They are produced by the symptomatic nature of the subject as this "subject function" interacts with the material of social discourse.

Many subject components begin as internalized nodules of social discourse and later become uniquely configured and relatively stable structures within a particular subject. Thus, while it is true that the "boundaries" of subjects contain some structures that merely reflect discourse systems external to the subject, it is also true that subject "boundaries" contain things—both discourse and subject functions— unique to a particular subject. These "things" are often not shared or even understood between subjects except through the psychoanalytic experience, but they have important effects. They have been produced by unique relationships of meaning within the subject, they structure characteristic subject functions that define the particular repetitive work- ings of a particular singular subject, and, in so doing, they can produce new discourse meanings—both for the subject and for others.[28]

For example, when trauma (as Lacan describes it) contributes to the erasure of the Real and the institution of the *objet petit a,* this event is particularly configured within each singular subject. It is an effect of the particular personal history and linguistic history of the subject. This event influences the unique discourse of the subject and contributes to a singular rather than a common discourse pattern that defines the subject and its symptom. When the subject comes to the analyst with a symp- tom, analysis requires recognition of what Lacan calls the "singularity of a case."[29] Through analysis the patient comes to understand the effects of the singular nature of his or her speech and thus gains access to a new speech that represents and in some measure changes his or her nature.

At times discourse can be contained in the subject as a "package" that does not affect subject functions. At other times discourse can be considered an agency that forms or directs subject functions. Lacan argues that a subject can take different "positions" in respect to its reception of discourse. In his theory of the four discourses Lacan shows how four distinct discourse systems—discourse of the university, dis- course of the master, discourse of the hysteric, and discourse of the analyst—are produced by differing subject positions that the subject takes in relation to discourse. These different subject positions are not for Lacan mere metaphors describing different perspectives toward discourse, but are careful analytic descriptions of possible orientations of the subject toward its own self structure. These descriptions provide important clues for understanding how subjects respond to and process discourse.

Lacan uses his particular knowledge of the subject to show how "the function of the speaking subject" produces four different kinds of discourse. He also explains how each of these four forms of discourse affects subjects. This account of relations between discourse and the subject gives Lacan's system tremendous resilience. He is able, for example, to explain those conditions that allow knowledge to be easily transferred from one subject to another. Knowledge passes easily when the subject adopts a passive attitude toward discourse and empties itself of any preexisting knowledge that might interfere with the new knowledge taken in. In other cases a subject participating in discourse can not only retain its awareness of its preexisting knowledge but also use an awareness of knowledge conflict to produce new knowledge. When this project is carried out in analysis, the subject, by participating in the discourse of the analyst, produces, in a small measure, a new variation upon the discourse structures that determine its nature.

Neither the poststructuralist nor the Marxist subject can in any sense produce itself. Nor can the poststructuralist or the Marxist subject in any real sense be a source of social meanings. Lacan's subject can do both. Lacan's subject, by producing discourse in response to discourse conflict, can (though in a restricted sense) constitute itself. It can also produce singular instances of social discourse that can have "originary" social effects. These originary "meanings" are never fully mastered or controlled. But they can be produced, and their production is important.

If these things are true, Lacan's ideas should have far-ranging effects upon our understanding of ideology and rhetoric. It might seem, for example, that the state requires ISAs (ideological state apparatuses, i.e., the church, schools) not so much, as Althusser argues, to fully interpellate unified subjects as to defend ideology from the constant ravages of subject abuse.[30] Rote learning and group recitation of nationalistic allegiances are modes of repetition needed by ISAs because subjects, left to themselves, are never fully positioned by the discourse patterns they repeat. Indeed, the patterned repetitions produced by subjects are very different from the patterned repetitions demanded by social ritual. Conflictual discourse processes within the subject continually threaten to unravel the structural unity of social discourse. If the conflicts that cause such unraveling can be "spoken" and if they are rhetorically effective (if they deform or recombine discourse systems within the subject in such a way as to modify subjectivity according to a more desirable pattern), they can be preserved, idealized, and "carried over" to others. Institutions can be formed for the generation, preservation, and idealization (through writing) of these subject-produced texts. Because collective action is necessary to produce the collective preservation and idealization of these texts, Marxist theorists would be correct in asserting that subjects, in and of themselves, cannot produce ideology. Volosinov insists, "Ideology cannot be derived from consciousness" (13).[31] Indeed, ideology is not created ex nihilo from a unitary subject. But subjects, driven by internalizations of social conflict and suffering from singular instances of discourse contradiction, can be the origins of new ideological formations. Such an origin is, of course, both directed by concrete historical events and motivated by an imagined participation in social consequence. Nonetheless it is enunciated at the level of the individual biological subject, according to that subject's particular style and symptom.

This originating power is not inconsequential. Certain components of subjects, motivated by desire, can "intend" the production of ideology. These intentions can even have the desired effects, though such intentions can never *guarantee* these effects. Speech, because it is produced by the subject, can never assure the unity and purity of such intentions. This is true because the subject, as I have been trying to demonstrate throughout the course of this essay, can never fully "contain" discourse, and discourse can never fully "contain" the subject.

Notes

1. Fredric Jameson, *The Political Unconscious* (Ithaca, NY: Cornell University Press, 1981), 153.
2. Eve Tavor Bannet, *Structuralism and the Logic of Dissent* (Urbana: University of Illinois Press, 1989), 14.

3. Jacques Lacan, *The Seminar of Jacques Lacan, Book II,* ed. Jacques-Alain Miller (New York: Norton, 1988), 291.
4. Ibid., 286.
5. Ibid., 287.
6. Ibid.
7. Ibid.
8. Ibid.
9. Ibid., 287–89.
10. Ibid., 307–8.
11. Ibid., 314.
12. Lacan, *The Seminar of Jacques Lacan, Book I,* ed. Jacques-Alain Miller (New York: Norton, 1988), 1.
13. Bannet, 20.
14. Ibid., 21.
15. Culler, "In Pursuit of Signs," *Daedalus* 106 (1977): 104.
16. Diane Macdonell, *Theories of Discourse* (Oxford: Blackwell, 1986), 42.
17. Jacques-Alain Miller, "How Psychoanalysis Cures According to Lacan," *Newsletter of the Freudian Field* 1 (1987): 6.
18. Paul Smith, *Discerning the Subject* (Minneapolis: University of Minnesota Press, 1988), 39.
19. Ibid., 41.
20. Ibid., 32.
21. Lacan, *Book II,* 325–26.
22. Lacan, *Ecrits: A Selection,* tr. Alan Sheridan (New York: Norton, 1977), 81.
23. Ibid.
24. Jacques Lacan, *The Four Fundamental Concepts of Psycho-Analysis,* ed. Jacques-Alain Miller (New York: Norton, 1978), 51.
25. Lacan, *Book I,* 26.
26. Lacan, *Book II,* 285.
27. Lacan, *Book I,* 23.
28. Ibid., 12.
29. Ibid.
30. Louis Althusser, "Ideology and Ideological State Apparatuses," in *Lenin and Philosophy* (New York: Monthly Review Press, 1971).
31. V. N. Volosinov, *Marxism and the Philosophy of Language* (Cambridge: Harvard University Press, 1986).

2. A Hair of the Dog That Bit You

Slavoj Žižek

Jacques Lacan formulates the elementary dialectical structure of the symbolic order by stating that "speech is able to recover the debt that it engenders,"[1] a thesis in which one must recognize all its Hegelian connotation. The debt, the "wound," opened up by the symbolic order is a philosophical commonplace, at least from Hegel onward: with entry into the symbolic order, our immersion into the immediacy of the real is forever lost, we are forced to assume an irreducible loss, the word entails the (symbolic) murder of the thing, etc. In short, what we are dealing with here is the negative-abstractive power that pertains to what Hegel called *Verstand* (the analytical mortification-dismembering of what organically belongs together). How, then, precisely, are we to conceive the thesis that *logos* is able to recover its own constitutive debt, or, even more pointedly, that it is only speech itself, the very tool of disintegration, that can heal the wound it incises into the real ("only the spear that smote you / can heal your wound," as Wagner puts it in *Parsifal*)? It would be easy to provide examples here, first among them the ecological crisis: if there is one thing that is clear today, it is that a return to any kind of natural balance is forever precluded; only technology and science themselves can get us out of the deadlock into which they brought us. Let us, however, remain at the level of the notion. According to the postmodern *doxa,* the very idea that the symbolic order is able to square its debt in full epitomizes the illusion of the Hegelian *Aufhebung*: language compensates us for the loss of immediate reality (the replacement of "things" with "words") with sense, which renders present the essence of things, that is, in which reality is preserved in its notion. However—so the *doxa* goes on—the problem consists in the fact that the symbolic debt is constitutive and as such unredeemable: the emergence of the symbolic order opens up a *béance* that can never be wholly filled up by sense; for that reason, sense is never "all"; it is always truncated, marked by a stain of non-sense.

46

Yet contrary to the common opinion, Lacan does not follow this path; the most appropriate way to track down his orientation is to take as our starting point the relationship between "empty speech" *(parole vide)* and "full speech" *(parole pleine)*. Here, we immediately encounter one of the standard misapprehensions of the Lacanian theory: as a rule, empty speech is conceived as empty, nonauthentic prattle in which the speaker's subjective position of enunciation is not disclosed, whereas in full speech, the subject is supposed to express his/her authentic existential position of enunciation; the relationship between empty and full speech is thus conceived as homologous to the duality of "subject of the enunciated" and "subject of the enunciation." Such a reading, however (even if it does not absolutely devalue empty speech but conceives it also as "free associations" in the psychoanalytical process, i.e., as a speech emptied of imaginary identifications), misses entirely Lacan's point, which becomes manifest the moment we take into account the crucial fact that for Lacan the exemplary case of empty speech is the password *(mot-de-passage)*. How does a password function? As a pure gesture of recognition, of admission into a certain symbolic space, whose enunciated content is totally indifferent. If, say, I arrange with my gangster-colleague that the password that gives me access to his hideout is "Aunt has baked the apple pie," it can easily be changed into "Long live comrade Stalin!" or whatever else. Therein consists the "emptiness" of empty speech: in this ultimate nullity of its enunciated content. And Lacan's point is that human speech in its most radical, fundamental dimension functions as a password: prior to its being a means of communication, of transmitting the signified content, speech is the medium of the mutual recognition of the speakers. In other words, it is precisely the password qua empty speech that reduces the subject to the punctuality of the "subject of the enunciation": in it, he is present qua a pure symbolic point freed of all enunciated content. For that reason, full speech is never to be conceived as a simple and immediate filling out of the void that characterizes the empty speech (as in the usual opposition of "authentic" and "nonauthentic" speech). Quite the contrary, one must say that it is only empty speech that, by way of its very emptiness (of its distance toward the enunciated content that is posited in it as totally indifferent), creates the space for "full speech," for speech in which the subject can articulate his/her position of enunciation. Or, in Hegelese: it is only the subject's radical estrangement from immediate substantial wealth that opens up the space for the articulation of his/her subjective content. In order to posit the substantial content as "my own," I must first establish myself as a pure, empty form of subjectivity devoid of all positive content.

And insofar as the symbolic wound is the ultimate paradigm of Evil, the same holds also for the relationship between Evil and Good: radical Evil opens up the space for Good precisely the same way as empty speech opens up the space for full speech. What we come across here, of course, is the problem of "radical Evil" first articulated by Kant in his *Religion within the Limits of Reason Alone*. By conceiving the relationship Evil-Good as contrary, as "real opposition," Kant is forced to accept a hypothesis on "radical Evil," on the presence, in man, of a positive counterforce to his tendency toward Good. The ultimate proof of the positive existence of this counterforce is the fact that the subject experiences moral Law in himself as an unbearable traumatic pressure that humiliates his self-esteem and self-love—so there must be something in the very nature of the Self that resists the moral Law, that is, that gives preference to the egotistical, "pathological" leanings over following the moral Law. Kant emphasizes the a priori character of this propensity toward Evil (the moment that was later developed by Schelling): insofar as I am a free being, I cannot simply objectify that which in me resists the Good (by saying, for example, that it is part of my nature for which I am not responsible). The very fact that I feel morally responsible for my evil bears witness to the fact that, in a timeless transcendental act, I had to choose freely my eternal character by giving preference to Evil over Good. This is how Kant conceives "radical Evil": as an a priori, not just an empirical, contingent propensity of human nature toward Evil. However, by rejecting the hypothesis of "diabolical Evil," Kant recoils from the ultimate paradox of radical Evil, from the uncanny domain of those acts that, although "evil" as to their content, thoroughly fulfill the formal criteria of an ethical act: they are not motivated by any pathological considerations, that is, their sole motivating ground is Evil as a principle, which is why they can involve the radical abrogation of one's pathological interests, up to the sacrifice of one's life.

Let us recall Mozart's *Don Giovanni:* when, in the final confrontation with the statue of the Commendatore, Don Giovanni refuses to repent, to renounce his sinful past, he accomplishes something the only proper designation of which is a radical ethical stance. It is as if his tenacity mockingly reverses Kant's own example from the *Critique of Practical Reason,* wherein the libertine is quickly prepared to renounce the satisfaction of his passion as soon as he learns that the price to be paid for it is the gallows: Don Giovanni persists in his libertine attitude at the very moment when he knows very well that what awaits him is *only* the gallows and none of the satisfactions. That is to say, from the standpoint of pathological interests, the thing to do would be to accomplish the formal gesture of penitence: Don Giovanni knows that death is close, so that by atoning for his deeds he stands to lose nothing, only to gain (i.e., to save himself from posthumous torments), and yet "on principle" he chooses to persist in his defiant stance of the libertine. How can one avoid experiencing Don Giovanni's unyielding "No!" to the statue, to this living dead, as the model of an intransigent *ethical* attitude, notwithstanding its "evil" content?

If we accept the possibility of such an "evil" ethical act, then it is not sufficient to conceive radical Evil as something that pertains to the very notion of subjectivity on a par with a disposition toward Good; one is compelled to advance a step further and to conceive radical Evil as something that ontologically precedes Good by way of opening up the space for it. That is to say, in what, precisely, does Evil consist? Evil is another name for the "death drive," for the fixation on some Thing that derails our customary life circuit. By way of Evil, man wrests himself from the animal instinctual rhythm; that is, Evil introduces the radical reversal of the "natural" relationship.[2] Here, therefore, is revealed the insufficiency of Kant's and Schelling's standard formula (the possibility of Evil is grounded in man's freedom of choice, on account of which he can invert the "normal" relationship between universal principles of Reason and his pathological nature by way of subordinating his supra-sensible nature to his egotistical inclinations). Hegel, who, in his *Lectures on the Philosophy of Religion,* conceives the very act of becoming human, of passage from animal into man, as the Fall into sin, is here more penetrating: the possible space for Good is opened up by the original choice of radical Evil, which disrupts the pattern of the organic substantial Whole. The choice between Good and Evil is thus in a sense not the true, original choice. The truly first choice is the choice between (what will later be perceived as) yielding to one's pathological leanings or embracing radical Evil, an act of suicidal egoism that "makes place" for the Good, that is, that overcomes the domination of pathological natural impulses by way of a purely negative gesture of suspending the life circuit. Or, to refer to Kierkegaard's terms, Evil is Good itself "in the mode of becoming." It "becomes" as a radical disruption of the life circuit; the difference between them concerns a purely formal conversion from the mode of "becoming" into the mode of "being."[3] This is how "only the spear that smote you can heal the wound": the wound is healed when the place of Evil is filled out by a "good" content. Good qua "the mask of the Thing (i.e., of the radical Evil)" (Lacan) is thus an ontologically secondary, supplementary attempt to reestablish the lost balance. Its ultimate paradigm in the social sphere is the corporatist endeavor to (re)construct society as a harmonious, organic, nonantagonistic edifice.

The thesis according to which the possibility to choose Evil pertains to the very notion of subjectivity has therefore to be radicalized by a kind of self-reflective inversion: *the status of the subject as such is evil.* That is, insofar as we are "human," in a sense we *always already* have chosen Evil. Far more than by his direct references to Hegel, the Hegelian stance of the early Lacan is attested to by the rhetorical figures that give body to this logic of the "negation of negation." Lacan's answer to the ego-psychological notion of the ego's "maturity" as the capability to endure frustrations, for example, is that "the ego as such is frustration in its essence":[4] insofar as the ego emerges in the process of imaginary identification with its mirror double who is at the same time its rival, its potential paranoid persecutor, the frustration on the part of the mirror double is constitutive of the ego. The logic of this reversal is strictly Hegelian: what first appears as an external hindrance frustrating the ego's striving for satisfaction is thereupon experienced as the ultimate support of its being.[5]

Why, then, does Kant hold back from bringing out all the consequences of the thesis on radical Evil? The answer is here clear, albeit paradoxical: what prevents him is the very logic that compelled him to articulate the thesis on radical Evil in the first place, namely, the logic of "real opposition," which, as suggested by Monique David-Menard, constitutes a kind of ultimate fantasmatic frame of Kant's thought. If moral struggle is conceived as the conflict of two opposing positive forces striving for mutual annihilation, it becomes unthinkable for one of the forces, Evil, not only to oppose the other, endeavoring to annihilate it, but also to undermine it from within, by way of assuming the very form of its opposite. Whenever Kant approaches this possibility (apropos of "diabolical Evil" in practical philosophy; apropos of the trial against the monarch in the doctrine of law), he quickly dismisses it as unthinkable, as an object of ultimate abhorrence. It is only with Hegel's logic of negative self-relating that this step can be accomplished.

This dialectical coincidence of Good and radical Evil that is the "un-thought" of Kant can be further clarified by reference to the relationship between the Beautiful and the Sublime. That is to say, Kant, as is well known, conceives beauty as the symbol of the Good. At the same time, in his *Critique of Judgment,* he points out that what is truly sublime is not the object that arouses the feeling of sublimity but the moral Law in us, our suprasensible nature. Are then beauty and sublimity simply to be conceived as two different symbols of the Good? Is it not, on the contrary, that this duality points toward a certain chasm that must pertain to the moral Law itself? Lacan draws a line of demarcation between the two facets of law. On the one hand, there is Law qua symbolic Ego-Ideal, that is, Law in its pacifying function, Law qua guarantee of the social pact, qua the intermediating Third that dissolves the impasse of imaginary aggressivity. On the other hand, there is law in its superego dimension, that is, law qua "irrational" pressure, the force of culpability totally incommensurable with our actual responsibility, the agency in the eyes of which we are a priori guilty and that gives body to the impossible imperative of enjoyment. It is this distinction between Ego-Ideal and superego that enables us to specify the difference in the way Beauty and Sublimity are related to the domain of ethics. Beauty is the symbol of the Good, that is, of the moral Law as the pacifying agency that bridles our egotism and renders possible harmonious social coexistence. The dynamical sublime, on the contrary—volcanic erup-tions, stormy seas, mountain precipices, etc.—by its very failure to symbolize (to represent symbolically) the suprasensible moral Law, evokes its superego dimension. The logic at work in the experience of the dynamical sublime is therefore as follows: true, I may be powerless in face of the raging forces of nature, a tiny particle of dust thrown around by wind and sea, yet all this fury of nature pales in comparison with the absolute pressure exerted on me by the superego, which humili-ates me and compels me to act contrary to my fundamental interests!

(What we encounter here is the basic paradox of the Kantian autonomy: I am a free and autonomous subject, delivered from the constraints of my pathological nature precisely and only insofar as my feeling of self-esteem is crushed by the humiliating pressure of the moral Law.) Therein consists also the superego dimension of the Jewish God evoked by the high priest Abner in Racine's *Athalie:* "Je crains Dieu et n'ai point d'autre crainte." The fear of raging nature and of the pain other men can inflict on me converts into sublime peace not simply by my becoming aware of the suprasensible nature in me out of reach of the forces of nature but by my taking cognizance of how the pressure of the moral law is stronger than even the mightiest exercise of the forces of nature.

The unavoidable conclusion to be drawn from all this is that if Beauty is the symbol of the Good, the Sublime is the symbol of.... Here, already, the homology gets stuck. The problem with the sublime object (more precisely: with the object that arouses in us the feeling of the sublime) is that it *fails* as a symbol—it evokes its Beyond by the very failure of its symbolic representation. So, if Beauty is the symbol of the Good, the Sublime evokes—what? There is only one answer possible: the nonpathological, ethical, suprasensible dimension, for sure, but *that dimension precisely insofar as it eludes the domain of the Good*—in short: radical Evil, Evil as an ethical attitude. In today's popular ideology, this paradox of the Kantian Sublime is what perhaps enables us to detect the roots of the public fascination with figures like Hannibal Lecter, the cannibal serial killer from Thomas Harris's novels: what this fascination ultimately bears witness to is a deep longing for a Lacanian psychoanalyst. That is to say, Hannibal Lecter is a sublime figure in the strict Kantian sense: a desperate, ultimately failed attempt of the popular imagination to represent to itself the idea of a Lacanian analyst. The relationship between Lecter and the Lacanian analyst corresponds perfectly to the relationship that, according to Kant, defines the experience of the "dynamic sublime": the relationship between wild, chaotic, untamed, raging nature and the suprasensible Idea of Reason beyond any natural constraints. True, Lecter's evil—he not only kills his victims but then goes on to eat parts of their entrails—strains to its limits our capacity to imagine the horrors we can inflict on our fellow creatures; yet even the utmost effort to represent Lecter's cruelty to ourselves fails to capture the true dimension of the act of the analyst: by bringing about *la traversée du fantasme* (the going-through of our fundamental fantasy), he literally "steals the kernel of our being," the object *a*, the secret treasure, *agalma*, what we consider most precious in ourselves, denouncing it as a mere semblance. Lacan defines the object *a* as the fantasmatic "stuff of the I," as that which confers on the $, on the fissure in the symbolic order, on the ontological void that we call "subject," the ontological consistency of a "person," the semblance of a fullness of being. And it is precisely this "stuff" that the analyst "swallows," pulverizes. This is the reason for the unexpected "eucharistic" element at work in Lacan's definition of the analyst, namely, his repeated ironic allusion to Heidegger: "Mange ton *Dasein!*" ("Eat your being there!") Therein consists the power of fascination that pertains to the figure of Hannibal Lecter: by its very failure to attain the absolute limit of what Lacan calls "subjective destitution," it enables us to get a presentiment of the Idea of the analyst. So, in *The Silence of the Lambs*, Lecter is truly cannibalistic not in relation to his victims but also in relation to Clarice Sterling: their relationship is a mocking imitation of the analytic situation, since in exchange for his helping her to capture "Buffalo Bill," he wants her to confide in him—what? Precisely what the analysand confides to the analyst, the kernel of her being, her fundamental fantasy (the crying of the lambs). The quid pro quo proposed by Lecter to Clarice is therefore, "I'll help you if you let me eat your *Dasein!*" The inversion of the proper analytic relation consists in the fact that Lecter compensates her for it by helping her in tracking down "Buffalo Bill." As such, he is not cruel enough to be a Lacanian analyst, since in psychoanalysis, we must pay the analyst so that he or she will allow us to offer him or her our *Dasein* on a plate.

What opens up the space for such sublime monstrous apparitions is the breakdown of the logic of representation, that is, the radical incommensurability between the field of representation and the unrepresentable Thing, which emerges with Kant. The pages that describe the first encounter of Madame Bovary and her lover [6] condense the entire problematic that, according to Foucault, determines the post-Kantian episteme of the nineteenth century: the new configuration of the axis power-knowledge caused by the incommensurability between the field of representation and the Thing, as well as the elevation of sexuality to the dignity of the unrepresentable Thing. After the two lovers enter the coach and tell the driver just to circulate around the city, we hear nothing about what goes on behind its safely closed curtains: with an attention to detail reminiscent of the later *nouveau roman,* Flaubert limits himself to lengthy descriptions of the city environment through which the coach wanders aimlessly, the stone-paved streets, the church arches, etc.; only in one short sentence does he mention that, for a brief moment, a naked hand pierces through the curtain. This scene is made as if to illustrate Foucault's thesis, from the first volume of his *History of Sexuality,* that the very speech whose "official" function is to conceal sexuality engenders the appearance of its secret, that is, that (to make use of the very terms of psychoanalysis against which Foucault's thesis is aimed) the "repressed" content is an effect of repression. The more the writer's gaze is restricted to boring architectural details, the more we, the readers, are tormented, greedy to learn what goes on in the closed space behind the curtains of the coach. The public prosecutor walked into this trap in the trial against *Madame Bovary* in which it was precisely this passage that was quoted as one of the proofs of the obscene character of the book: it was easy for Flaubert's defense lawyer to point out that there is nothing obscene in the neutral descriptions of paved streets and old house—the obscenity is entirely constrained to the reader's (in this case the prosecutor's) imagination obsessed by the "real thing" behind the curtain. It is perhaps no mere accident that today this procedure of Flaubert cannot but strike us as eminently *cinematic:* it is as if it plays upon what cinema theory designates as *hors-champ,* the externality of the field of vision, which, in its very absence, organizes the economy of what can be seen: if (as was long ago proven by the classical analyses of Eisenstein) Dickens introduced into the literary discourse the correlates of what later became the elementary cinematic procedures— the triad of establishing shots, "American" pans and closeups, the parallel montage, etc.—Flaubert went a step further toward an externality that eludes the standard exchange of field and counterfield, that is, that has to remain excluded if the field of what can be represented is to retain its consistency.[7]

The crucial point, however, is not to mistake *this* incommensurability between the field of representation and sexuality for the censorship in the description of sexuality already at work in the preceding epochs. If *Madame Bovary* had been written a century earlier, the details of sexual activity would also have remained unmentioned, for sure, yet what we would have got after the two lovers' entry into the secluded space of the coach would have been a simple, short statement like: "Finally alone and hidden behind the curtains of the coach, the lovers were able to gratify their passion." The lengthy descriptions of streets and buildings would have been totally out of place; they would have been perceived as lacking any function, since, in this pre-Kantian universe of representations, no radical tension could arise between the represented content and the traumatic Thing behind the curtain. Against this background, one is tempted to propose one of the possible definitions of "realism": a naive belief that, behind the curtain of representations, there actually exists some full, substantial reality (in the case of *Madame Bovary,* the reality of sexual superfluity). "Postrealism" begins when a doubt emerges as to the existence of this reality "behind the curtain," that is, when the foreboding arises that the very gesture of concealment creates what it pretends to conceal.

An exemplary case of such a "postrealist" playing, of course, is found in the paintings of René Magritte. His notorious *Ceci n'est pas une pipe* is today part of common knowledge: a drawing of a pipe with an inscription below it stating, "This is not a pipe." Taking as a starting point the paradoxes implied by this painting, Michel Foucault wrote a perspicacious little book of the same title.[8] Yet perhaps there is another of Margritte's paintings that can serve even more appropriately to establish the elementary matrix that generates the uncanny effects that pertain to his work: *La lunette d'approche* from 1963, the painting of a half-open window where, through the windowpane, we see the external reality (blue sky with some dispersed white clouds). Yet what we see in the narrow opening that gives direct access to the reality beyond the pane is nothing, just nondescript black mass. The translation of this painting into Lacanese goes by itself: the frame of the windowpane is the fantasy frame that constitutes reality, whereas through the crack we get an insight into the "impossible" Real, the Thing-in-itself.[9]

This painting renders the elementary matrix of the Magrittean paradoxes by way of staging the "Kantian" split between (symbolized, categorized, transcendentally constituted) reality and the void of the Thing-in-itself, of the Real, which gapes in the midst of reality and confers upon it a fantasmatic character. The first variation that can be generated from this matrix is the presence of some strange, inconsistent element that is "extraneous" to the depicted reality, that is, that, uncannily, has its place in it, although it does not "fit" in it: the gigantic rock that floats in the air close to a cloud as its heavy counterpart, its double, in *La Bataille de l'Argonne* (1959); or the unnaturally large bloom that fills out the entire room in *Tombeau des lutteurs* (1960). This strange element "out of joint" is precisely the fantasy object filling out the blackness of the real that we perceived in the crack of the open window in *La lunette d'approche*. The effect of uncanniness is even stronger when the "same" object is redoubled, as in *Les deux mystères,* a later variation (from 1966) on the famous *Ceci n'est pas une pipe:* the pipe and the inscription underneath it, "Ceci n'est pas une pipe," are both depicted as drawings on a blackboard; yet on the left of the blackboard, the apparition of another gigantic and massive pipe floats freely in a nonspecified space. The title of this painting could also have been "A pipe is a pipe," for what is it if not a perfect illustration of the Hegelian thesis on tautology as the ultimate contradiction: the coincidence between the pipe located in a clearly defined symbolic reality and its fantasmatic, uncanny, shadowy double. The inscription under the pipe on the blackboard bears witness to the fact that the split between the two pipes, the pipe that forms part of reality and the pipe as real, that is, as a fantasy apparition, results from the intervention of the symbolic order: it is the emergence of the symbolic order that splits reality into itself and the enigmatic surplus of the real, each of them "derealizing" its counterpart. (The Marx brothers version of this painting would be something like, "This looks like a pipe and works like a pipe, but this should not deceive you—this *is* a pipe!"[10]) The massive presence of the free-floating pipe, of course, turns the depicted pipe into a "mere painting," yet, simultaneously, the free-floating pipe is opposed to the "domesticated" symbolic reality of the pipe on the blackboard and as such acquires a phantomlike, "surreal" presence, like the emergence of the "real" Laura in Otto Preminger's *Laura:* the police detective (Dana Andrews) falls asleep staring at the portrait of the allegedly dead Laura; upon awakening, he finds at the side of the portrait the "real" Laura, alive and well. This presence of the "real" Laura accentuates the fact that the portrait is a mere "imitation"; on the other hand, the very "real" Laura emerges as a nonsymbolized fantasmatic surplus, a ghost— like the inscription, "This is not Laura." A somewhat homologous effect of the real occurs at the beginning of Sergio Leone's *Once upon a Time in America:* a phone goes on ringing endlessly; when, finally, a hand picks up the receiver, it continues to ring. The first sound belongs to "reality," whereas the ringing that goes on even after the receiver is picked up comes out of the nonspecified void of the real.[11]

This splitting between symbolized reality and the surplus of the Real, however, renders only the most elementary matrix of the way the Symbolic and the Real are intertwined; a further dialectical "turn of the screw" is introduced by what Freud called *Vorstellungs-Repraesentanz,* the symbolic representative of an originally missing, excluded ("primordially repressed") representation. This paradox of the *Vorstellungs-Repraesentanz* is perfectly staged by Magritte's *Personnage marchant vers l'horizon* (1928–29): the portrait of his usual elder gentleman in a bowler hat, seen from behind, situated near five thick, formless blobs that bear the italicized words "nuage," "cheval," "fusil," etc. Words are here signifiers' representatives that stand in for the absent representation of the things. Foucault is quite right in remarking that this painting functions as a kind of inverted rebus: in a rebus, pictorial representations of things stand for the words that designate these things, whereas here words themselves fill out the void of absent things. It would be possible for us to continue ad infinitum with the variations generated by the elementary matrix (one thinks of *The Fall of the Evening,* for example, where the evening literally falls through the window and breaks the pane—a case of realized metaphor, i.e., of the intrusion of the Symbolic into the Real). Yet it suffices to ascertain how behind all these paradoxes the same matrix can be discerned, the same basic fissure whose nature is ultimately Kantian: reality is never given in its totality; there is always a void gaping in its midst, filled out by monstrous apparitions.

The impenetrable blackness that can be glimpsed through the crack of the half-opened window thus opens up the space for the uncanny apparitions of an Other who precedes the Other of "normal" intersubjectivity. Let us recall here a detail from Hitchcock's *Frenzy* that bears witness to his genius. In a scene that leads to the second murder, Babs, its victim, a young girl who works in a Covent Garden pub, leaves her workplace after a quarrel with the owner and steps out onto the busy market street. The street noise that hits us for a brief moment is quickly suspended (in a totally "nonrealistic" way) when the camera approaches Babs for a closeup, and the mysterious silence is then broken by an uncanny voice coming from an indefinite point of absolute proximity, as if from behind her and at the same time from within her, a man's voice softly saying,

"Need a place to stay?" Babs moves off and looks back. Standing behind her is her old acquaintance who, unbeknownst to her, is the "necktie murderer." After a couple of seconds, the magic again evaporates and we hear the sound tapestry of "reality," of the market street bustling with life. This voice that emerges on the suspension of reality is none other than the *objet petit a,* and the figure that appears behind Babs is experienced by the spectator as supplementary with regard to this voice: it gives body to it, and, simultaneously, it is strangely intertwined with Babs's body, as its shadowy protuberance (not unlike the strange double body of Leonardo's Madonna, analyzed by Freud; or, in *Total Recall,* the body of the leader of the underground resistance movement on Mars, a kind of parasitic protuberance on another person's belly). It would be easy to produce a long list of homologous effects. For instance, in one of the key scenes of *Silence of the Lambs,* Clarice and Lecter occupy the same positions when engaged in a conversation in Lecter's prison: in the foreground, the closeup of Clarice staring into the camera, and on the glass partition wall behind her, the reflection of Lecter's head germinating behind—out of her—as her shadowy double, simultaneously less and more real than she. The supreme case of this effect, however, is found in one of the most mysterious shots of Hitchcock's *Vertigo,* when Scottie peers at Madeleine through the crack in the half-opened back door of the florist's shop. For a brief moment, Madeleine watches herself in a mirror close to this door, so that the screen is vertically split: the left half is occupied by the mirror in which we see Madeleine's reflection, while the right half is carved by a series of vertical lines (the doors); in the vertical dark band (the crack of the half-opened door) we see a fragment of Scottie, his gaze transfixed on the "original" whose mirror reflection we see in the left half. There is a truly "Magrittean" quality to this unique shot. Although, as to the disposition of the diegetic space, Scottie is here "in reality," whereas what we see of Madeleine is only her mirror image, the effect of the shot is exactly the reverse: Madeline is perceived as part of reality and Scottie as a phantomlike protuberance who (like the legendary dwarf in the Grimms' *Snow White*) lurks from behind the mirror. This shot is Magrittean in a very precise sense: the dwarflike mirage of Scottie peeps out of the very impenetrable darkness that gapes in the crack of the half-open window in *La lunette d'approche* (the mirror in *Vertigo,* of course, corresponds to the windowpane in Magritte's painting). In both cases, the framed space of the mirrored reality is traversed by a vertical black rift.[12] As Kant puts it, there is no positive knowledge of the Thing-in-itself; one can only designate its place, "make room" for it. This is what Magritte accomplishes on a quite literal level: the crack of the half-open door, its impenetrable blackness, makes room for the Thing. And by locating in this crack a gaze, Hitchcock supplements Magritte in a Hegelian-Lacanian way: the Thing-in-itself beyond appearance is ultimately the gaze itself, as Lacan puts it in his *Four Fundamental Concepts.*

In his Bayreuth production of *Tristan und Isolde,* Jean-Pierre Ponelle changed Wagner's original plot, interpreting all that follows Tristan's death—the arrival of Isolde and King Mark, Isolde's death—as Tristan's mortal delirium: the final appearance of Isolde is staged so that the dazzlingly illuminated Isolde grows luxuriantly *behind* him, while Tristan stares at us, the spectators, who are able to perceive his sublime double, the protuberance of his lethal enjoyment. This is also how Bergman, in his version of *The Magic Flute,* often shot Pamina and Monostatos: a closeup of Pamina, who stares intensely into the camera, with Monostatos appearing behind her as her shadowy double, as if belonging to a different level of reality (illuminated with pointedly "unnatural" dark violet colors), with his gaze also directed into the camera. This disposition, in which the subject and his/her shadowy, extimate double stare into a common third point (materialized in us, spectators), epitomizes the relationship of the subject to an Otherness that is prior to intersubjectivity. The field of intersubjectivity wherein subjects, within their shared *reality,* "look into each other's eyes," is sustained by the paternal metaphor, whereas the reference to the absent third point that attracts the two gazes changes the status of one of the two partners— the one in the background—into the sublime embodiment of the *real* of enjoyment.

What all these scenes have in common on the level of purely cinematic procedure is a kind of formal correlate of the reversal of face-to-face intersubjectivity into the relationship of the subject to his shadowy double that emerges behind him/her as a kind of sublime protuberance: the condensation of the field and counterfield within the same shot. What we have here is a paradoxical kind of communication: not a "direct" communication of the subject with his fellow creature *in front of* him, but a communication with the excrescence *behind* him, mediated by a third gaze, as if the counterfield were to be mirrored back into the field itself. It is this third gaze that confers upon the scene its hypnotic dimension: the subject is enthralled by the gaze that sees "what is in himself more than himself." And the analytical situation itself—the relationship between analyst and analysand—does it not ultimately also designate a kind of return to this preintersubjective relationship of the subject (analysand) to his shadowy other, to the externalized object in himself? Is not this the whole point of its spatial disposition: after the so-called preliminary encounters, that is, with the beginning of the analysis proper, the analyst and the analysand are *not* confronted face to face, but the analyst sits *behind* the analysand who, stretched on the divan, stares into the void in front of him? Does not this very disposition locate the analyst as the analysand's object *a*, not his dialogical partner, not another subject?

At this point, we should return to Kant: in his philosophy, this crack, this space where such monstrous apparitions can emerge, is opened up by the distinction between negative and indefinite judgment. The very example used by Kant to illustrate this distinction is telling: the positive judgment by means of which a predicate is ascribed to the (logical) subject—"The soul is mortal"; the negative judgment by means of which a predicate is denied to the subject—"The soul is not mortal"; the indefinite judgment by means of which, instead of negating a predicate (i.e., the copula that ascribes it to the subject), we affirm a certain nonpredicate—"The soul is not-mortal." (In German also, the difference is solely a matter of spacing: "Die Seele ist nicht sterbliche" versus "Die Seele ist nichtsterbliche"; Kant enigmatically does not use the standard "unsterbliche.")

In this line of thought, Kant introduces in the second edition of the *Critique of Pure Reason* the distinction between positive and negative meanings of "noumenon": in the positive meaning of the term, "noumenon" is "an object of a nonsensible intuition," whereas in the negative meaning, it is "a thing insofar as it is not an object of our sensible intuition" (B307). The grammatical form should not deceive us here: the positive meaning is expressed by the negative judgment and the negative meaning by the indefinite judgment. In other words, when one determines the Thing as "an object of a nonsensible intuition," one immediately negates the positive judgment that determines the Thing as "an object of a sensible intuition": one accepts intuition as the unquestioned base or genus; against this background, one opposes its two species, sensible and nonsensible intuition. Negative judgment is thus not only limiting; it also delineates a domain beyond phenomena where it locates the Thing—the domain of the nonsensible intuition—whereas in the case of the negative determination, the Thing is excluded from the domain of our sensible intuition, without being posited in an implicit way as the object of a nonsensible intuition; by leaving in suspense the positive status of the Thing, negative determination saps the very genus common to affirmation and negation of the predicate.

Therein consists also the difference between "is not mortal" and "is not-mortal": what we have in the first case is a simple negation, whereas in the second case, a *nonpredicate is affirmed*. The only "legitimate" definition of the noumenon is that it is "not an object of our sensible intuition," that is, a wholly negative definition that excludes it from the phenomenal domain; this judgment is "infinite" since it does not imply any conclusions as to where, in the infinite space of what remains outside the phenomenal domain, the noumenon is located. What Kant calls "transcendental illusion" ultimately consists in the very (mis)reading of infinite judgment as negative judgment: when we conceive the noumenon as an "object of a nonsensible intuition," the subject of the judgment remains the same (the "object of an intuition"); what changes is only the character (nonsensible instead of sensible) of this intuition, so that a minimal "commensurability" between the subject and the predicate (i.e., in this case, between the noumenon and its phenomenal determinations) is still maintained.

A Hegelian corollary to Kant here is that limitation is to be conceived as prior to what lies "beyond" it, so that it is ultimately Kant himself whose notion of Thing-in-itself remains too "reified." Hegel's position as to this point is subtle: what he claims by stating that the Suprasensible is "appearance qua appearance" is precisely that the Thing-in-itself is *the limitation of the phenomena as such*. "Suprasensible objects (objects of suprasensible intuition)" belong to the chimerical "topsy-turvy world." They are nothing but an inverted presentation, a projection, of the very content of sensible intuition in the form of another, nonsensible intuition. Or, to recall Marx's ironic critique of Proudhon in *The Poverty of Philosophy:* "Instead of the ordinary individual with his ordinary way of speech and thought, we get this same ordinary way of speech and thought, without the individual." (The double irony of it, of course, is that Marx intended these lines as a mocking rejection of Proudhon's Hegelianism, i.e., of his effort to supply economic theory with the form of speculative dialectics!) This is what the chimera of "nonsensible intuition" is about: instead of ordinary objects of sensible intuition, we get the same ordinary objects of intuition, without their sensible character.

This subtle difference between negative and indefinite judgment is at work in a certain type of witticism wherein the second part does not immediately invert the first part by negating its predicate but instead repeats it with the negation displaced onto the subject. The judgment, "He is an individual full of idiotic features," for example, can be negated in a standard mirror way, that is, replaced by its contrary, "He is an individual with no idiotic features"; yet its negation can also be given the form of, "He is full of idiotic features without being an individual." This displacement of the negation from the predicate onto the subject provides the logical matrix of what is often the unforeseen result of our educational efforts to liberate the pupil from the constraint of prejudices and cliches: not a person capable of expressing himself/herself in a relaxed, unconstrained way, but an automatized bundle of (new) cliches behind which we no longer sense the presence of a "real person." Let us just recall the usual outcome of psychological training intended to deliver the individual from the constraints of his/her everyday frame of mind and to set free his/her "true self," its authentic creative potentials (transcendental meditation, etc.): once s/he gets rid of the old cliches that were still able to sustain the dialectical tension between themselves and the "personality" behind them, what take their place are new cliches that abrogate the very "depth" of personality behind them. In short, s/he becomes a true monster, a kind of "living dead." Samuel Goldwyn, the old Hollywood mogul, was right: what we need are indeed some new, original cliches.

The mention of the "living dead" is by no means accidental here: in our ordinary language, we resort to indefinite judgments precisely when we endeavor to comprehend those borderline phenomena that undermine established differences such as that between living and being dead. In the texts of popular culture, the uncanny creatures that are neither alive nor dead, the "living dead" (vampires, etc.), are referred to as "the undead": although they are not dead, they are clearly not alive like us ordinary mortals. The judgment, "he is undead," is therefore an indefinite-limiting judgment in the precise sense of a purely negative gesture of excluding vampires from the domain of the dead, without for that reason locating them in the domain of the living (as in the case of the simple negation, "he is not dead"). The fact that vampires and other "living dead" are usually referred to as "things" has to be rendered with its full Kantian meaning: a vampire is a Thing that looks and acts like us, yet is not one of us. In short, the difference between the vampire and the living person is that between indefinite and negative judgment: a dead person loses the predicates of a living being, yet s/he remains the same person. An undead, on the contrary, retains all the predicates of a living being without being one. As in the above-quoted Marxian joke, what we get with the vampire is "the same ordinary way of speech and thought, without the individual."

This intermediate space of the unrepresentable Thing, filled out by the "undead," is what Lacan has in mind when he speaks of "l'entre-deux-morts." To delineate more precisely the contours of this uncanny space, let us take as our starting point a new book on Lacan, Richard Boothby's *Death and Desire*.[13] Its central thesis, although ultimately false, is very consequent and at the same time deeply satisfying in the sense of fulfilling a demand for symmetry: it is as if it provides the missing element of a puzzle. The triad Imaginary-Real-Symbolic renders the fundamental coordinates of the Lacanian theoretical space. But these three dimensions can never be conceived simultaneously, in pure synchronicity. One is always forced to choose between two of them (as with Kierkegaard's triad of the esthetical-ethical-religious): Symbolic versus Imaginary, Real versus Symbolic. The hitherto predominating interpretations of Lacan in effect put the accent on one of these axes: symbolization (Symbolic realization) against Imaginary self-deception in the Lacan of the fifties; the traumatic encounter of the Real as the point at which symbolization fails in the late Lacan. What Boothby offers as a key to the entire Lacanian theoretical edifice is simply the third, not yet exploited, axis: Imaginary versus Real. That is to say, according to Boothby, the theory of the mirror stage not only is chronologically Lacan's first contribution to psychoanalysis but also designates the original fact that defines the status of man. The alienation in the mirror image due to man's premature birth and his/her ensuing helplessness in the first years of life, this fixation on an imago, interrupts the supple life flow, introducing an irreducible *beance*, a gap, separating forever the

Imaginary ego—the wholesome yet immobile mirror image, a kind of halted cinematic picture—from the polymorphous, chaotic sprout of bodily drives, the Real Id. In this perspective, the Symbolic is of a strictly secondary nature with regard to the original tension between Imaginary and Real: its place is the void opened up by the exclusion of the polymorphous wealth of bodily drives. Symbolization designates the subject's endeavor, always fragmentary and ultimately doomed to fail, to bring into the light of the day, by way of Symbolic representatives, the Real of bodily drives excluded by Imaginary identification; it is therefore a kind of compromise formation by way of which the subject integrates fragments of the ostracized Real. In this sense, Boothby interprets the death drive as the reemergence of what was ostracized when the ego constituted itself by way of imaginary identification: the return of the polymorphous impulses is experienced by the ego as a mortal threat, since it actually entails the dissolution of its Imaginary identity. The foreclosed Real thus returns in two modes: either as a wild, destructive, nonsymbolized raging or in the form of Symbolic mediation, that is, "sublated" *(aufgehoben)* in the Symbolic medium. The elegance of Boothby is here to interpret the death drive as its very opposite: as the return of life force, of the part of it excluded by the imposition of the petrified mask of the ego. What reemerges in the "death drive" is ultimately *life itself,* and the fact that the ego perceives this return as a death threat precisely confirms its perverted "repressive" character. The "death drive" means that life itself rebels against the ego: the true representative of death is Ego itself, as the petrified imago that interrupts the flow of life. Boothby also reinterprets against this background Lacan's distinction between the two deaths: the first death is the death of the ego, the dissolution of its imaginary identifications, whereas the second death designates the interruption of the presymbolic life flow itself. Here, however, problems begin with this otherwise simple and elegant construct: the price to be paid for it is that Lacan's theoretical edifice is ultimately reduced to the opposition between an original polymorphous life force and its later coagulation, confining to the Procrustean bed of imagos the opposition that characterizes the field of *Lebensphilosophie.* For that reason, there is no place in Boothby's scheme for the fundamental Lacanian insight according to which the Symbolic order "stands for death" in the precise sense of "mortifying" the real of the body, of subordinating it to a foreign automatism, of perturbing its "natural" instinctual rhythm, thereby producing the surplus of desire, that is, desire *as* a surplus: the very Symbolic machine that "mortifies" the living body produces by the same token its opposite, the immortal desire, the Real of "pure life" that eludes symbolization. To clarify this point, let us bring to mind an example that, in a first approach, may appear to confirm Boothby's thesis: Wagner's *Tristan und Isolde*. In what, precisely, consists the effect on the (future) lovers of the philtre provided by Isolde's faithful maid Brangaene?

Wagner never intends to imply that the love of Tristan and Isolde is the *physical consequence* of the philtre, but only that the pair, having drunk what they imagine to be the draught of Death and believing that they have looked upon earth and sea and sky for the last time, feel themselves free to confess, when the potion begins its work within them, the love they have so long felt but have concealed from each other and almost from themselves.[14]

The point is therefore that after drinking the philtre, Tristan and Isolde find themselves in the domain "between the two deaths," alive, yet delivered of all symbolic ties. *In this domain,* they are able to confess their love. In other words, the "magical effect" of the philtre is simply to suspend the "big Other," the Symbolic reality of social obligations (honors, vows). Does this not fully accord with Boothby's thesis on the domain "between the two deaths" as the space where Imaginary identification, as well as the Symbolic identities attached to it, are all invalidated, so that the excluded Real (pure life drive) can emerge in all its force, although in the form of its opposite, the death drive? According to Wagner himself, the passion of Tristan and Isolde expresses the longing for the "eternal peace" of death. The trap to be avoided here, however, is that of conceiving this pure life drive as a substantial entity subsisting prior to its being captured in the Symbolic network: this "optical illusion" renders invisible that it is the very mediation of the Symbolic order that transforms the organic "instinct" into an unquenchable longing that can find solace only in death. In other words, this "pure life" beyond death, this longing that reaches beyond the circuit of generation and corruption, is it not the *product* of symbolization, so that symbolization itself engenders the surplus that escapes it? By conceiving the Symbolic order as an agency that fills out the gap between the Imaginary and the Real opened up by the mirror identification, Boothby avoids its constitutive paradox: the Symbolic itself opens up the wound it professes to heal.

In lieu of a more detailed theoretical elaboration, it is appropriate at this point to approach the relationship of Lacan to Heidegger in a new way. In the fifties, Lacan endeavored to read "death drive" against the background of Heidegger's "being-toward-death" *(Sein-zum-Tode)*, conceiving death as the inherent and ultimate limit of symbolization that provides for its irreducible temporal character. With the shift of accent toward the Real from the sixties onward, however, it is rather the "undead" lamella, the indestructible-immortal life that dwells in the domain "between the two deaths," that emerges as the ultimate object of horror. Lacan delineates the contours of this "undead" object toward the end of chapter 15 of his *Four Fundamental Concepts,* where he proposes his own myth, constructed upon the model of Aristophanes' fable from Plato's *Symposium,* the myth of *l'hommelette* (little female-man omelette):

Whenever the membranes of the egg in which the foetus emerges on its way to becoming a new-born, are broken, imagine for a moment that something flies off, and that one can do it with an egg as easily as with a man, namely the *hommelette,* or the lamella.

The lamella is something extra-flat, which moves like the amoeba. It is just a little more complicated. But it goes everywhere. And as it is something . . . that is related to what the sexed being loses in sexuality, it is, like the amoeba in relation to sexed beings, immortal—because it survives any division, any scissiparous intervention. And it can run around.

Well! This is not very reassuring. But suppose it comes and envelops your face while you are quietly asleep. . . .

I can't see how we would not join battle with a being capable of these properties. But it would not be a very convenient battle. This lamella, this organ, whose characteristic is not to exist, but which is nevertheless an organ . . . is the libido.

It is the libido, *qua* pure life instinct, that is to say, immortal life, or irrepressible life, life that has need of no organ, simplified, indestructible life. It is precisely what is subtracted from the living being by virtue of the fact that it is subject to the cycle of sexed reproduction. And it is of this that all the forms of the *objet a* that can be enumerated are the representatives, the equivalents. The *objets a* are merely its representatives, its figures. The breast—as equivocal, as an element characteristic of the mammiferous organization, the placenta for example—certainly represents that part of himself that the individual loses at birth, and which may serve to symbolize the most profound lost object.[15]

What we have here, again, is an Otherness prior to intersubjectivity: the subject's "impossible" relationship to this amoebalike creature is what Lacan is ultimately aiming at by way of his formula $ \$ \diamondsuit a $. The best way to clarify this point is perhaps to allow ourselves the string of associations that Lacan's description must evoke insofar as we like horror movies. Is not the alien from Ridley Scott's film of that title the "lamella" in its purest form? Are not all the key elements of Lacan's myth contained already in the first truly horrifying scene of the film when, in the womblike cave of the unknown planet, the "alien" leaps from the egglike globe when its lid splits off and sticks to John Hurt's face? This amoebalike flattened creature that envelops the subject's face stands for the irrepressible life beyond all the finite forms that are merely its representatives, its figures (later in the film, the "alien" is able to assume a multitude of different shapes), immortal and indestructible. It suffices to recall the unpleasant thrill of the moment when a scientist cuts with a scalpel into a leg of the creature that envelops Hurt's face: the liquid that drips from it falls onto the metal floor and corrodes it immediately; nothing can resist it.[16]

The second association here, of course, is to a detail from Syberberg's film version of *Parsifal,* in which Syberberg depicts Amfortas's wound—externalized, carried by the servants on a pillow in front of him, in the form of a vagina-like partial object out of which blood is dripping in a continuous flow (like, *vulgari eloquentia,* a vagina in an unending period). This palpitating opening—an organ that is at the same time the entire organism (let us just recall a homologous motif in a series of science-fiction stories, like the gigantic eye living a life of its own)—epitomizes life in its indestructibility: Amfortas's pain consists in the very fact that he is unable to die, that he is condemned to an eternal life of suffering; when, at the end, Parsifal heals his wound with "the spear that smote it," Amfortas is finally able to rest and die. This wound of Amfortas's, which persists outside himself as an *undead* thing, is the "object of psychoanalysis."

And—to conclude—it is precisely the reference to this indestructible, mythical object-libido that enables us to throw some light on one of the most obscure points of Lacanian theory: what, precisely, is the role of *objet petit a* in a drive—say, in the scopic drive—as opposed to desire? The key is provided by Lacan's clarification, in his *Four Fundamental*

Concepts, that the essential feature of the scopic drive consists in *"making oneself seen (se faire voir)."*[17] However, as Lacan immediately points out, this "making oneself seen" that characterizes the circularity, the constitutive loop, of the drive, is in no way to be confused with the narcissistic "looking at oneself through the other," that is, through the eyes of the big Other, from the point of the Ego-Ideal in the Other, in the form in which I appear to myself worthy of love: what is lost when I "look at myself through the other" is the radical heterogeneity of the object qua gaze to whom I expose myself in "making oneself seen." In the ideological space proper, an exemplary case of this narcissistic satisfaction provided by "looking at oneself through the other" (Ego-Ideal) is the reporting on one's own country as seen through the foreign gaze (see the obsession of American media today by the way America is perceived—admired or despised—by the Other: Japanese, Russians, etc.). The first exemplary case of it, of course, is Aeschylus's *Persians,* where the Persian defeat is rendered as seen through the eyes of the Persian royal court: the amazement of King Darius at what a magnificent people the Greeks are, etc., provides for the deep narcissistic satisfaction of the Greek spectators. Yet this is not what "making oneself seen" is about. In what, then, does it consist?

Let us recall Hitchcock's *Rear Window,* which is often quoted as an exemplary staging of the scopic drive. Throughout most of the film, it is the logic of desire that predominates: this desire is fascinated, propelled, by its object-cause, the dark window opposite the courtyard that gazes back at the subject. When, in the course of the film, does "the arrow come back toward the subject"? At the moment, of course, when the murderer in the house opposite Stewart's rear window returns the gaze and catches him red-handed in his act of voyeurism: at this precise moment when James Stewart does not "see himself seeing himself," but *makes himself seen to the object of his seeing,* that is, to that stain that attracted his gaze in the dark room across the courtyard, we pass from the register of desire into that of drive. That is to say, we remain within the register of desire as long as, by way of assuming the inquisitive attitude of a voyeur, we are looking in what we see for the fascinating X, for some trace of what is hidden "behind the curtain"; we "change the gear" into drive the moment we make ourselves seen to this stain in the picture, to this impervious foreign body in it, to this point that attracted our gaze. Therein consists the reversal that defines drive: insofar as I cannot see the point in the other from which I'm gazed at, the only thing that remains for me to do is to make myself visible to that point. The difference between this and the narcissistic looking at oneself from the point of the Ego-Ideal is clear: the point to which the subject makes himself seen retains its traumatic heterogeneity and nontransparency; it remains an object in a strict Lacanian sense, not a symbolic feature. This point to which I make myself visible in my very capacity of looking is the object of drive, and in this way, one can perhaps clarify a little bit the difference between the status of object *a* in desire and in drive. (As we all know, when Jacques-Alain Miller asks Lacan about this point in the *Four Fundamental Concepts*, the answer he gets is chiaroscuro at its best.)

What can further clarify this crucial distinction is another feature of the final scene of *Rear Window* that stages in its purest this transmutation of desire into drive: the desperate defense of Jefferies, who attempts to stop the murderer's advance by lighting the flashbulbs. This apparently nonsensical gesture must be read precisely as a *defense against drive*, against "making oneself seen." Jefferies endeavors frantically to blur the other's gaze.[18] What befalls him when the murderer throws him through the window is precisely the inversion that defines drive: by falling through the window, Jefferies in a radical sense falls into his own picture, into the field of his own visibility. In Lacanian terms, he changes into a stain in his own picture, he makes himself seen in it, that is, within the space defined as his own field of vision.[19]

Those magnificent scenes toward the end of *Who Framed Roger Rabbit* are another variant on the same motif, where the hardboiled detective falls into the universe of cartoons: he is thereby confined to the domain "between the two deaths" where there is no death proper, just unending devouring and/or destruction. Yet another left-paranoiac variant of it is to be found in *Dreamscape*, a sci-fi movie about an American president troubled by bad dreams about the nuclear catastrophe he may trigger: the dark militarist plotters try to prevent his pacifist plans by making use of a criminal with a paranormal capacity to transpose himself into another person's dream and act in it. The idea is to scare the president so much in his dream that he dies of a heart attack.

The apparent melodramatic simplicity of the final scene of Chaplin's *Limelight* should not deceive us: here, also, we have the reversal of desire into drive. This scene is centered around a magnificent backward tracking shot that moves from the closeup of the dead clown Calvero behind the stage to the establishing shot of the entire stage where the young girl, now a successful ballerina and his great love, is performing. Just before this scene, the dying Calvero expresses to the attending doctor his desire to see his love dancing; the doctor taps him gently on the shoulders and comforts him: "You shall see her!" Thereupon Calvero dies, his body is covered by a white sheet, and the camera withdraws so that it comprises the dancing girl on the stage, while Calvero is reduced to a tiny, barely visible white stain in the background. What is here of special significance is the way the ballerina enters the frame: from behind the camera, like the birds in the famous "God's-view" shot of Bodega Bay in Hitchcock's *Birds*—yet another white stain that materializes out of the mysterious intermediate space separating the spectator from the diegetic reality on the screen. We encounter here the function of the gaze qua object-stain in its purest: the doctor's forecast is fulfilled, precisely as dead—that is, insofar as he cannot *see* her anymore—Calvero *looks at her*. For that reason, the logic of this backward tracking shot is thoroughly Hitchcockian: by way of it, a piece of reality is transformed into an amorphous stain (a white blot in the background), yet a stain around which the entire field of vision turns, a stain that "smears over" the entire field (as in the backward tracking shot in *Frenzy*). In other words, what confers upon this scene its melodramatic beauty is our—the spectators'—awareness that without knowing that he is already dead, the ballerina is dancing for it, for that stain (the melodramatic effect always hinges on such an ignorance of the agent). It is this stain, this white smudge in the background, that guarantees the sense of the scene. Where, precisely, is the transmutation of desire into drive here? We remain within the register of desire as long as the field of vision is organized, supported, by Calvero's desire to see for the last time his love dancing; we enter the register of drive the moment Calvero is reduced to a stain-object in his own picture. For that precise reason, it is not sufficient to say that it is simply she, the ballerina, his love, who makes herself seen to him; the point is rather that, simultaneously, he acquires the presence of a stain, so that both of them appear within the same field of vision.[20]

The scopic drive always designates such a closing of the loop whereby I get caught in the picture I'm looking at, lose distance toward it; as such, it is never a simple reversal of desire to see into a passive mode.

"Making oneself seen" is inherent to the very act of seeing: drive is the loop that connects them. The ultimate exemplifications of drive are therefore the visual and temporal paradoxes that materialize the nonsensical, "impossible" vicious circle: Escher's two hands drawing each other, or the waterfall that runs in a closed perpetuum-mobile, or the time-travel loop whereby I visit the past in order to create myself (to couple my parents).

Perhaps even better than with the arrow mentioned by Lacan, this "loop formed by the outward and return movement of the drive" can be exemplified by the first free association that this formulation resuscitates, namely, the boomerang, where "hitting the animal" changes over into "making oneself hit." That is to say, when I throw the boomerang, the "goal" of it, of course, is to hit the animal; yet the true artifice of it consists in being able to catch it when, upon my missing the goal, the boomerang flies back—the true aim is precisely to miss the goal, so that the boomerang returns to me (the most difficult part of learning how to handle the boomerang is therefore to master the art of catching it properly, i.e., of avoiding being hit by it, of blocking the potentially suicidal dimension of throwing it). The boomerang thus designates the very moment of the emergence of "culture," the moment when instinct is transformed into drive: the moment of splitting between goal and aim, the moment when the true aim is no longer to hit the goal but to maintain the very circular movement of repeatedly missing it.

Notes

1. Jacques Lacan, *Ecrits: A Selection* (New York: Norton, 1977), 144.
2. In this sense, the femme fatale who, in the film noir universe, derails man's daily routine, is one of the personifications of Evil: the sexual relationship becomes impossible the moment woman is elevated to the dignity of the Thing.
3. We must be careful here to avoid the trap of retroactive projection: Milton's Satan in his *Paradise Lost* is not yet the Kantian radical Evil—it appeared as such only to the Romantic gaze of Shelley and Blake. When Satan says, "Evil, be thou my Good," this is not yet the radical Evil, but remains simply a case of wrongly putting some Evil at the place of Good. The logic of radical Evil consists rather in its exact opposite, that is, in saying "Good, be thou my Evil"—in filling out the place of Evil, of the Thing, of the trau-

matic element that derails the closed circuit of organic life, by some (second-ary) Good.

4. Lacan, *Ecrits*, 42.

5. Lacan often makes use of the same rhetorical inversion to delineate the relationship of the ego to its symptoms: it is not sufficient to say that ego forms its symptoms in order to maintain its precarious balance with the forces of Id. Ego itself is, as to its essence, a symptom, a compromise-formation, a tool enabling the subject to regulate his/her desire. In other words, the subject desires by means of his/her ego-symptom.

6. Cf. Alain Abelhauser's analysis "D'un manque à saisir" in *Razpol* 3 (1987).

7. One can imagine how the cinematic version of this scene would be able to rely on the contrapuntal use of sound: the camera would show the coach running along the empty streets, the fronts of old palaces and churches, whereas the soundtrack would be allowed to retain the absolute proximity to the Thing and to render the real of what goes on in the coach: the gasping and groaning that bear witness to the intensity of the sexual encounter.

8. Cf. Michel Foucault, *This Is Not a Pipe* (Berkeley and Los Angeles: University of California Press, 1982).

9. One encounters the same paradox in Robert Heinlein's science-fiction novel *The Unpleasant Profession of Jonathan Hoag:* upon opening a window, the reality previously seen through it dissolves and all we see is the dense, nontransparent slime of the Real; for a more detailed Lacanian reading of this scene, cf. chapter 1 of Slavoj Žižek, *Looking Awry* (Cambridge, MA: MIT Press, 1991).

10. In Marx brothers films, we encounter three variations on this paradox of identity, that is, of the uncanny relationship between existence and attribute. (1) Groucho Marx, upon being introduced to a stranger: "Say, you remind me of Emmanuel Ravelli. 'But I *am* Emmanuel Ravelli.' No wonder, then, that you look like him!" (2) Groucho, defending a client in court: "This man looks like an idiot and acts as an idiot, yet all this should not deceive you—he *is* an idiot!" (3) Groucho, courting a lady: "Everything on you reminds me of you, your nose, your eyes, your lips, your hands—everything except you!"

11. What we have in this scene, of course, is a kind of reflective redoubling of the external stimulus (sound, organic need, etc.), which triggers the activity of dreaming: one invents a dream integrating this element in order to prolong the sleep, yet the content encountered in the dream is so traumatic that, finally, one escapes into reality and awakens. The ringing of the phone while we are asleep is such a stimulus par excellence; its duration even after the source in reality ceased to emit it exemplifies what Lacan calls the insistence of the Real.

12. A similar shot is found in Fritz Lang's *Blue Gardenia*, when Anne Baxter peeps out of the crack of half-opened doors.

13. Richard Boothby, *Death and Desire* (New York: Routledge, 1991).

14. Ernest Newman, *Wagner Nights* (London: Bodley Head, 1988), 221.

15. Jacques Lacan, *The Four Fundamental Concepts of Psycho-Analysis* (New York: Norton, 1979), 197–98.
16. It is precisely this physical, tangible impact of "lamella" that gets lost in *Aliens II*, which is why this sequel is infinitely inferior to *Alien*.
17. Lacan, *Four Fundamental Concepts*, 195.
18. The same defense against the drive is at work in the famous tracking shot from Hitchcock's *Young and Innocent:* the nervous blinking of the drummer is ultimately a defense-reaction to being seen, an attempt to avoid being seen, a resistance to being drawn into the picture. The paradox, of course, is that by his very defense-reaction he inadvertently draws attention to himself and thus exposes himself, divulges, that is, literally "renders public by beat of drum," his guilt. He is unable to endure the other's (camera's) gaze.
19. We get a hint of this even in the first scene of the film where we see for a brief moment the last snapshot taken by Jefferies prior to his accident, depicting the cause of his broken leg. This shot is a true Hitchcockian counterpart to Holbein's *Ambassadors:* the oblique stain in its center is a racing-car wheel flying toward the camera, captured the split second before Jefferies was hit by it. The moment rendered by this shot is the very moment when Jefferies lost his distance and was, so to speak, caught into his own picture; cf. Miran Bozovic's article on *Rear Window* in *Everything You Always Wanted to Know about Lacan (But Were Afraid to Ask Hitchcock)* (London: Verso, 1992).
20. What we encounter here, again, is the condensation of field and counterfield within the same shot. Desire delineates the field of ordinary intersubjectivity in which we look at each other face to face, whereas we enter the register of drive when, together with our shadowy double, we find ourselves on the same side, both of us staring at the same third point. Where here is the "making oneself seen" constitutive of the drive? One makes oneself seen precisely to this third point, to the gaze capable of embracing field in counterfield, that is, capable of perceiving in me also my shadowy double, what is in me more than myself, the object *a*.

3. Extimité

Jacques-Alain Miller

The term "extimacy"[a] *(extimité)*, coined by Lacan from the term "intimacy" *(intimité)*, occurs two or three times in the *Seminar*. Our task will be to transform this term into an articulation, a structure, to produce it as an S_1 that would allow us to go beyond and over the confusion that we first experience when faced with such a signifier.

1. $

For analysts, referring only to the analytic experience is illusory, for Freud's and Lacan's works are also part of our relation to psychoanalysis. And our common reading of the commentary on Freudian texts that forms the subject of the first ten years of Lacan's *Seminar* is not unlike the *lectio* of the Middle Ages. At that time, the lesson of a master was to be divided into three parts: *littera, sensus,* and *sententia. Littera* is the level of the construction of the text, the most grammatical level; *sensus* is the level of the signified, of the explicit and easy meaning; and *sententia* is the deep understanding of meaning. Only this level of *sententia* can justify the discipline of commentary.

The problem posed by Lacan's teaching is precisely that one of its constants is a commentary on Freud. Moreover, of his own sayings, Lacan makes maxims, or *sententiae* (in the Middle Ages, the word also meant "commonplace"). Thus, he does not allow the Other to choose what of Lacan must be repeated—because he formalizes his own thought by expressing it in formulas that are simple, or that at least seem simple. Thus, "The unconscious is structured like a language," "Desire is the desire of the Other," and "The signifier represents the subject for another signifier," are *sententiae* of Lacan. At present, part of our task lies in culling these *sententiae,* in gathering them into a florilegium.[b] This we do with Lacan, because he seems to present himself

74

as an author in the medieval sense of the word, that is, as the one who knows what he says.

Despite his *sententiae*, however, Lacan is not an author. His work is a teaching. We must take this into consideration; we must know that following his star requires that we do not synchronize and dogmatize this teaching, that we do not hide but rather stress its contradictions, its antinomies, its deadlocks, its difficulties. For a teaching on the analytic experience is like a *work in progress* [c] and implies a back-and-forth motion between text and experience.

2. Extimacy *(Extimité)*

Why this title? First, because last year I gave my attention to gathering, developing, and articulating the quaternary structures in Lacan's teaching; and as a result it seems to me that extimacy must be formalized and dealt with apart from these structures. Second, I could not disregard this question of extimacy, because I am particularly devoting myself to the question of the real in the symbolic. It so happens that "extimacy" is a term used by Lacan to designate in a problematic manner the real in the symbolic. Third, it seems to me that this term has a great potential for crystallization. When reconsidering the problems of analytic experience and of Lacan's teaching from the standpoint of this term, one realizes indeed that a number of scattered questions raised by our practice fall into place. Fourth, this expression "extimacy" is necessary in order to escape the common ravings about a psychism supposedly located in a bipartition between interior and exterior.

Let us qualify this last point, however, for it is not enough to say that this bipartition is unsatisfactory. We must also elaborate a relation in its stead. Indeed, it is so easy to slide into this interior-exterior bipartition that we need, for our own use, to substitute for it another relation, the simplest possible, which we will represent with the following drawing:

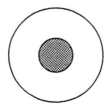

This very simple diagram of Lacan's means that the exterior is present in the interior. The most interior—this is how the dictionary defines "intimate" *(l'intime)*—has, in the analytic experience, a quality of exteriority. This is why Lacan invented the term "extimate." The word indeed is not current yet. But with a little effort and luck, it will perhaps come to exist—in a few centuries—in the *Académie française* dictionary![d]

It should be observed that the term "interior" is a comparative that comes to us from Latin and of which *intimus* is the superlative. This word is like an effort on the part of language to reach the deepest point in the interior. Let us note as well that quotations from literary works given by dictionaries show that one says commonly, constantly, that the most intimate is at the same time the most hidden. Therefore, paradoxically, the most intimate is not a point of transparency but rather a point of opacity. And this point of opacity is generally used to found the necessity of certain covers, the most common being the religious cover, as we are going to see.

3. A → $

Extimacy is not the contrary of intimacy. Extimacy says that the intimate is Other—like a foreign body, a parasite. In French, the date of birth of the term "intimacy" can be located in the seventeenth century; it is found for instance in Madame de Sévigné's *Correspondance,* a model of intimacy, from which comes this sentence: "I could not help telling you all this detail, in the intimacy and love of my heart, like someone who unburdens herself to a maid whose tenderness is without parallel." Is it not charming that one of the first occurrences in the French language of the term "intimacy" already has a relation to a kind of confession of the heart to someone full of tenderness?

In psychoanalysis, it seems to us natural from the start to place ourselves in the register of intimacy, for there is no experience more intimate than that of analysis, which takes place in private and requires trust, the most complete lack of restraint possible, to the point that in our consulting rooms—these places reserved for the confessions of intimacy—analysands, though in the house of someone else, sometimes act as if they were at home. This is confirmed when such an analysand takes out of his pocket the key to his own house as he is reaching the doorstep of his analyst.

However, in no way can one say that the analyst is an intimate friend of his analysand. The analyst, on the contrary, is precisely extimate to this intimacy. Perhaps this shows that one cannot have one's own house. Perhaps also it is this position of the psychoanalyst's extimacy that makes so distinct and so constant the role of the Jew in the history of psychoanalysis.

If we use the term "extimacy" in this way, we can consequently make it be equivalent to the unconscious itself. In this sense, the extimacy of the subject is the Other. This is what we find in "The Agency of the Letter," when Lacan speaks of "this other to whom I am more attached than to myself, since, at the heart of my assent to my identity to myself, it is he who stirs me" (*Ecrits: A Selection,* 172; translation modified)— where the extimacy of the Other is tied to the vacillation of the subject's identity to himself. Thus the writing A → $ is justified.

There are several covers of this point of extimacy, one of which is the religious cover. Thus Saint Augustine speaks of God as *interior intimo meo,* "more interior than my innermost being." "God" here is thus a word that covers this point of extimacy that in itself has nothing likeable. This implies this schema—

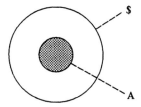

—where the circle of the subject contains as the most intimate *(intime)* of its intimacy the extimacy of the Other. In a certain way, this is what Lacan is commenting on when he speaks of the unconscious as discourse of the Other, of this Other who, more intimate than my intimacy, stirs me. And this intimate that is radically Other, Lacan expressed with a single word: "extimacy."

We could apply this term to the psychiatric clinic and call mental automatism "extimate automatism" insofar as it manifests in an obvious fashion the presence of the Other and of its discourse at the very center of intimacy. In the analytic clinic, it is interesting to note that it is always when extimacy is punctualized that an analyst's hesitations about the diagnosis occur—between obsession and psychosis, for example—despite the very clear distinctions that he makes in other respects between one and the other. Extimacy indeed is so structural for the speaking being that no analyst can say he has never encountered it, if only in the experience of his own hesitations.

4. a ◇ A

Let us introduce now a dimension other than the one from our previous schema, by posing the small *a* as part of the Other. The structure is the same, but this time the exterior circle is that of the Other, and the central area, the area of extimacy, is occupied by *a*.

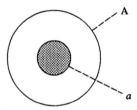

This is not the negation of the preceding schema but a new use of the same structure, which responds to another consideration. Up to this point in our argument, we have used the concept of the Other as something obvious. Now, the question of extimacy leads us to problematize this concept, to ask the question of the alterity of the Other, that is, of why the Other is really other.

"What is the Other of the Other?" is the very simple question asked by Lacan in order to ground the alterity of the Other. To say that the Other of the Other is the subject would not take us very far, for the precise reason that the subject of the analytic experience is nothing, is a barred function.

The first attempt made by Lacan was to posit that the Other of the Other of the signifier was the Other of the law. This hypothesis concludes his essay on psychoses.[1] There would exist an Other who lays down the law to the Other. This would imply the existence of a metalanguage that would be the Law, for the Law as absolute is a metalanguage.

Later, Lacan, thinking against Lacan, says on the contrary that "there is no Other of the Other," that "there is no metalanguage." To whom does he say this? He says it to the previous Lacan. Thus, there is no reason to confuse an effort at rationality with a dogmatization. Let us note that this famous *sententia*, "There is no Other of the Other," implies a devalorization and a pluralization of the Name-of-the-Father. But it also implies a problem in grounding the alterity of the Other. Indeed, what is it, this Other, if not a universal function, an abstraction? Father Takatsuga Sasaki's reaction, for example, testifies to this when he tells us that this kind of abstraction seems impossible in the Japanese language, in which there is no Other but various categories of alterity, of plurality.

The Other that we experience through the religious cover is omnivalent. It is precisely what is called, in Christianity, the neighbor.[e] It is a way to nullify extimacy; it grounds what is common, what conforms, conformity. It belongs fundamentally, as universal, to this conformity. But if there is no Other of the Other, what is the ground of his alterity?

Jouissance is precisely what grounds the alterity of the Other when there is no Other of the Other. It is in its relation to *jouissance* that the Other is really Other. This means that no one can ground the alterity of the Other in the signifier, since the very law of the signifier implies that one can always be substituted for the other and vice versa. The law of the signifier is indeed the very law of 1-2, and in this dimension, there is a kind of democracy, an equality, a community, a principle of peace.

Now, what we are attempting to see is what makes the Other other, that is, what makes it particular, different, and in this dimension of alterity of the Other, we find war. Racism, for example, is precisely a question of the relation to an Other as such, conceived in its difference. And it does not seem to me that any of the generous and universal discourses on the theme of "we are all fellow beings" have had any effectiveness concerning this question. Why? Because racism calls into play a hatred that is directed precisely toward what grounds the Other's alterity, in other words, its *jouissance*. If no decision, no will, no amount of reasoning is sufficient to wipe out racism, this is indeed because it is founded on the point of extimacy of the Other.

It is not simply a matter of an imaginary aggressivity that, itself, is directed at fellow beings. Racism is founded on what one imagines about the Other's *jouissance*; it is hatred of the particular way, of the Other's own way, of experiencing *jouissance*. We may well think that racism exists because our Islamic neighbor is too noisy when he has parties. However, what is really at stake is that he takes his *jouissance* in a way different from ours. Thus the Other's proximity exacerbates racism: as soon as there is closeness, there is a confrontation of incompatible modes of *jouissance*. For it is simple to love one's neighbor when he is distant, but it is a different matter in proximity.

Racist stories are always about the way in which the Other obtains a *plus-de-jouir:*[f] either he does not work or he does not work enough, or he is useless or a little too useful, but whatever the case may be, he is always endowed with a part of *jouissance* that he does not deserve. Thus true intolerance is the intolerance of the Other's *jouissance*. Of course, we cannot deny that races do exist, but they exist insofar as they are, in Lacan's words, races of discourse, that is, traditions of subjective positions.

5. *a* ⊂ A

One usually stresses what, of the Other, is subject. When Lacan speaks, for example, of the subject assumed to know, there seems to be no difficulty: there is a way of the Other that is to be a subject. However, we must point out something else—that is, what in the Other is object. We will develop this point from two seminars by Lacan, *The Ethics* and *Transference*.

The opposition between *das Ding*, the Thing, and the Other is laid out in the seminar on *The Ethics*. This antinomy is worked out enigmatically—which explains the fact that *das Ding* has long remained wrapped in mystery. But it is the case that, in the seminar on transference, which comes immediately after *The Ethics*, this opposition is transformed into a relation that can be written in this way: *a* ⊂ A. Lacan makes this transformation from a metaphor borrowed from philosophy that is nowadays known as that of Silenus, which contains the object, *agalma*, inside itself. Here we see a revolution in Lacan's teaching, for this relation, established in a literary, mythical, nonformalist way, appears to be completely antagonistic to earlier developments. The Other, in the seminar on transference, is no longer only the place of the signifier; there the object is included in the Other—which appears somewhat mystical because the Seminar works only with the idea of interior and exterior. Plato's model is nothing more: a cover that looks like a Silenus and inside which something else is found. We must therefore formalize this model of interior and exterior.

Something has been introduced in Lacan's teaching that has only been understood recently, that is, the devalorization of the Other of the signifier. He could thus say, "The Other does not exist," which does not prevent the Other from functioning, for many things function without existing. However, the sentence, "The Other does not exist," is meaningless if it does not imply that *a*, on the contrary, does exist. The Lacanian Other, the Other that functions, is not real. That is what allows us to understand that *a* is real, to understand how this *a* as *plus-de-jouir* founds not only the Other's alterity but also what is real in the symbolic Other. It is not a matter of a link of integration, of interiorization, but of an articulation of extimacy.

Let us illustrate this with the incident that interrupted my class: a bomb scare.[2] The bomb did not exist. However, we had the proof that, without existing, it could produce its effect. My class is of the order of the signifier and is held in a place devoted to teaching, where was introduced an object that, by the way, had a great effect, but that no one knew the location of. This object was impossible to locate. Thus did we prove that at the very moment when this object crops up via the signifier "Bomb!" the Other is emptied, disappears. Only the object remains, the object in a desert.

This is a good example of the antinomy existing between A and *a*. And this antinomy is compatible with the formula that we write $a \subset A$. For this object, the bomb—an object that is perfectly efficacious without existing or that perhaps will explode tomorrow or next week—is the result of the discourse of the Other. It is not a natural phenomenon, neither a seism nor an earthquake; it is not a substance but on the contrary a result, a product of the discourse of science. The sentence "Bomb!" is located on the level of intersections that Lacan studied to prove that the presence of the subject of the enunciation does not need the presence of the *énoncé*. At the same time, this sentence gives a clear indication of the relation between signifier and object. Indeed, if the signifier "Bomb!" is truly a reference to the bomb, it still does not represent this bomb; it does not say where the bomb is. There is thus a link between this signifier and the object, but we cannot say that "Bomb!" is the signifier of this bomb. The best proof of this is that no one will get the idea to go speak to the bomb so that it will not blow up.

To be done with this point, which has a paradigmatic value, my own position is to say that the young woman who burst into the room shouting "Bomb!" should have written this on a sheet of paper and handed it to me. At that time, I would have asked the people from one part of the room to leave, then from another part, then from a third one. That is, I would have tried to do things in the most orderly way. This indicates a clinical difference between her and me, and the importance of the way a subject situates itself in a moment of crisis. When I asked this person why she had not warned me in writing, she answered: "But the bomb could have exploded any moment!" Of course, but identifying with the bomb may not be the best way to get out of such a situation.

6. *Quod* without *Quid*

This part of my development concerns the type of the object and what makes its localization in the place of the Other difficult. When we speak of the object *a*, we are not speaking about an object summoned opposite the subject of the representation. If we take the bomb, for example, no one is there to gaze at it. It is really an object incompatible with the presence of the subject; it implies a physical disappearance of bodies and persons that, in this example, represent the subject. While you can sit down opposite a painting and chat with the people next to you, it is not so with the bomb; when you speak about this type of object, the subject disappears.

The object *a* is not a chapter of ontology. Indeed, ontology says what is common to all objects. It consists in gathering several features of the object of representation before the object itself is experienced. This is what Heidegger called "ontological precomprehension": we can know a priori that an object is an object if it has such and such a feature. We can also enumerate the object's criteria. An ontology tells a priori what can be said about objects. These are Aristotle's categories, where the said is already placed on the object. An ontology is indeed always a doctrine of categories. It can be said that there the structure of objects is already the same as that of the *énoncé*.

But when we speak of object *a*, we speak of another objectivity—let's say of another "objectity," an objectity that is not summoned opposite the subject of representation. For representation is not an imaginary function. In the seminar on *The Ethics*, *Vorstellung* is the symbolic itself—what Lacan will formalize a few years later with the representation of the subject by the signifier. The definition, in the Lacanian sense, of *Vorstellung* refers thus to the symbolic and not to the imaginary. However, this new objectity is such that one cannot avoid experiencing it. It is an object articulated not to the subject but to its division, to a subject that does not represent to itself the objects of the world but that is itself represented. For this reason, we cannot say that the structure of this object is identical to that of the *énoncé*. There is no specificity of the object in the Other, where nonetheless, the object *a* does not dissolve. It escapes categories because it does not have the same structure as the *énoncé*. By using the medieval reference reactualized by Yankélévich, we can say that here it is a matter of a *quod,* in the sense of difference between *quodity* and *quidity*. We could also say that it is a question of the difference between existence and essence, of something that there is, but the essence of which one cannot define in the Other.

One can say that it is—that is, *quodity*—but one cannot say what it is. There we have a kind of paradox of the *quod:* something exists but without *quid*. In this way no one can describe the bomb I was speaking about earlier, except the person who would encounter it, but then, he would not live long! This *quod* without *quid* is a "being without essence" (this expression is found once or twice in Lacan).

7. $\dfrac{A}{a}$, $\dfrac{i(a)}{a}$

$\dfrac{A}{a}$ is constructed on the model of another formula of Lacan, $\dfrac{i(a)}{a}$, which means that in reality, the image of the other clothes or covers the real of the object. But this can also be said of capital A. $\dfrac{A}{a}$ is a formula that implies the devalorization of the Other. It indicates that the Other does not exist, that it has no other status than that of illusion. For this reason, Lacan was able to characterize the end of an analysis as "cynical." Cynicism means here the end of the illusion of the Other. And sometimes, this fall allows a new access to *jouissance,* to a *jouissance* that Lacan terms perverse because it does not involve the relation to the Other. Sometimes, in fact, this is what someone gains at the end of an analysis—which is then nothing more that the naiveté of this cynicism.

Cynicism as such is indeed a form of naiveté, because it consists in thinking that the fact that the Other does not exist means that it does not function. However, it is naive to deduce from the fact that the Other does not exist that we can erase its universal function and that only *jouissance* is real. Thus Lacan could say that psychoanalysis made scoundrels stupid.[g] They become so because they think, after an analysis, that the values of the Other do not function.

Due to lack of time, we won't develop here the analyst's position between cynicism and sublimation. Let us only specify that sublimation can be written $\frac{a}{A}$. This does not mean that the analyst is only a semblance of the object—which would imply that the ultimate truth of the object *a* is that it is real. The apparatus of analytic discourse involves something more difficult: the object *a* is a semblance as such. In the expression "semblance of the object" that we often use, we find the naive belief that the object *a* is real. However, the object *a* as such, as I must emphasize, is a semblance. And the A that is below the bar can function perfectly well as a supposition. The fact that it does not exist, as we have seen, does not at all prevent it from functioning as such.

8. $a \diamondsuit \Phi$

We are going to introduce here a case that was presented in Barcelona [3] and in which we can see a way to refer to the guarantee in order to try to make sure of the absolute risk.[h] The case concerns a woman who gets married, then goes to a lawyer to establish a deed stipulating that she will give up all her rights the day her husband ceases to desire her. This case seems to me paradigmatic for explaining the antinomy between these two terms, since it concerns the very inversion of marriage, marriage being precisely what can permit one to insure oneself against the cause of desire. Marriage implies that the cause of desire is inscribed in the signifier, whereas this woman goes to her lawyer to inscribe in the law the risk of desire.

9. $\dfrac{A}{-\varphi}$

This case concerns what I call, in Lacan, the formula of the second paternal metaphor. It corresponds point by point to the formula of the Name-of-the-Father (NF $\dfrac{\text{other}}{\text{phallus}}$), which we must absolutely not forget, but in the clinic itself we must refer to the second formula, which poses the signification of the phallus as minus phi ($-\varphi$) and which forces us to operate with the inexistence and the inconsistency of the Other, and not with the function of its consistency. This seems to me to have important consequences for analytic practice.

10. The Object *a*

The real, when it concerns the object *a*, is thus a semblance. It is so because it is a lie. Where does the object *a* come from in Lacan? It comes from the partial object of Karl Abraham, that is, from a corporeal consistency. The interesting thing is to see that Lacan transforms this corporeal consistency into a logical consistency. It is a fact, and a significant one: Lacan reduces the object *a*, which is not a signifier, to a logical consistency. This is why we can read out in full, in *Book XX* of his *Seminar*, that the object *a* introduces a semblance of being. Note that he does not say that there is an opposition between semblance and real; quite the opposite. But it is not enough to develop the logical consistency of the Other; it is also necessary to articulate it with the logical consistency of the object *a*. It is only from there that one can understand that the real can be situated only in relation to the deadlocks of logic. Lacan introduces this use of the category of the real in "L'étourdit."[4] If there were an ontic in psychoanalysis, it would be the ontic of the object *a*. But this is precisely not the road taken by Lacan. The one he took is the road of logical consistency. It is only in this way that we can conceive of the analyst as the object *a*. The analyst is not only a corporeal consistency. He is so also, obviously, as presence, but his value comes especially from logic. And this does not allow sitting quietly between the signifier and the object, but requires on the contrary seeing in what sense the object *a* is a logical consistency. To speak in this way is perhaps equivalent to think counter to what we said previously, but you know now that thinking counter to oneself is also the lesson of Lacan.

I will add as a final note that this festival of mathemes that I have given here rests on the in-depth work that is done in my class in a looser, more entertaining way, where I make it more palatable by using stories. But these stories are not, for all that, more valuable than the in-depth work of which the present text is the result.

—Text established by Elisabeth Doisneau,
translated by Françoise Massardier-Kenney

Notes

This exposition is a condensed version of the course on "Extimacy" that Jacques-Alain Miller gave during the 1985–86 academic year in the department of psychoanalysis at the University of Paris VIII. It was delivered in Spanish for the Sixth International Convention of the *Champ Freudien,* which took place in February 1986.

1. "Of a Question Preliminary to Any Possible Treatment of Psychosis," in *Ecrits: A Selection,* translated by Alan Sheridan (New York: Norton, 1977), 179–225.
2. The class of February 19, 1986, was interrupted by a bomb scare and was rescheduled the same evening in another location.
3. Published subsequently in *Ornicar?* 43 (1987–88): 107.
4. *Scilicet* 4 (1983): 5.

Translator's Notes

a. Although the established translation of *"intimité"* in Lacan is "intimacy," this translation does not do justice to the full semantic value of the term. In French, *"intimité"* means "intimacy" but also the deepest, innermost part, as in the *"intimité"* of one's being, one's thoughts. Perhaps a more satisfying translation would be "intimateness."
b. Or a medieval anthology.
c. In English in the French text.
d. Very conservative dictionary.
e. In French, *"le prochain,"* that is, the one who is close.
f. *"Plus-de-jouir"* indicates a "more than," but the structure *"plus de"* + infinitive reminds one of the Marxist notion of "surplus value." *"Plus-de-*

jouir" would thus be the surplus value, or surplus *jouissance*, in the economy of pleasure.

g. In French, "*rend les canailles bêtes*." Here Lacan is performing a linguistic dance: "*canaille*" means "scoundrel," but the word comes from the Greek and Latin for "dog," as does the word "cynicism." Moreover, "*bête*" means "beast, animal" as well as "stupid."

h. Here the pun revolves around the dual use of the verb "*s'assurer*." "*S'assurer de*" means "to make sure of," whereas "*s'assurer contre*" means "to get insured against." By using the term "*garantie*" (guarantee, warranty) next to "*s'assurer*," Miller insures that we will combine the two uses of the term.

4. Otherness of the Body

Serge André

The debate Lacan pursues with Freud throughout the seminar *Encore* offers a way out of the impasse over the problematic of femininity that Freud ran into by reducing it to the impossible satisfaction of penis envy. By basing the feminine position on a division that is more radical than castration, since castration forms one of its two branches, Lacan succeeds in overcoming the stumbling block that castration represented at termination in the Freudian doctrine. For Lacan, castration is no longer the obstacle that a woman has to confront. On the contrary, castration becomes a path that itself indicates its beyond. To grasp this articulation, we must now direct our attention to chapter 5 of the seminar *Encore*, where Lacan holds a discussion not only with Freud but also with Aristotle.

This lesson opens with a sentence that straightaway places the debate in the context of *jouissance,* and of *jouissance* of a being defined as speaking—Lacan will sometimes call it *parlêtre*—who, by the very fact of this *jouissance,* is said to *have* a body: "All the needs of the speaking being are contaminated by the fact of being implicated in another satisfaction . . . which they can be missing."[1] This other satisfaction is that which is supported by language; it is a satisfaction not of the need of the organism, but of speech, of what is said and of what is not said. We have already noted that the need to be fed, for example, is for man totally subverted by the *jouissance* of eating some signifier: the statement on the menu alone makes us desire and opens our appetite beyond appetence. This other satisfaction is born when the object of need is transmuted into object cause of desire: the maternal breast, filled with milk, becomes the void around which the mouth starts to call. This incidence is manifest in sexuality. Certain hysteric women, for example, tolerate sexual relations only with those who declare their love to them. Thus, they testify that sexuality is something other than a need to have an orgasm and that it only acquires its human specificity beyond need.

Lacan does not hesitate to submit this other satisfaction to Aristotle and to his *Ethics*, which was already emphasized in the first lesson of *Encore*. If we can be lacking, that is to say be at fault, with respect to this other satisfaction, it is appropriate to clarify that the latter reaches its full importance only in the absence of another *jouissance* that itself does not depend on speech. Lacan thus summarizes in a few words the approach in the *Nicomachean Ethics*. If this work is attempting to determine what *jouissance* is all about and what should be the behavior of the man of means toward it, it nevertheless leaves us in the dark as to how Aristotle, in writing his text, himself takes up a certain position regarding *jouissance*. What was he enjoying and what did he abstain from enjoying in writing the *Nicomachean Ethics?* In seeking, page after page, to define *jouissance* of being, Aristotle slides into another satisfaction: speaking of *jouissance* is inevitably to displace *jouissance* into speech; it is to indulge in a *jouissance* that consists in the very articulation of signifiers.

This example allows us to identify a stratification at three levels: satisfaction of needs, *jouissance* of speech, and *jouissance* of being.

From one level to the other, a certain failure is entailed. The satisfaction of needs fails with respect to *jouissance* of speech, which itself fails relative to *jouissance* of being. This failure is inescapable: it is inherent in speech, in the mechanisms of the signifier, where the signified is always failing relative to the referent. The *jouissance* of speech—which is our only tool for approaching reality—is thus affected by a central vice: it is an obstacle to the existence of the sexual relation. *Jouissance* of speech, in other words, includes the failure of another *jouissance*. This is what Lacan clarifies when he says, "The universe is where, from saying, everything succeeds," adding immediately, "succeeds at making the sexual relation fail, in a male manner."[2] Thus the *jouissance* that Aristotle experiences in articulating the signifier in the discourse of the *Nicomachean Ethics* constitutes the very cause of his inability to grasp the *jouissance* of being by these same signifiers.

The division that is introduced here lies at the heart of our interrogation of femininity. Lacan in fact specifies that there are two ways of making the sexual relation fail: a male manner, and another manner that is elaborated from the not-all (and not from the universe, or the all) and that he will explore in questioning the relation of woman to God.

The male manner of failing the sexual relation, thus of falling short of the *jouissance* of the Other or of the body as such, comes from the fact that the exercise of speech that the male enjoys can produce, as sexual partner, only a phallicized object, the object *a*—and not a sexed Other, nonexistent at the level of the signifier. "The failure is the object," notes Lacan.[3] One might as well say that the phallic function Φx is confused, on the masculine side, with the function of the fantasm. This is why on this side the phallic *jouissance* is at the same time that which is a must (it is an imperative signifier), and that which is not (it is a failure regarding another *jouissance*). The register of "must" being confused with that of "failing" [*falloir* and *faillir* are almost homonyms], phallic *jouissance* thus ultimately renders woman ungraspable for man. However, as we noted in the previous chapter, this Other *jouissance*, which does not depend on the function of speech, is only a pure supposition: there is no other one, says Lacan. Consequently, on the male side, the relation between these two registers is organized as follows: it is false [*faux*] that there exists another *jouissance;* therefore, in the absence of [*faute de*] this other, the phallic *jouissance* must [*il faut;* the three words in brackets are homonyms] exist—this "must" taking the tone of a superego command.

That Lacan founds this phallic *jouissance* in the *jouissance* of speech indicates that sexual *jouissance* is not as easy to define as one might think. In fact it is systematically unrecognized, and notably in the sexual act. Lacan even goes so far as to suggest that the sexual act is only a misunderstanding with respect to *jouissance!* This constitutes, let us agree, an extreme point of view in this sexological century:

It is the speaking body insofar as it can only succeed in reproducing due to a misunderstanding of its *jouissance.* That is to say, that the speaking body only reproduces owing to a failure of what it wants to say, since what it wants to say—that is to say, its sense, as one says in French—is in effect its *jouissance.* And it is in failing its *jouissance* that the speaking body reproduces—that is to say, in fucking. It is precisely this that it does not want to do, after all. The proof is that when left alone, the speaking body sublimates all the time prolifically.[4]

Phallic *jouissance* should not be confused with what happens in the lovers' bed—in any case it cannot be restricted to it. One of the fundamental revelations of the analytic experience consists in this recentering of the *jouissance* called sexual: its space is less the *bed [lit]* than the *said [dit].* This is the reason why *jouissance* is repressed and unrecognized by the subject: *jouissance* does not even fulfill the requirement that the subject properly meet its partner in bed! Quite the contrary, the subject is the principle of failure of the bed: "Implying what I just said, repression is only produced to attest in all the statements, in the least of the statements, that *jouissance* is not suited—*non decet*—to the sexual relation. Because of the fact that it, the so-called *jouissance,* speaks, it, the sexual relation is not."[5]

A woman is no less dissatisfied with this absence of sexual relation than a man. But on the feminine side, something other than the object of the fantasm comes to make up for this lack. What takes the place of what Lacan writes as S(A) in his sexuation table? It is God, he suggests. Still, one has to understand what Lacan means by this term, which is certainly not reducible to the God of Christian faith. Here, "God" designates the Other, unsignifiable as such by speech, and concerns what Lacan calls *jouissance* of the Other. For the Other in question in this *jouissance* is not the Other of speech—which would be one way to situate phallic *jouissance*—but the Other insofar as it would have—in the conditional—*real* consistency beyond its dimension of language. The feminine *jouissance*—or at least that supposed for women—is thus linked to another side of the Other, to the Other that is nonexistent at the level of the signifier, to the sexed Other. Thus, Lacan proposes a real reversal in identifying God with this face of the Other as the sexed Other:

For me, it appears evident that the Other, suggested at the time of "The Agency of the Letter" as the place of speech, was a way, I do not want to say to secularize, but to exorcize the good old God. . . . Maybe I am instead going to show you how he exists, this good old God. The mode in which he exists may not please everyone, and particularly not the theologians who are, as I have said for a long time, much more able than I to do without his existence. . . . This other, if there is only one alone, should have some relation with what appears of the other sex.[6]

At this place in the text, Lacan makes an allusion, not so explicit, to his seminar on *The Ethics* and to what he suggested therein about courtly love. Now, relative to this, what was the lesson of this seminar if not that the knight or the poet gave a special status to the Lady? The Lady of courtly love is elevated, beyond her function as an object, to the rank of what Lacan calls "the Thing," which is nothing but a first approximation of what he designates thereafter by S(A). In other words, courtly love elevates the Lady to the level of the absolute real Other, which in itself is inaccessible; but it should also be perceived that this Other is at the same time perfectly empty, devoid of consistency. It occupies the place of what would be the global object, not the partial object, of the object that is lacking in order for us to be able to speak of a complete sexual drive (instead of several partial drives). The construction of this figure of the absolute Lady, of Woman, is only possible if it is left empty of all specification. We recognize there the notion of "being of *signifiance*," which Lacan opposes to the being already there, prior to the signifier, in which an entire school of philosophy has believed, beginning with Aristotle. The signifier engenders the being, as the courtly poet engenders the Lady, and as in sexuation the feminine position engenders "God." By following this model of engendering, rather than of an antinomy, we will attempt to resolve the problem that interests us here, that of the relation between phallic *jouissance* and feminine *jouissance,* or between the Other as the place of speech and the Other as the Other sex. The reasoning followed by Lacan is articulated in this sequence: because there exists in the Other, as the place of speech, a signifier S(A) that says that there is some hole, this hole can be assumed to be real and can be identified as such. For example, because language includes words such as "unutterable" and "unnameable," a place is hollowed out where something unutterable or something unnameable can really exist. This is why feminine *jouissance* is conceived by Lacan as *supplementary* relative to phallic *jouissance,* that is, to *jouissance* of speech.

The complexity of this relation of an Other (as symbolic place) to the Other (as supposed real starting from the symbolic) is difficult to conceive, since it is true, otherwise, that there is no Other of the Other. Lacan does not hide this difficulty, which can only revive the fundamental questioning about the nature of the signifier. Thus he writes in conclusion, "Since all this is produced thanks to the being of *signifiance,* and since this being has no other place than the place of the Other, which I designate by big A [*Autre*], one can see the play of what goes on. And as it is also there that the function of the father is inscribed, insofar as it relates to castration, one can see that it does not make two Gods, but that it does not make only one either."[7] This whole development thus relies on the ambiguity of the status of the Other, and on the status of femininity relative to this Other. This ambiguity implies that the Other, as place of the signifier, contains a signifier, S(A), which means that it does not contain all, that all cannot be said. Does this imply that there may actually be something else? That is the question. Now, femininity would be defined precisely relative to S(A), relative to this hole in the symbolic Other, letting us think that it can be Other than what the unconscious says, Other than what can be named by the signifying chain organized in A by the law of the phallus and of castration. It is what places Woman at the level of the radical Other, of the sexed real Other, of which the unconscious can say nothing except the lack. Therefore, we do not have two Others—since only one exists—nor do we only have one—since the symbolic nonexistence of the second has as much importance as the existence of the first.

If "God" is involved, according to Lacan, it is because the ambiguous status of femininity carries the weight of an appeal to being—to a being that would find its foundation elsewhere than in the place of speech, and that would, therefore, have a different consistency than that of the being of *significance*. In short, femininity inescapably leads to the question of the Other. How to sustain this empty appeal? How can a woman content herself with an inconsistency? In fact, in her *jouissance,* or at least in that part of her *jouissance* that transcends the phallic reference, a woman can only want as a partner a being who is himself placed beyond the law of the phallus. This wish leads her to slip from her position of *not all* castrated toward the point where there would be someone who would be *not at all* castrated ($\exists x.\overline{\Phi x}$), that is to say, the place where man becomes God and consequently a woman becomes Woman. It is by way of the dream of a supreme Being who would make her all Woman that a woman tends to respond to the hole that opens in S(A), in the same way that a man, for his part, responds to the hole with the object of his fantasm.

This tension between Woman and the Other can be analyzed, we shall try to show, as that of the relation of the subject to the body. The apprehension of the body by the subject reveals, in fact, the same polarities that we have identified regarding the Other: the place where the signifier is inscribed and as such exists and is identifiable as a being of *significance,* and on the other hand, as a real sexed consistency that is unnameable as such. This disjunction between the Other of desire, which exists, and the Other of *jouissance,* which does not exist, is thus reproduced at the level of the body.

One will not be surprised if one perceives that, in the final analysis, the Other that Lacan speaks about is, in all senses of the term, fundamentally the body for the subject. Such a formula will surprise only those who thought they understood that, for Lacan, the Other would be the unconscious. But Lacan never suggested such a formulation: he said that the Other is *the place* of the unconscious, and he talked about the *place of the Other*. One should not see there a simple turn of phrase, or even gratuitous preciosities attributed to a style that one considers "bombastic." The preciosities of Lacan are no more gratuitous than those of the *Précieuses;* they are all important. What is meant by the statement that the Other is a place, and only a place? And what is this place?

This question leads us to the very foundation of the dependence of man on the signifier, and to the effects of the signifier on his being. It is clear that the fact of being caught in language implies a loss for the human being at the level of the body—as much of his body as of the body of the Other. This loss appears as a *loss of being* whose tongue carries its trace: one does not say of man that he *is* a body, but rather that he *has* a body. By the fact that he speaks, the human being is no longer a body: a disjunction is introduced between the subject and his body, the latter becoming an external entity from whom the subject feels more or less separated. The subject that the effect of language brings into existence is as such distinct from the body. What remains for him is to inhabit it or to reach that of the Other. But he can only do so by way of the signifier, since it is the signifier that, to start with, tells us that we have a body, indeed, induces in us the illusion of a primordial body, of a being-body prior to language. Language intervenes between subject and body. This intervention constitutes at the same time an access and a barrier: access to the body insofar as it is symbolized, and a barrier to the body insofar as it is real.

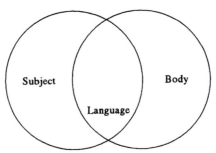

Subject   Body

Language

The corporeal being of the human animal thus becomes inaccessible, or at least beyond reach of a direct, nonmediated access. We have no idea of the "enjoyment" of the body, except indirectly through the imaginary that we project on animals or plants, or by a logical deduction from language. We only understand what a body is insofar as we cut it up and organize it with the signifier—a mechanism that the hysterical conversion pushes to its caricature. This does not mean that the body has no reality. The real body subsists, of course, but we have to face the fact: we are not really *in* it. On the contrary, more often we hit this real of the body as an external and impenetrable wall: we hit an obstacle, we get hurt, we fall, we learn about the existence of an unsuspected illness through a test, etc. Only these occasional encounters reveal that our body is also an organism foreign to the idea that we have of it.

This disjunction has its consequence. If language brings about an emptying of the being of the body, the latter becomes, due to this very fact, a place empty of substance where a series of signifying inscriptions operate. The psychoanalytic clinic thus allows us to bring to the fore a principle operating in culture at all times: the notion of erogenous zones, the process of conversion symptoms, and psychosomatic illness rejoin in their singularizations the generality of symbolic practices like circumcision, tattooing, etc. In this way, one can suggest that Lacan's Other is confounded with the body as place of inscription: on the one hand as a web of signifiers, and on the other as unsymbolizable real being, remaining out of reach of the nameable. This distinction between the two faces of the body is coherent with the dialectic of the two *jouissances*. It is not that the Other or the body does not *exist* as real, that it can be eliminated: its signifying nonexistence constitutes a mode of being that is singularly irreducible. In fact, the subject does not have a relation with the body as such that can be formulated: the latter is always a left-over beyond what can be said of the body. The relation between subject and body thus appears analogous to that of Achilles and the tortoise evoked by Lacan at the beginning of his Seminar.[8]

Thus one can see that strict parallels are established between three pairs of terms: man and woman, subject and Other, subject and body— these relations being illustrated by the paradox of Zeno. That Achilles never rejoins the tortoise, that the subject never rejoins the body, does not mean that either the tortoise or the body is not there. They are real, but are situated in a different dimension than the one in which Achilles moves: beyond the step, beyond the signifying and increasingly meticulous path by which he attempts to rejoin them. What is this dimension, other than that of the step? It is that which is evoked by the notion of real numbers, namely, the limit: "A number has a limit, and it is to this extent that it is infinite. It is clear that Achilles can only get ahead of the tortoise, he cannot rejoin it. He only rejoins it in infinity."[9] This limit is exactly what Lacan designates in the gathering of the signifiers of the Other as symbolic place, by S(A̶). S(A̶) says that there is some unnameable, some hole, some outside-language, in short, some radical otherness. This signifier thus counterbalances another key signifier that Lacan evokes several times in *Encore* and to which he devoted nearly his entire seminar of the preceding year,[10] namely, the signifier "One." These two terms, S(A̶) and One, form the two poles between which it is impossible to write a relation, the two points irremediably distinct in *signifiance* that found the impossibility of the sexual relation. Why does Achilles pursue the tortoise, why does a man relentlessly seek Woman, why does the subject drive himself crazy to rejoin his body? Because the *signifiance*, on which they depend, offers the signifier "One"—this signifier for which there is no other signified than what Lacan explains by the enigmatic affirmation, "There is some One." While S(A̶), the signifier of the unnameable, leaves being outside language, the signifier One, for its part, suggests to the subject that it could *unite* with this outside-language, that it could, or even should (the commanding effect of the master-signifier) become one with women or with the body. This bipolarity feeds an irreducible conflict inherent in the symbolic order. The speaking being can only be torn between these two vanishing points presented by language, between the signifier of division and that of unity: a part of being ineluctably escapes, and yet the subject sees itself ordered to fade into being. That being the case, what can Achilles do with his tortoise, man with woman, subject with body? Put to the challenge of division, the wish for unity can only diffract according to the equivocations on One. In the absence of becoming One with women, man can only take women one by one like Don Juan (the universe scatters into an infinity of units), or identify with, that is to say, become uniform with a woman, like the parrot in love with Picasso's jacket[11] (the union is transformed into imaginary standardization).

The heterogeneity of the two *jouissances* recovers that of the subject and the body. If a woman can incarnate the body that the subject tries in vain to unite with, it is because woman, or the body of woman, has the value of the metaphor of the Other to which there is no signifiable relation: like the Other, the woman is discompleted, not-all subjected to the signifying law.[12] Nevertheless, and let us insist again on this point, the idea of a *jouissance* of the body as such, or a specifically feminine *jouissance*, remains an *idea*, that is to say, an effect of the signifier. The body is a product of language; the *jouissance* of the body is a product of speech. Nature, in short, does not preexist culture: cells, atoms, proteins, lipids were there no doubt before language, but they only make a body due to language, that is to say, from the moment when the signified of a body as entity comes to be formulated. If the signifier interdicts access to the body as such, if it expels the body from the field of what we can enjoy as subjects, it is, nonetheless, at the origin of this body and its assumed *jouissance*. In short, the signifier creates the body while at the same time forbidding it. This contradiction follows from the conflict, internal to the symbolic order, between One and Other, between the requirement of unity and that of otherness. One should make One with the Other . . . but in the case of success, there would be no Other, and in the case of failure, it is unity that falls apart.

This principle of irreducible heterogeneity leads to the fundamental failure of the sexual act. Lacan had already given a radical definition of the latter in his seminar on "The Logic of the Fantasm": "All in all, sexuality, such as it is experienced and as it operates, can be fundamentally presented starting from what we find in the analytic experience as a 'defense' against following up on this truth that there is no Other of the Other."[13] If men and women sleep together, it is because, in fact, they want "*encore*" [again] to unite with the real Other, even if they are supposed to know that the latter is out of reach. For the horizon of *jouissance* is to enjoy the Other, the body of the Other as such. The *jouissance* called sexual opposes it; sexual *jouissance* is a defense against *jouissance* of the Other or of the body, inasmuch as the sexual comes to us from language, where it gets its phallic determination. The latter is plastered on the real body, whatever the anatomy, with more or less happiness. What is called the genital [*le sexe*], that is to say the phallus, should be identified as outside-body (since it is of signifying nature): it is a signifier inscribed on the body from outside. Thus it acts as a screen over our wish to enjoy the body of the Other as such. "One only enjoys [the body]," says Lacan, "by corporealizing it in a signifying manner."[14] The *jouissance* of the signifier that comes between the subject and the body of the Other bars the subject from it: such is the law of castration, the function Φx to which every subject is submitted. The sexual act of coitus takes on then the figure of an eternal missed act where repeatedly the absence of the sexual relation, the failure to reunite the subject with the Other to form one body, is verified. The resulting satisfaction can only be defined as the failure of the *jouissance* of the body and the return to the *jouissance* of the organ. Lacan gives to it a pretty name: *jouissance* of the idiot—"idiot" should be understood according to its Greek root—that is to say, *jouissance* that can do without the Other.

Post coitum omne animal triste, the saying goes. But it should be corrected in the sense that only the speaking being has a fundamental reason to experience some sadness. In fact, only for him alone can aiming toward the Other and failing to reach it make any sense. Language, in short, does not keep its promises: it makes us believe in the Other and by the same token takes it away from us; it evokes the horizon of a *jouissance* of the body, but makes it inaccessible to us. Sexual *jouissance* can only connote dissatisfaction. The pleasure that we get from it in passing is no doubt not negligible, but one still has to acknowledge its paradox: it is also what forbids us to really satisfy ourselves. The *jouissance* of the body of the Other remains, then, beyond the limits of the sexual act. One only enjoys this *jouissance* "mentally," says Lacan.[15]

And yet this Other, this fleeing body like the tortoise of Achilles, is really there and is very real! Let us take up our questioning another way, no longer starting from the subject, but starting from the Other itself. In this displacement of the question, the term "feminine *jouissance*" can find its only reality. Achilles, it is understood, does not rejoin his tortoise, he only approaches it by little steps in infinity. The subject can only unite with the body, can only introduce himself to it, signifier by signifier. Man, finally, is not able to enjoy the body of woman, which he cannot take all: he can only catch her one by one, and each one piece by piece, a part of the body by a part of the body. The One of unity, the One-All, is forced to dissolve in the One of difference, the singular One. But in the meantime, what is happening on the side of the tortoise? While her partner is wearing himself out to join her, what does the woman's body experience? If the subject cannot enjoy the Other, would the latter enjoy, in its turn, a *jouissance* that the former does not succeed in appropriating? Formulated in these terms, our questioning uses the equivocation that hangs over the expression "*jouissance* of the Other." Up to now, we had understood it in the sense of the objective genitive. Let us take it now in its subjective sense, that is to say, in the sense of the Other who enjoys.

Perversion offers the most convenient tool to approach this question: does that which is enjoyed enjoy also, does it enjoy a greater *jouissance?* The problematic of perversion, in its aim of corrupting the Other, does not cease to articulate and verify the supposition that true *jouissance* follows from the position of being enjoyed rather than that of enjoying. If one reads Sade again, one will see that the point of his work designates *jouissance* on the side of the victim rather than on the side of the torturer, who distinguishes himself by his strange apathy. A passage from an admirable book by Pierre Klossowski, *Sade My Neighbor,* appears to shed on the position of the pervert a light that we will use in a more general manner. He defines perversion as an attempt at *subjectification* of the Other:

The representation of having a proper body is most clearly specific to perversion: although the pervert feels the otherness of the foreign body, what he feels the best is the body of the other as being his; and that which is his in a normative and institutional fashion, as being really *foreign to himself,* that is to say, foreign to this insubordinated function which defines him. He lives *in another person beforehand* so he can manage to conceive the effect of his own violence over others; he verifies this strangeness in the reflexes of the body of others: the irruption of a foreign force inside "self." It is at the same time inside and outside.[16]

In other words, the *jouissance* of the Sadian torturer is located less in the final discharge by which "the posture breaks" than in the moment, during the torture, when the torturer seeks to put himself in the place of the victim. The scene has the function of allowing the torturer to enjoy the body of the victim, of course, but in the subjective sense of the expression rather than in the objective sense. We shall deduce that the sadistic act, from this point of view, is supported by a masochistic fantasm.

This subjectification of the Other appears still more obvious in the masochistic scenario. The man who lets himself be humiliated, insulted, whipped by his associate seeks in reality to take the place of the woman.

He only offers himself as the object of a staging typical of the masculine fantasm to experience what would subsist of a *jouissance* not mastered by this fantasm. The question that the masochist puts to the test through his practice is that of knowing what is experienced by the body that the other enjoys through whiplashes or signifiers: does this body enjoy as well? and does it enjoy beyond what is provided by the instrument that marks him? Yes, answers the masochist. But this *jouissance* that he attests to is certainly not transmittable to his female partner, who occupies the usual position devolved to the man, that is to say, the position of Achilles vis-à-vis the tortoise. The *jouissance* of the Other, if it is sustained from a *subjective* point of view, thus remains impossible from an objective point of view: the sexual nonrelation is thus verified.

It may appear paradoxical that we approach the field of feminine *jouissance* by way of masculine perversion. This detour is, however, imposed on us by the fact that of this *jouissance* of the body—in the subjective sense of the genitive—women tell us nothing, as Lacan does not cease to insist on, with undisguised pique. In the absence of revelations coming from the mouths of women themselves, we have no other choice than to turn to the discourse of perverts, who propose a sort of mimetic caricature of feminine *jouissance*. Moreover, we shall note that the first time that Lacan approaches this question of the *jouissance* of the body, he situates it by using the *jouissance* of the slave as a tool.[17] He suggests elsewhere, in *Television*, this statement of principle: "If Man [*L'homme*] wants Woman [*La femme*], he cannot reach her without finding himself run aground on the field of perversion."[18] Even if Man [*L'homme*] reaches Woman [*La femme*], this reaching thus remains a failure since it is limited to a simple permutation of positions. That the masochist plays the Other, or the Woman, does not for all that institute the sexual relation.[19]

This similarity between the aim of the perverse position—especially that of the masochist—and the subjective feminine position in *jouissance* clarifies the misunderstanding of post-Freudian psychoanalysis around the notion of a *specifically feminine masochism*. As if women particularly like to suffer and be humiliated! This idea, commonly accepted by a good number of psychoanalysts, cannot in any case be retained as a concept of Freud himself. The latter cites "feminine masochism" as one of three forms of masochism, but he does it within a reasoning that should be restored. Thus, masochism is presented, according to Freud, "as a mode of sexual stimulation, as an expression of the being of woman, and as a norm of behavior within existence (behavior). As a function of this, one can distinguish between an *erogenous* masochism, a *feminine* masochism, and a *moral* masochism."[20] But it should be noted that, as in "A Child Is Being Beaten," it is the analysis of the pervert's fantasm that Freud is referring to. It is in the perverse scenario of the masochist that he identifies an "expression of the being of woman," but he does not find an expression of the being of the masochist in the behavior of woman. The subjective position of the masochist in his fantasm is indeed a "characteristic position of femininity," says Freud, the reason for which he is said to have named this form of masochism "feminine masochism." Thus, in Freud's mind, it is not a question of insisting that women find pleasure in pain—an idea whose development can be found in the writings of Helene Deutsch or Jeanne Lampl de Groot—but rather of pinpointing in what way the masochistic man manifests something on the order of a feminine position: it is his position as subject that is feminine, and not the intermix of pain and pleasure. The sense of the expression "feminine masochism" is thus not that woman is masochistic, but really that the masochist is woman or tries hard to be one.

From this reordering, what distinction should be made between the two forms of cleavage that are implied by the perverse position and the feminine position? In both cases, the subject sees itself divided between two sides: one where castration is recognized and subjectified, the other where it is neither recognized nor subjectified. In what does the nonrecognition (the denial) of castration by the pervert differ from a woman's nonsubjectification (the not-all)? This question is equivalent to asking what *logical* distinction separates the two parts of the Lacanian table of sexuation. This table shows us indeed that on one side a cleavage is made between subjection to castration ($\forall x.\overline{\Phi x}$) and the negation of castration ($\exists x.\overline{\Phi x}$), while on the other side, the cleavage operates between the affirmation of a partial nonsubjection ($\overline{\forall x.\Phi x}$) and the negation of the negation of castration ($\overline{\exists x.\overline{\Phi x}}$). The masochistic position, whatever it may have in common with the feminine position regarding its aim, thus remains distinct from it: it is only a caricature of it. This difference becomes more apparent if we note that the pervert himself believes in the Other, in the subjective *jouissance* of the Other, while a woman does not have to believe it—she simply finds herself in the place where the question of the Other is formulated. For the masochist, the bar is never really inscribed on the Other and must, consequently, replay incessantly the scenario in which the Other receives this mark from his partner, while what woman attests to is actually the irremovable character of this bar—that is to say, the *impossible subjectification of the body as Other.* The pervert appears able to slide into the skin of this Other body like a hand into a glove; women themselves repeatedly say that this body does not fit them like a glove, that it is Other to them as well, and that the *jouissance* that can be produced here is foreign to them and is not subjectifiable. Hence, the anxiety of depersonalization—or, to use the term that appears pertinent here, of *desubjectification*—that invades a woman, one does not know why, when she happens to experience this *jouissance.* It is because, as *subject,* she can only say and subjectify her relation to Φ, and not to the body as such.

The mystical discourse of a Saint Teresa of Avila, when she describes herself being "carried away," "delighted," taken up in an irresistible "abduction," is no doubt no less caricatural than the masochistic scenario. Pushed to this point of desubjectification, a woman has no other point of reference than to address herself to God, to the supreme Being who is located beyond Φx. This appeal to God—which in the case of Teresa of Avila gets a response—allows us to grasp this formula of *Television,* which matches the one according to which "*Man* cannot reach *Woman* without finding himself run aground on the field of perversion": "A woman only encounters Man [L'*homme*] in psychosis." Applied to Teresa of Avila, this statement clarifies the function that religion has played for her: the function of a symptom that allows, with a certain success, containing a psychosis of which she has all the signs. But we must here take up again in its entirety the passage in *Television* where this formula is introduced:

A woman only encounters Man [L'*homme*] in psychosis. Let's state the axiom, not that Man [L'*homme*] doesn't ex-sist, which is the case for Woman [La *femme*], but that a woman forbids Him for herself, not because He would be the Other, but because "there is no Other of the Other," as I put it. Hence the universal of what women desire is sheer madness: all women are mad, they say. That's precisely why they are not-all, that is to say not-at-all-mad-about-the-whole [*folles-du-tout*]; accommodating rather: to the point where there is no limit to the concessions made by any woman for *a* man: of her body, her soul, her possessions.[21]

To the appeal that arises in S(A̶)—that is the appeal to a partner for the *jouissance* of the body—a woman, in general, abstains from answering. Except in the case of psychosis, a woman does not meet God, nor the superman: she interdicts it to herself, says Lacan; she renounces the existence of an Other of the Other that she herself incarnates.

This function of prohibition laid upon Man had already been noted by Freud as a key element of the female amorous life.[22] If women thus renounce Man, with a capital M, it is to preserve, all in all, their position of subject, in order not to slide on the slope of desubjectification (which Freud points to as sexual *subjection*).[23] They appear willing to do anything so that their man remains *a* man, and not Man [L'*homme*]. This leads them, at the end, to give their support to the male fantasm and to marry the phallic domination. Thus the rest of the text of *Television:* "She is party to the perversion which I take to be Man's [L'*homme*]. Which leads her into the familiar masquerade that is not just the lie of which some ingrates, themselves clinging to the role of Man [L'*homme*], accuse her."[24]

What is the reach of this reversal of the feminine position? It means that if sexual *jouissance* contributes to the failure of the *jouissance* of the body of the Other, women are well placed to know that it would be worse if it did not fail. Sexual *jouissance,* since it is first of all the *jouissance* of the signifier, implies no doubt a painful disjunction between the subject and the body, but the subject at least finds a place here that the *jouissance* of the body could abolish. It is normal that a woman wants to preserve her division and that correlatively she longs for the castration of man, since it is the condition of her subjectivity as woman. In so doing, she engages in masquerade, acts as the Other who does not exist, and allows man to misunderstand the object of her fantasm. Thus "acting as the Other" would be the best definition of the feminine position, just as "acting as Man" specifies the hysterical position. Finally, we expect of a woman to collaborate so there would be no sexual relation, except in the seeming, since she knows, herself, that if men were not castrated and women not divided, if the sexual relation could be tied, it would be the subjective catastrophe.

—Translated by Aida Der Hovanessian

Notes

1. Jacques Lacan, *Le séminaire de Jacques Lacan, Livre XX: Encore, 1972–1973*, text established by Jacques-Alain Miller (Paris: Seuil, 1975), 49.
2. Ibid., 53.
3. Ibid., 55.
4. Ibid., 109.
5. Ibid., 57.
6. Ibid., 65.
7. Ibid., 71.
8. Ibid., 13.
9. Ibid., 13.
10. Jacques Lacan, " . . . *Ou pire*," unpublished seminar, 1972.
11. See *Encore*, 12.
12. It will be noted that this thesis is already emerging between the lines of the seminar on "The Purloined Letter," a text much earlier than *Encore*. See Jacques Lacan, *Ecrits* (Paris: Seuil, 1966), 11–61.
13. Jacques Lacan, *The Logic of the Fantasm*, unpublished seminar, 1966–67.
14. *Encore*, 26.
15. " . . . *Ou pire*."
16. P. Klossowski, *Sade mon prochain* (Paris: Seuil, 1967), 47.
17. *Logic of the Fantasm*.
18. Jacques Lacan, "Television," *October* 40 (1987): 41–42.
19. An illustration of this impasse of the perverse position can be found in Philippe Sollers's book *Femmes*, where the hero, believing that by acting like a woman he could pass over to the side of the Other sex, is seen to be constantly led back to the *jouissance* of the idiot. There remains to him the path of decreeing that the Other is death, and that the rest is only imposture, or else of believing in God: a way of retorting to the women that the truth about femininity is not less deceiving than the belief in God.
20. Sigmund Freud, "The Economic Problem of Masochism," *S.E.*, vol. 19, translated by James Strachey (London: Hogarth, 1961), 159–70.
21. "Television," 44.
22. See Sigmund Freud, "On the Universal Tendency to Debasement in the Sphere of Love," *S.E.*, vol. 11, translated by James Strachey (London: Hogarth, 1957), 179–90. See especially 186–87.
23. Literature gives us an example of a woman who doesn't renounce it and as a result becomes monstrously insane: Henreich von Kleist's Penthesilea. See Henreich von Kleist, *Penthesilea* (Leipzig: Poeschel & Trepte, 1927).
24. "Television," 44.

Part II

Discourse Structures and Subject Structures

5. On the Psychological and Social Functions of Language: Lacan's Theory of the Four Discourses

Mark Bracher

The Psychological and Social Significance of Discourse

"What I'm trying to articulate," Lacan says in his seminar on *L'envers de la psychanalyse*, "is that what dominates [society] is the practice of language" (239).* During the course of that year (1969–70), Lacan formulated his schemata of the four discourses—those of the university, the master, the hysteric, and the analyst—as an attempt to identify and analyze the crucial factors through which language exercises both formative and transformative power in human affairs. More precisely, his schemata of the four discourses offer the means, respectively, of understanding four key social phenomena: educating, governing, protesting, and revolutionizing.

Discourse, Lacan emphasizes, is "a necessary structure" that "subsists in certain fundamental relations" (11) and thus conditions every speech act (216) and the rest of our behavior and actions as well (11). These "fundamental relations" are of several different orders: intrasubjective or psychological relations, intersubjective or social relations, and relations with the nonhuman world. Discourse, according to Lacan, plays formative and transformative roles in each of these orders.

The constitutive role played by discourse in our relation to the external world is perhaps most clearly visible in the realm of science, which, Lacan says, is primarily an effect of discourse. Although we may normally think of science as the product of a progressively more intimate understanding of the world, Lacan points out that science as we know it greatly surpasses anything that could result from just an effective

---

* Page references are to Jacques Lacan, *Le seminaire, livre XVII: L'envers de la psychanalyse*, text established by Jacques-Alain Miller (Paris: Seuil, 1991).

107

understanding *[connaissance]* of things. Science involves not a better understanding of the world but rather the construction of realities that we previously had no awareness of, since they "didn't exist in any manner at the level of our perception" (184). What science constructs is not just a new model of the world, but a world in which there are new phenomena. And this constructed world occurs solely through the play of a logical truth, a strict combinatory (185): the system of signifiers that constitutes scientific knowledge (187). To grasp the validity and the significance of this effect of discourse, we have only to consider the results of nuclear physics (see 120).

Discourse is similarly constitutive of the social order, as can be seen, for instance, from the effects of law (17). But the reason discourse exercises force in the social order is that, as Marxism demonstrated, it is "linked to the interests of the subject" (105). Thus the real force of discourse in the social as well as the psychological order derives from the fact that "it is on discourse that every determination of the subject depends" (178), including thought, affect, enjoyment, meaning, and even one's identity and sense of being. Meaning, which is itself a function of the signifier, has custody of being in general (63–64)—that is, it determines what is and has being, by defining what it means to be. Specifically, it defines human identity (180)—what it means to be human—including sexual identity—what it means to be a man or a woman (62). Even affect is a function of discourse: it is produced by "the capture of the speaking being in a discourse insofar as this discourse determines [the speaking being] as object" (176)—in the first instance, as object of the *jouissance* of the Other (parents and society in general). As for *jouissance*, discourse originates there, rouses it anew, and aims to produce it (80). That is, the earliest intersubjective relations (e.g., between mother and infant) take shape within a context of the enjoyment of the Other—a discourse without speech. Linguistic discourse—discourse of speech—is at once an efflorescence or exfoliation of this *jouissance* of the Other, and an attempt to recover and repeat it. Since discourse figures fundamentally in all these phenomena, it is only logical that changes in discourse can produce changes in these psychological and social realities. The purpose of Lacan's schemata of the four discourses is to show what sorts of changes are possible and how they might be brought about.

The Four Positions

In his schemata of the four discourses, Lacan demonstrates how differently structured discourses mobilize, order, repress, and produce four key psychological factors—knowledge/belief, values/ideals, self-division/alienation, and *jouissance*/enjoyment—in ways that produce the four fundamental social effects of educating/indoctrinating, governing/brainwashing, desiring/protesting, and analyzing/revolutionizing. The differing effects produced by these discourses result from the differing roles or positions occupied by the four psychological functions. These positions are arranged in the following way:

$$\frac{\text{Agent}}{\text{Truth}} \rightarrow \frac{\text{Other}}{\text{Production}}$$

The left-hand positions are occupied by the factors active in the subject speaking or sending a message, and the right-hand positions are occupied by the factors that the subject receiving the message is summoned to assume. The top position on each side represents the overt or manifest factor, the bottom position the covert, latent, implicit, or repressed factor—the factor that acts or occurs beneath the surface. More specifically, the top left position is the place of agency or dominance; it is occupied by the factor in a discourse that is most active and obvious. The bottom left position is the place of (hidden) truth, the factor that underlies, supports, and gives rise to the dominant factor, or constitutes the condition of its possibility, but is repressed by it.

On the right, the side of the receiver, the top position is designated as that of the other, which is occupied by the factor called into action by the dominant factor in the message. The activation of this factor is a prerequisite for receiving and understanding a given message or discourse. For example, if systematic knowledge is the dominant element of a discourse (occupying the top left position), receivers, in order really to receive (i.e., understand) this discourse, must (for a moment, at least) be receptive to a preconstituted knowledge, which means emptying themselves of any knowledge that might interfere with the knowledge in the discourse and becoming an amorphous, nonarticulated substance, *a,* to be articulated by the discourse. What is produced as a result of their allowing themselves to be thus interpellated by the dominant factor of a discourse is represented by the position of production, the bottom right.

The Four Factors

Knowledge (S₂)

The four crucial factors in discourse include the system of knowledge (S_2), the master signifier(s) (S_1), the alienated/divided subject ($), and the *plus-de-jouir (a)*. Knowledge, S_2, is the diacritical, synchronic, systematic aspect of language. Although knowledge has two aspects—that of the articulated systematic apparatus and that of the more intuitive *savoir-faire* (21)—all knowledge is based on a signifying articulation, even if it can at first be approached only as *savoir-faire* (178). Even intuitive knowledge is articulated, that is, is constituted by a system of differentiated elements; it is "something that links, in a reasoned relation, one signifier, S_1, to another signifier, S_2" (32).

There are different types of knowledge, and they serve different functions in the various discourses (38). These functions are crucial in the constitution of the subject. In the first place, knowledge is necessary in establishing identity for the subject. When knowledge of any type articulates itself within a subject, the subject itself is caught up in the signifying apparatus in a position that is in certain ways unique, not common to all subjects. It is in the linking of one signifier to another (always in a somewhat singular way), Lacan says, "precisely insofar as [this linking] does not know itself, that resides the seat of what knows itself—of that which tranquilly articulates itself as little master, as ego, as that which knows a bit about it" (32). These invisible links, that is, make up the network of the subject's pleasure and pain, likes and dislikes, allies and enemies, etc., and thus constitute the subject's sense of itself. Knowledge thus also determines the nature of the enjoyment—*jouissance*—that the subject is able to obtain. This is the case because even the most elementary pleasures of the body are situated within a knowledge, that is, an articulation of signifiers, a network of relationships (associations and oppositions) with other sensations, perceptions, and affective states.

But there are conflicts among different systems (or subsystems) of knowledge, which sometimes cause the system of the ego to misfire, thus producing parapraxias in which the unconscious reveals itself (32). And the unconscious is nothing other than "knowledge that speaks all by itself" (80), independently of, and at times in conflict with, the ego.

Another way of putting this is to say that the unconscious is "a perfectly articulated knowledge for which no subject is properly responsible and which, when a subject happens to encounter it," throws the subject off course, acting with the subject's body against the subject's conscious will. One undergoes psychoanalysis in order to discover this knowledge that is the unconscious—that is, "in order to know what [one] doesn't know, all in knowing it" (130).

Master Signifiers (S₁)

The force then—psychological and social—of the articulated systems of knowledge derives from the systems' positioning the subject at certain points within them and thus establishing a certain "identity" for the subject. These positionings entail a certain sense of identity (or ego), a certain *jouissance,* and a certain structuring of the unconscious. The most significant factor in these positionings is the imposition of the *trait unaire,* or singular characteristic. This singular characteristic is the earliest significance through which the child experiences itself—as a result of significations attributed to it by the Other (mother, father, and ultimately society at large). This constitutes the subject's primary identification, and this primary identification continues throughout the subject's existence to exercise a decisive influence on the subject's desire, thought, perception, and behavior. But the *trait unaire* established by primary identification is supplemented and extended by various second-ary identifications that serve as its avatars. It is, in fact, only through these secondary identifications that the primary identification manifests itself. And these secondary identifications, which are certain (usually collective) values or ideals, play a crucial role in discourse. They are what Lacan calls master signifiers, S_1.

A master signifier is any signifier that a subject has invested his or her identity in—any signifier that the subject has identified with (or against) and that thus constitutes a powerful positive or negative value. Master signifiers are thus the factors that give the articulated system of signifiers (S_2)—that is, knowledge, belief, language—purchase on a subject: they are what make a message meaningful, what make it have an impact rather than being like a foreign language that one can't understand.

Lacan expresses this point by saying that master signifiers are what make a discourse readable (218–19). Because of this fact, master signifiers are absolutely necessary: "There is the necessity that, in knowledge, something be produced that functions as master signifier" (218).

We can recognize master signifiers by the way both senders and receivers of a message respond to them. Senders use them as the last word, the bottom line, the term that anchors, explains, or justifies the claims or demands contained in the message. Receivers respond to master signifiers with a similar attitude: whereas other terms and the values and assumptions they bear may be challenged, master signifiers are simply accepted as having a value or validity that goes without saying.

Lacan offers several examples of master signifiers. He indicates that Freud produced a number of them that analysts can't get clear of. "It is not so much Freud that they hold on to as a certain number of signifiers: the unconscious, seduction, trauma, fantasy, the ego, the id, and so on" (150–51). Other, quite common master signifiers would include words like "God," "Satan," "sin," "heaven," and "hell" in religious discourse and terms such as "American," "freedom," "democracy," and "communism" in political discourse.

Master signifiers are significant not only for the force they exert in messages (speech) but also for the larger role they play in structuring the subject—specifically, in giving the subject a sense of identity and direction. A master signifier is such because it fills the role Lacan attributes to all signifiers more completely and forcefully than do other signifiers—namely, it represents the subject for another signifier. The master signifier thus arises from "*m'être à moi-même*," Lacan says (178), from the urge to be myself to myself—that is, to have an identity in which I can recognize myself and be encountered and recognized by others. Given this suppressing, substantializing force of the master signifier—that is, its effect of producing identity, which is by definition self-same, static, frozen, and hence in a sense lifeless—Lacan says that the best way to pin the master signifier down is to identify it with death (198). It is for this same reason—that is, the fact that it is offered and accepted as the subject's identity, meaning, or even being—that the master signifier constitutes what Lacan calls the castration of the subject. "Castration," the loss of the capacity to enjoy certain body parts or activities, is said to occur because "the subject that [the master signifier] represents is not univocal. It is doubtless represented, but it is also not represented. Something at this level remains hidden in relation with this very signifier" (101).

The Divided/Alienated Subject (\$)

The fact that something remains hidden produces the divided subject, \$, whose division is the effect of the master signifier, and which the master signifier has the function of covering over. The \$, the divided subject, is operative in all of the various ways in which we fail to identify ourselves, grasp ourselves, or coincide with ourselves. These can all be conceptualized as relations among signifiers. One manifestation is the gap between thinking and being. The "I" that I think about never coincides completely with the "I" that does the thinking; the urges and characteristics that I take to be mine never exhaust or even adequately represent the forces that constitute my being and drive my thought and action— forces, moreover, that are themselves conflictual and self-contradictory. As Lacan puts it, " 'either I do not think, or I am not.' There where I think, I don't recognize myself, I am not, it is the unconscious; there where I am, it is only too clear that I stray from myself" (118).

Another manifestation of the divided subject can be seen in defenses, which are products of the position of the subject as determined by the signifying relation, S_1 to S_2 (101). What is defended against, that is, is being attached to or implicated in signifiers that are incompatible with the signifiers that one has identified with and that constitute the verbal core of the ego. The subject is the arena within which, or the ground upon which, these incompatible signifiers, associations, or systems can coexist and, on occasion, do battle.

The subject can thus be deduced from the relation between S_1, the master signifier that represents it, and S_2, knowledge, or the system of all the other signifiers in relation to which S_1 represents the subject. The subject, that is, is what must be assumed in order to explain why certain signifiers function as master signifiers and others don't. At the origin, S_1 is to be seen as intervening in S_2, the battery of signifiers, the network of knowledge. From this intervention of S_1 in S_2, the subject is established as the *hypokeimenon* of this intervention. There is no way, Lacan says, to escape the formula that "there is something beneath this." This "something," however, is not any delimitable, identifiable *thing* at all—"it is simply an underneath, a subject, a *hypokeimenon*" (53).

The Plus-de-Jouir (a)

When the divided subject, $, arises in the intervention of S_1 in S_2, another factor is produced as well: the object *a* (13), which Lacan says "designates precisely what of the effects of discourse presents itself as the most opaque and . . . misunderstood, and yet essential" (47). The object *a* is that part of the subject's being that is simultaneously left out of and produced by the identity established for the subject in the S_1-S_2 articulation. As such, the object *a* holds the key to understanding both the nature of *jouissance* and "what the incidence of the signifier in the destiny of the speaking being is all about" (57). The *a* thus figures the lack of being that causes all desire, and it underlies affect as well (154). And as the cause of desire and the ground of affect, the object *a* is what animates the psychology of the group or the masses (56).

The function of object *a* can be filled by various things—whatever, in fact, can appear to offer the possibility of stopping up the gap, filling the lack. Woman (i.e., Woman, object of male fantasy), insofar as she is desired by man, fills the role of object *a* (179), a role that can also be filled by a pet (194), by capital (207), and by other phenomena as well. Early in life the role is filled primarily by various body parts and functions—our own as well as those of other people. For the infant, the breast of the mother, as well as her voice and her gaze, come closest to filling the lack or stopping the gap (56). For the mother (and father), the baby itself may serve this function (207). In fact, Lacan says, we all begin life as the object *a* (187); that is, all our earliest experiences of ourselves (and of otherness) are determined by our being the objects of the desire of others, most notably our parents. The position we occupy in relation to the desire of our parents—at the most basic level, whether they desire that we exist or not—determines the fundamental parameters within which we experience ourselves and the world around us. We continue to fill the role of object *a* for each other throughout our lives. Students, for instance, continue to serve the role for their parents (and perhaps their teachers and society at large) insofar as they were (and are being) produced to stop a gap—for example, to be something that their progenitors were unable to be.

The Four Discourses

The Discourse of the University

Our first role in discourse is thus as the *a*. Before we learn to speak—and even before we are born—we occupy the position of the other or receiver of speech, and we do so in the form of the *a*, as the as-yet-unassimilated piece of the real that is the object of the desires of those around us, particularly our parents:

$$\frac{S_2}{S_1} \rightarrow \frac{a}{\textbf{\$}}$$

Subjected, in this position, to a dominating totalized system of knowledge/belief (S_2), we are made to produce ourselves as (alienated) subjects, \$, of this system. This means, in the first instance, that our preverbal experience of ourselves and the world, mediated as it is by the actions and demeanor of our primary caretakers, is partially determined by the system of knowledge/belief, or language, inhabited by them, and by the position they attribute to us within that system—when they speak and think of us, for example, as son or daughter, delicate or hearty, future beauty queen or athlete, etc. In the second instance, it means that when we begin to understand language and to speak it, we must fashion our sense of ourselves (our identity) out of the subject positions made available by the signifiers (i.e., categories) of the system, S_2.

This discursive structure and hence the totalizing and tyrannical effect of the S_2 are not limited, however, to our infancy. They are also present in several other realms—most notably in education and bureaucracy. Bureaucracy is perhaps the purest form of the discourse of the University; it is nothing but knowledge (34)—that is, pure impersonal system: The System, and nothing else. No provision is made for individual subjects and their desires and idiosyncracies. Individuals are to act, think, and desire only in ways that function to enact, reproduce, or extend The System. Bureaucracy thus functions to educate, in the root sense of that term: it forms particular types of subjects.

Education is of course the primary instance of the discourse of the University. Lacan emphasizes to his audience, many of whom are students, that it is through the structure of University discourse and their position within it that "many things can be explained regarding the singular phenomena that are occurring at the present time [May 13, 1970] throughout the world" (172). In the first place, the discursive position of students can explain why they were driven to protest and rebel. The student is in the position of the exploited (172), and what torments students, Lacan says, is not that the knowledge they are given isn't structured and solid, but that there is only one thing they can do: namely, weave themselves in with their teachers and thus serve as both the means of production and the surplus value (235) of The System. The surplus value that students are charged with producing is "culture," an elaboration or extension of The System. Insofar as they produce culture—by means of their theses, for example (220)—they simply nourish The System, because the function of a thesis is to add to society's knowledge—that is, to reinforce precisely the factor, S_2, by which the students are exploited and alienated. Science is a particularly obvious example.

Given the totalizing, tyrannical power of the discourse of the University, The System, it is important to know how one might oppose it. The answer, according to Lacan, does not lie in traditional revolutionary strategies, such as an alliance of workers and peasants, for as Lacan points out, this sort of alliance in the Soviet Union produced the reign of the discourse of the University (237)—that is, a society in which a totalizing, totalitarian system (S_2) was dominant. As long as students continue to speak, they remain within the (discourse of the) University (237), and they search for a new discourse of the Master. The only place that revolutionary desire can lead, Lacan says, is to a discourse of the Master (239), of which the discourse of the University is a perversion (212). "What you aspire to as revolutionaries," Lacan tells the students, "is a Master. You will have one!" (239).

One factor that makes the discourse of the University so powerful and tyrannical is the force of its master signifiers, which operate, for the most part, surreptitiously. In the field of science, for example, the major master signifier is knowledge itself. It is impossible, Lacan observes, not to obey the commandment—that is, the master signifier or ultimate value—that is at the place of truth in the discourse of science: "Continue always to know more" (120). All questioning about the value of this master signifier is simply crushed (120): that knowledge is valuable—especially scientific knowledge—goes without saying in this scientific age. Lacan, however, interrogates the ground of this master signifier and finds that it consists in an even more fundamental master signifier—that of an "I" that is identical to itself and transcendental. Thus the final, root operation that establishes the discourse of the University is the assumption of such an "I": "The myth of the ideal 'I,' of the 'I' that masters, of the 'I' by which at least something is identical to itself—i.e., the enunciator—is very precisely what the discourse of the university cannot eliminate from the place where its truth is found" (70–71). Anyone who enunciates scientific knowledge automatically assumes the position of subject of this coherent, totalized knowledge, a subject that must itself be stable, consistent, self-identical. And this assumption is neither more nor less than the assumption of the self-identical "I" as its master signifier, its ultimate value and truth (70–71).

Since the master signifier in this way dominates (surreptitiously) the discourse of the University, this discourse is in a way subservient to the discourse of the Master. The university, Lacan says, "has an extremely precise function which has a relation at each instant with the stage that one is at with the discourse of the master. . . . It is precisely because of the more and more extreme uncovering of the discourse of the master that the discourse of the university finds itself manifested" (172–73). These comments indicate that the university, insofar as master discourse of overt law and governance is suppressed, functions as an avatar of the Master discourse, promulgating master signifiers hidden beneath systematic knowledge. And this suggests that one step toward opposing the tyranny of University discourse would be to expose the master signifiers that underlie it and constitute its truth. Doing so makes overt the discourse of the Master that has been covert.

The Discourse of the Master

The discourse of the Master, Lacan says, is known by us today only in a considerably modified form (203), but it is nonetheless active and visible in the various discourses that promote mastery—that is, discourses that valorize and attempt to enact an autonomous, self-identical ego. The discourse of the Master promotes consciousness, synthesis (79), and self-equivalence (91) by instituting the dominance of master signifiers (S_1), which order knowledge (S_2) according to their own values and keep fantasy (i.e., $\$ \Diamond a$) in a subordinate and repressed position (124):

$$\frac{S_1}{\$} \quad \rightarrow \quad \frac{S_2}{a}$$

Lacan finds this basic disposition to be present in the discourses of a number of different fields and disciplines. Philosophy is a clear instance (20). As philosophers of the ordinary language school have realized for some time, philosophical works are ultimately nothing other than attempts to promote a certain way of speaking. What this school often fails to emphasize, however, is that such ways of speaking are never merely ways of speaking: they are also ways of thinking, feeling, desiring, and acting, and thus have real consequences for people's lives. Lacan's identification of philosophy as a discourse of the Master allows us to see that more specifically the basic function of philosophy is to articulate and promote certain master signifiers. Ontology, for instance, attempts to see all phenomena in terms of its central master signifier, "being," and specific ontologies establish other master signifiers, such as "permanence," "becoming," "entelechy," etc., which function as the bearers of ultimate meaning and which thus bestow meaning and value on all other signifiers. Ethics, similarly, is concerned with signifying all action in terms of the master signifiers that it establishes as either attributes or opposites of "good," the central master signifier. And epistemology views all phenomena in terms of master signifiers such as "knowledge," "truth," and "reality."

Other discourses are also characterized by the structure of the Master discourse. Teaching, for instance, begins as a discourse of mastery (79), with the imposition of the basic concepts of a discipline—master signifiers that serve to ground and explain the procedure or body of knowledge that constitutes the discipline. Lacan suggests that medical teaching, for example, sometimes consists basically of acts of reverence to terms considered sacred (25)—that is, to master signifiers.

Science, too, is in solidarity with the discourse of the Master. "At the present time," Lacan says, "our scientific discourse is on the side of the master" (174). Science, in Lacan's view, is not primarily a matter of the advance of understanding but is rather a force that constitutes and preserves the discourse of the Master. Although science claims to be devoted to understanding the real through empirical research, it effectively functions to promote the various master signifiers that dominate it. That is, rather than using its encounter with the real (in empirical research) to challenge the dominant paradigms (S_1) of knowledge (S_2), science uses this encounter to annex more and more of the real into the territory ruled by the already established master signifiers. And these master signifiers are not limited to those that structure the explanatory paradigms of the scientific disciplines themselves; they also include the master signifiers that guide the larger social and political agendas of our society. These master signifiers—for instance, "strength," "freedom," "independence," "individuality," "family," etc.—not only determine which scientific enterprises receive major funding; they also determine what issues are identified in the first place as questions to be asked or problems to be solved. And above all, the discourse of science makes no provision for fantasy and desire, or for the *jouissance* they seek.

We can also see the discourse of the Master operating in the realm of politics (99). "What I mean by that," Lacan says, "is that [the discourse of the master] encompasses everything, even what is believed to be revolution, or more exactly, what is romantically called Revolution with a capital R. The discourse of the master accomplishes its revolution, in the other sense of the turning that buckles itself" (99). This revolution, that is, is not a military or governmental phenomenon but rather a revolving of the elements of discourse into the structure of the discourse of the Master, where the master signifier is dominant and buckles the other elements of discourse so they can't move and disrupt its dominance. In the late sixties, when Lacan made this comment, almost everything was politicized—particularly in Paris—producing a totalizing, totalitarian discourse of the Master. This effect was promoted above all by those advocating revolution, for it was precisely they who annexed all aspects of life into the discourse of politics, seeing all phenomena in terms of master signifiers like "imperialism," "domination," "freedom," "oppression"—and "Revolution" itself. The elevation of "Revolution" to the rank of a master signifier, however, ironically served to promote not radical change but rather reinforcement—"buckling"—of the S_1-S_2 articulation of the discourse of the Master that underlay the tyranny of the present system (S_2).

The discourse of the Master, then, exercises an extremely powerful force in all spheres of human life, from the most intimate and subjective realms to the most common and collective. Its force is nothing less than imperialistic, and at times it can be murderous (207). The question, then, is "how to stop this little mechanism" (207). It must be possible to stop it or at least reduce its power, since primitive societies are not dominated by it to the extent we are (105). But the answer does not lie in the rhetoric of revolution; the effect of Marx's discourse, for instance, has changed nothing concerning the stability of the discourse of the Master. One telling indication of the power of the discourse of the Master even under Marxism is "the fact that exploited or not, the workers work. Work has never been so highly honored since humanity has existed. It is even excluded that one not work" (195). Marxism has succeeded not in overthrowing the imperialism of the discourse of the Master but rather in simply altering slightly the distribution of its force—by, for example, replacing a master signifier like "individual" (in capitalism) or "master" (in feudalism) with that of "worker." Hence Lacan's warning that calling for political revolution is only asking for a master (239). The reason is that any mass movement, as Freud demonstrated, is based on idealization, and thus reproduces, Lacan says, the resurgence of the discourse of the Master. That is, the idealized object or its attributes function as master signifiers around which a new (totalizing, imperialistic) system is constituted.

But if rhetoric and political movements simply repeat the discourse of the Master and its imperialism, how could it ever be possible to overturn this tyranny? The answer, according to Lacan, lies in promoting a discourse with the opposite structure—what Lacan calls the discourse of the Analyst. But before we can consider this discourse and how it can produce psychological restructuring and thereby political restructuring as well, we must first examine the structure of the discourse of the Master, and then the discourse of the Hysteric, which represents a discourse midway between that of the Master and that of the Analyst, and which is also the discursive structure of the desiring, alienated, protesting subject.

The most salient structural feature of the discourse of the Master is, as we have seen, the dominance of the master signifier, S_1. When one reads or hears such a discourse, one is forced, in order to understand the message, to accord full explanatory power and/or moral authority to the proffered master signifiers and to refer all other signifiers (objects, concepts, or issues) back to them. In doing this, the receiver of the message enacts the function of knowledge, S_2. And as a result of enacting this function, the receiver produces *a*, the *plus-de-jouir*—that is, the suppressed (i.e., beneath the bar) excess of enjoyment, no longer to be enjoyed, for which there is no place in the system of knowledge or belief (S_2) enacted by the receiver in response to the master's S_1. It is this *a*, this *plus-de-jouir*, that carries the power of resistance and revolution.

The discourse of the Master, however, restricts this *a*, the unsymbolized cause of desire, to the receiver (the slave, the one in the position of powerlessness), who has no voice (no legitimation of his own subjectivity). The speaker, or master, is oblivious to the cause of his own desire (*a*), and has even repressed his own self-division, S (124), as experienced in such subjective states as shame, anxiety, meaninglessness, and unsatisfied desire. The speaker, that is, has so successfully identified with his master signifiers that he actually believes himself to be whole, undivided, self-identical (101–2, 178). But in thus filling the function of the master—that is, in being *m'être à moi-même*—the speaker loses something (123–24): the *a*, the cause of his or her desire. There is no relation between what constitutes the truth of the master—S, the (repressed) division or deficiency in its various forms, which underlies and motivates the master's promotion of the unifying master signifier—and the cause of the master's desire. Thus the essence of the position of the master, Lacan says, is to be castrated: *jouissance* is forbidden to him (123).

The discourse of the Master is unique in this regard; it is the only one of the four discourses to exclude fantasy, which consists precisely in the taking into account by the symbolic order, or signifier, of the relation of *a*, nonsymbolized being, with the subject that is subjected to the signifier in ways discussed above. Fantasy, that is, articulates the relation of the subject to what is not captured directly by the signifiers of the articulated system. Fantasy does this not by naming the *a* directly (which is impossible) but by evoking it through image and narration, functions by which discourse can evoke what it can't name. The exclusion of this function of fantasy makes the discourse of the Master completely blind in its foundation (124): that is, its speaker is totally unaware of the reason for promulgating its master signifiers—namely, of the lack of being, or cause of desire, that the master signifier attempts to plaster over. It is only by confronting this lack in its relation to the cause of desire (*a*) that the impetus behind the S_1 can be understood and, perhaps, redirected, displaced. It is around this something that remains hidden, Lacan says, that takes place not only psychoanalytic discovery (101) but also the transformation of the social order. By interrogating the something of the subject that is left out by the master signifier, it becomes possible to reclaim that which has been suppressed and repressed and thus institute a new economy of both the psychological and the social structure. If one wants to be subversive, Lacan suggests, one might do worse than to approach "the hole from which the master signifier gushes" (218).

The Discourse of the Hysteric

We have a clear view of this divided, lacking subject in the discourse of the Hysteric, where the division, $, assumes the position of dominance:

$$\frac{\$}{a} \rightarrow \frac{S_1}{S_2}$$

This discourse takes its name from the fact that its most striking instance is hysterical neurosis, whose physical symptoms manifest in the most striking way possible the subject's refusal to embody—literally to give its body over to—the master signifiers that constitute the subject positions that society, through language, makes available to individuals (107). In hysterical neurosis this refusal of the body to follow the master signifier manifests itself in symptoms like anaesthesia, paralysis, or tics—disorders whose basis, Freud discovered, lay not in neurological dysfunction but rather in a conflict involving representations of the body. The divided subject, $, is thus a manifestation of the alienation that occurs as a result of the subject's accession to language—an alienation that is suppressed in the discourses of the Master and of the University, but which gains expression and dominance in the discourse of the Hysteric.

The hysterical structure of discourse also characterizes other instances of resistance, protest, and complaint—from the plaintive anthems of slaves to the yearning lyrics of lovesick poets to the iconoclastic rhetoric of revolutionaries. The hysterical structure is in force whenever a discourse is dominated by the speaker's symptom—that is, his or her unique mode of experiencing *jouissance,* a uniqueness that is manifested (in experiences such as shame, meaninglessness, anxiety, and desire) as a failure of the subject, $, to coincide with or be satisfied by the master signifiers offered by society and embraced as the subject's ideals.

Despite its refusal to follow the master signifier, however, the hysterical subject remains in solidarity with it (107). This solidarity manifests itself in the wish of anxiety for security and stability, the search of meaninglessness for a meaning or identity, and the urge of shame to coincide with the ideal. This is the meaning of Lacan's warning to revolutionary students that what they were really asking for—and would get—was a master.

It is this quest to which the receiver of the hysterical subject's message is summoned to respond by providing a master signifier, S_1, in the form of a secure meaning that will overcome anxiety, meaninglessness, and shame and give a sense of stable, meaningful, respectable identity. Such responses are given by counselors, therapists, and priests to distraught individuals; by advertisements and political speeches to the desiring masses; and by all sympathetic people to needy friends. And as the schema indicates, such a provision of master signifiers covertly entails or produces a system (S_2) of knowledge/belief within which the master signifiers take their bearings and assume their force, and within which the hysterical subject can thus find its stability. Despite its expression of alienation and division, then, the discourse of the Hysteric remains in thrall to master signifiers (S_1) and a system of knowledge/belief (S_2) that it has not itself embodied and produced. It is only with the discourse of the Analyst that the subject is in a position to assume its own alienation and desire and, on the basis of that assumption, separate from the given master signifiers and produce its own, new master signifiers—identity and values less antithetical to its fundamental fantasy and the desires arising from that fantasy.

The Discourse of the Analyst

It is thus the discourse of the Analyst that, according to Lacan, offers the only ultimately effective means of countering the psychological and social tyranny exercised through language. It does so because it puts receivers of its message in the position of assuming and enacting the $\$$— that is, their own alienation, anxiety, shame, desire, symptom—and of responding to this $\$$ by producing new master signifiers (S_1), ultimate values, formulations of their identity or being:

$$\frac{a}{S_2} \rightarrow \frac{\$}{S_1}$$

Such production does not constitute a radical break with tyranny and an accession to freedom, for the subject remains in thrall to a master signifier. This means that what is produced in the discourse of the

Analyst is another discourse of the Master, thus rendering the process circular rather than progressive.

There is a crucial difference, however, in this new discourse of the Master: its master signifiers are produced by the subject rather than imposed upon the subject from the outside. In this way, one "shifts gears," as Lacan puts it. The analytic discourse, that is, makes it possible to produce a master signifier that is a little less oppressive, because it is of a different style (205), a style that, we might surmise, is less absolute, exclusive, and rigid in its establishment of the subject's identity, and more open, fluid, processual—constituted, in a word, by relativity and textuality.

The discourse of the Analyst is able to promote such a response and production because it is opposed to all will of mastery (79), engaging in a continuous flight from meaning and closure, in a displacement that never ceases (171) (which does not mean, however, that the *analysand* never reaches any kind of closure). The discourse of the Analyst does this by placing in the dominant position the *a*, precisely what has been excluded from symbolization (48) and suppressed by the discourse of the Master. The analyst, that is, works first to elicit from the patient a discourse with a hysterical structure (35–36), that is, a discourse in which the alienated subject—the subject of shame, anxiety, meaningless, or desire—is revealed. This manifestation of the divided subject occurs not only in the thematic content of the patient's discourse—that is, in confessions about desire, frustration, anxiety, shame, or other symptoms—but also in the style of the patient's speech, that is, in the particular nature of the images, the syntax, the self-reference, and the other-reference employed by the patient, and also in whatever ellipses and parapraxias might occur. The analyst responds to this hysterical discourse of the patient in such a way as to illuminate and emphasize what has been left out, repressed—that is, the *a*. This response of the analyst may not involve any explicit interpretation at all; it may consist simply in a punctuation of the patient's speech produced by ending the session or uttering an exclamation at a particular point in the patient's speech. Or it may occur as the forebearance of naming—as the silent witness that the analyst bears to the patient's speech and to the transference elicited by the fact that the patient supposes the analyst to have knowledge of why the patient suffers, what the patient desires, and what will answer to this suffering and/or desire. Whatever the specific response of the analyst, it is efficacious to the extent that it represents to the patient the effect of what has been left out of discourse—that is, the *a* (48), the cause of the patient's desire (205). It is being confronted with this rejected element that produces the depth and intensity of self-division or alienation necessary for patients to want to separate themselves from some of the alienating master signifiers (which embody these patients' symbolic identifications) and produce new master signifiers/identifications that are less exclusive, restrictive, and conflictual.

The analyst's activity of interpretation—that is, of representing the *a*, cause of the patient's desire—is sustained by the analyst's implicit knowledge, S_2, in the place of truth. This knowledge, Lacan says, can be either the analyst's already acquired knowledge (38)—for example, of the Oedipus complex (113)—which functions as the basis of analytic *savior-faire,* or it may be knowledge acquired from listening to the analysand (38)—that is, specific knowledge of the analysand's particular psychic economy and of the nature of the analysand's *a*. In either case, this knowledge is very different from those found in the discourses of the University and of the Master. It is what Lacan calls a mythic knowledge. While the knowledge of Master and University discourses—or mathematical knowledge, as Lacan characterizes it—emphasizes identities as absolute and self-referential, mythic knowledge emphasizes relationships (102–4). Logical, mathematical knowledge thus forms a completely coherent but static, tautological (i.e., self-referential, self-enclosed) system, and it is precisely such a knowledge/system that, rejecting truth as dynamic, produces the *a*. Mythic knowledge, on the other hand—that is, the form of the knowledge that constitutes the truth of the discourse of the Analyst, and is repressed by the patient—is a disjoint knowledge, a form that is completely alien to the discourse of science (103–4). In the mythic knowledge of the discourse of the Analyst, that is, "the truth only shows itself in an alternation of things that are strictly opposed, which it is necessary to make turn around each other" (127). It is only the mythic form of knowledge that can avoid excluding the *a*, because it offers not absolute, clearly established, self-referential identities, but rather a system of oppositions embodied in images and fantasies that offer no unequivocal identities, meanings, or values.

It is this basis in the mythic, unconscious knowledge that allows the enactor of the discourse of the Analyst to discover and express the *a*, cause of desire, to which this knowledge bears mute witness. And this position of the analyst, Lacan indicates, can be taken up with regard not only to individual subjects but also in relation to society as a whole. Taking up such a position provides the only real chance, in Lacan's view, to produce a real revolution in relation to the discourse of the Master. The best thing to do to bring about revolution is to be not anarchists but analysts, Lacan says. Operating from the position of an analyst with regard to culture means reading the various, mutually disjoint and even contradictory discourses of a culture in order to reveal the *a*, unconscious fantasy, cause of desire, which operates from behind the facade of the master signifiers and the entire signifying apparatus. By exposing the real that the system of signifiers, and particularly the master signifiers, fail to grasp, one can interpellate subjects to an activation of their alienated condition, their nonidentity with their master signifiers, and thus create an impetus for the production of new master signifiers. What must be done, essentially, is to reveal to the subjects of a society that what they are asking for (and perhaps think they are getting) in their values, ideals, conscious desires, and identifications is not the only expression or even the most truthful embodiment of what they really want—that what they really want is not, per se, the actualization of a particular ideal, the satisfaction of a specific desire, the realization of a certain identity, or the establishment of a given value, but rather the enactment of a particular fantasy, which ultimately means occupying a particular position as object of the Other's desire and *jouissance*.

The Uses of Lacan's Schema of Discourse

The value of Lacan's theory of the four discourses should be evident. Its greatest contribution should be in the area of ideology critique or cultural criticism, for more than any other rhetorical theory, Lacan's model provides the means for explaining how a given text *moves* people. One reason it is able to surpass other approaches on this score is that its formulation of four cardinal factors of discourse—knowledge-system, master signifier, alienated subject, and remainder—unites psychic structure, the ground of motivation, with semiotic phenomena and discursive structure in a single model. This synthesis allows for an analysis of discourse that views every linguistic and discursive phenomenon in terms of the role it might play in the full range of psychological and social functions and structures that underlie human motivation on various planes—including identity, identification, ideals, values, alienation, anxiety, shame, desire, and fantasy.

A second advantage of Lacan's model is its rigorously dialogical structure, which establishes definite, determinative links between the dominant and subordinate linguistic-psychological factors of the sender of a message and the dominant and subordinate factors that a given discourse summons forth in the receiver. In prompting us to identify the dominant element in a discourse (i.e., S_2, S_1, S, or a), Lacan's model immediately tells us where to look for (1) the repressed factor in the sender of the discourse and (2) the elements that the receivers of the discourse are called upon (a) to assume or enact and (b) to produce. In short, Lacan's theory can provide the means of determining the dialogical discursive structure of any given speech act, text, or discourse, and on that basis, the means for gauging the psychological and (thereby) social-political functions it might serve for its producers, as well as the psychological and (thereby) social-political impact it might have on various types of receiving subjects. In doing this, Lacan's schema not only allows us to expose the ideological force of a discourse; it also puts us in a position to intervene more effectively either to counter or to promote that force.

The implications for the study of discourse are thus profound and wide ranging. Lacan's model offers the means for a clearer understanding, for example, of how sermons and political speeches can stir some people to a frenzy and even change radically their behavior, or, conversely, leave people unmoved. Lacan's model can guide the way to a clearer understanding of how the discourses of science (physical and social) work to reinforce a sense of identity and security or, conversely, induce a state of anxiety. It can help us understand how education works, and why it often doesn't, at least not in the intended manner. In brief, Lacan's schema of discourse puts us in a position both to understand and to alter the effects not only of obviously moving, hortatory forms of discourse, such as sermons, political speeches, and other forms of propaganda, but also the more expository (and often seemingly objective) discourses of science, history, and biography. In doing so, Lacan's schema offers us a basis for making some crucial distinctions and interventions in what still remains, for rhetoricians as well as the general populace, the largely amorphous and invisible sea of discourse in which we spend most of our days swimming blindly, carried along by massive currents of which we are ignorant.

6. Hysterical Discourse: Between the Belief in Man and the Cult of Woman

Julien Quackelbeen
with L. Billiet, J-M. de Wulf, L. Jonckheere, D. Lorré,
L. Van de Vijver, H. Van Hoorde, and P. Verhaeghe

A certain reading of Freud's beginnings allows us to observe that his innovation in the area of neurosis leaves us with many problems. He shows, vis-à-vis the question of hysteria, that a typical form of defense, repression and its return (conversion and phobia), is determinative. Furthermore, he shows that free association is the mechanism that makes it possible for this defense to be demonstrated as well as treated. Thus, diagnosis and treatment now constitute but a single path; they are indistinguishable in the practice of treatment.

However, repression is not a characteristic of the hysteric only. If this mechanism can be generalized, any distinction between hysteria and the rest falls apart. It is true that this generalization has been justified and useful for renewing psychoanalytic treatment. That the distinction between Anna O's hysteria and common hysteria does not pose a problem from a phenomenological point of view does not obviate the fact that, from a theoretical point of view, still nothing is solved. What is easily distinguished on the phenomenological level should lead to distinctions based on structural criteria.

From his early works on, Freud mentions normal repression and pathological repression, which he attempts to define clearly. In his first answer, he supposes a hereditary or individual predisposition in pathological hysteria, a predisposition that explains the exaggeratedly intense character of repression. The answer does not satisfy him for long. He looks for a new explanation in the direction of the trauma, an actual experience that reactualizes a traumatic experience from childhood. Again, this theory is abandoned with the discovery of infantile sexuality, which forces him to modify the whole theory of trauma proceeding from

129

the experience of pleasure. Freud then goes back to his first proposition: the difference is a question of intensity and can be explained by factors of constitution. He goes back, with Moebius, to the acknowledgment that every man is slightly hysterical.[1] Thus, he leaves intact the problem of differential diagnosis.

This problem returns with the teaching of Lacan, who first emphasizes the hysterical component of desire and then takes the hysterical discourse as one of the social bonds of the speaking being *[parlêtre]*. The problem of the dividing line of the pathological comes up again here; and it is not as if answers had not been provided. Some thought that a solution could be found on the descriptive level, without recognizing that such an attempt would entail importing foreign elements; an example of this is found in Zetzel, with her true good hysteric and pseudo-oedipal and pseudo-genital hysteric.[2] Others did not go beyond designating degrees of intensity, ranging from "mild hysterical reactions" to the other extreme of "hysterical psychosis," going through a series of ill-defined concepts such as "conversion reaction," "infantile personality," "hysteroid character," "hysteroid personality," and "hysterical personality."[3] A little more rigor is required of psychoanalysts, unless they are willing to perpetuate forever what Freud called in 1893 the "transforming of hysterical misery into common unhappiness."[4] Don't we need to ask the question of the dividing line between pathological hysteria and the hysteria that is common to any speaking being *[parlêtre]* in order to understand what expressions such as "hysterization of the analysand in treatment" could ever mean? We do not intend to place psychoanalytic treatment in the teleological perspective of normality, nor constitute a diagnosis prior to treatment; rather, we hope that clarifying this point could shed some light on the handling of treatment, on its finality, its end, on the crossing of the fundamental fantasy.

When listing a few possible solutions, we are tempted to start off with two mathemes—the matheme of the four discourses and that of the fantasy—because they each include, in a more general framework, a specific form for the hysteric.

The Discourse of the Hysteric

There are the four discourses. Changing the existing formulas is out of the question; and so is proposing new ones for pathological hysteria;

rather, we propose to work with those that already exist and to show how they help us understand psychoanalytic treatment.

Let us first define pathological hysteria as an attempt to undermine always the same disjunctions that are constitutive of the discourse of the hysteric:

$$\begin{array}{c} \text{Impossible} \\ \underline{\$} \;\; \rightarrow \;\; \underline{S_1} \\ a \;\; // \;\; S_2 \\ \text{Impotence} \end{array}$$

The impotence between a and S_2 is ceaselessly negated by a belief in an Other without flaw, which prevents the disjunction from fulfilling its founding function. The hysteric does <u>not</u> only confine herself to the exception that determines the rule $\exists x.\overline{\Phi x}$—to the Freudian father of *Totem and Taboo;* she also demands that every man be its embodiment. She never stops confronting every man with this norm. She makes a category of this exception. In this matter, her prescription is imperative. She believes in the hidden existence of a totalizing knowing about the truth of her object a, although she has never had the least experience of it.

An analogous attempt is observable with regard to the other disjunction, the impossible between $\$$ and S_1. Where the first disjunction, impotence, is undermined, it neither founds nor hides nor protects the second one. The impossible—that the other possesses the unifying signifier for Woman—is made possible. The hysteric madly claims this signifier. In the meantime, she becomes devoted to the cult of Woman, sometimes with other women, sometimes by acting like a man, in the hope that this signifier will someday appear.

The structure of the discourse shows the deficit of the symbolic when it is a matter of totally recovering the real. Its symbolic character, given in the metonymic $(x \rightarrow y)$ and metaphoric $(\frac{x}{y})$ play, reveals its function: to order the impossible of the social bond, the nonexistence of sexual relation and the resulting impotence of everyone vis-à-vis *jouissance.* This humility, which the discourse requires of the subject, is refused by the neurotic. He attempts to cover up the humiliation that the symbolic finally brings, by means of his imaginary terms.

Approaching the distinction between the pathological and the normal state by way of the matheme has the advantage of going beyond individual solutions without being trapped in the Freudian myth of the primordial father of *Totem and Taboo,* without limiting us with the question "What does woman want?" Moreover, it allows us to situate a set of clinical facts that we grouped as "the belief in man" and "the cult of woman" with their specific splits. One can see the easy slope that the headings of these two groups of facts contain, a slope that easily leads to imaginarization. The matheme can keep us from it; it can reduce knowing to its purely symbolic form, freed from its imaginary scales. For the analyst, the matheme represents a knowledge according to the image of the S_2 in the analytic discourse, the only discourse where the S_2 in the place of truth, has no relation to the S_1.

The problem of the social bond that is expressed in discourse revolves around impotence and the impossible, and even finds its dynamics there. This is where we situate Freud's hysterical confusion. When we progress from the universal to the particular, we run up against the impossible, the impossibility of saying something of the particular; the way from the particular to the universal leads to impotence, the impotence to generalize. All would be resolved if we possessed a unit of measurement, or that exception that outlines a delineation of a group. This is where we place hysteria as a solution that does not hold, but that encloses the neurotic: to abandon oneself to the intense cult of Woman and to unceasingly look for this nonexistent signifier are as contradictory as the belief in Man, in the Other without flaw, in the primordial father, a measure applied to every man, who is always impotent to embody this model imposed on him.

The sabotage of the two disjunctions, necessary to the dialectics of discourse, situates pathological hysteria on a chiasmus formed by these two pairs of opposition that are mutually exclusive and isolated from each other. This is the famous *Spaltung* that Freud discovered early in hysteria and that never ceased to haunt him, sometimes as specific to hysteria, sometimes as characteristic of the subject. The decommissioning of the two disjunctions constitutes the fixation on one single type of discourse. It is an attempt to put all the terms of a single type of discourse in continuity above the flaw of impotence, whereas it is precisely the characteristic of the four discourses to actualize this contact intermittently. It is a fixation on one discourse, thus defined as contrary to the dialectics that lead the subject into the rotation of the four discourses, as loss of the possibilities of permutation between the elements and the places of the discourse. The pathological choice prefers the wheel of the hysterical chiasmus to the rotation of the discourses.

Where the hysteric fixates in her pathology on a single type of discourse, the terms can occupy only one and the same place. The terms can only be filled in one and the same way: at the place of the agent there is always the $, and at the place of truth only the *a* can be found.

The social bond is hysterical where the divided subject occupies, with its discord, its *Spaltung*, the place of the agent. A question looms there, which is repeated and modulated in many different ways, a question that interpellates the Other, the master. Every action there is a being acted upon, a passage into action, a formulation through symptoms, and thereby rendered opaque. The acting, in the sense of working, falls to the master. He is called, obliged, summoned to produce the response that the hysteric won't fail to invalidate. It is up to him to work; the responsibility—response/ability—is his business.

The hysteric does not work. She even often avoids professional work. Where the obligation to work is unavoidable, she will express her fundamental aversion by an opposition, occasionally a subtle opposition: "It is not that I want to be an obstacle. . . . It's not that I am recalcitrant, or that I want to oppose your business." The first idea appearing under the negative sign brands the hysterical bond.

The hysteric who successfully comes through a difficult selection process declares herself, in contrast with her performances, "incompetent for this job, not up to tackling this task. . . . Everything is the fault of the psychologist who organized this. . . . It was not what she was looking for." She asks that her divided search be recognized; she is not looking for a job. She is quite dominated by her question, while at the same time she makes of the master the slave of the work that she leaves him.

In analysis also, we find this refusal to do the work, the analytic work: they come for the sake of their friend, for their former therapist, for the analyst, victims of the social bond of which they keep bearing the yoke, which certainly they haven't created. They haven't designed the plan of their own labyrinth. "The others don't have any problem; they are allowed to do as they please." Every master who promises improvement, or even a cure, will bear the yoke in their place. The analyst must beware and keep to his discourse, remain "abject."

This probably forms the permanence of the relation of the hysteric to the master, $\mathcal{S} \rightarrow S_1$, a permanence that we can recognize in the most diverse clinical approaches that try to decide who is hysterical by looking at the phenomena.

In the hysteric's discourse, the object a is inscribed in the place of truth, under the divided subject. This is why the hysteric has a relation to truth that is quite unique. It is unique in the sense that what is in question here is the unconscious truth of the subject. It is not a question of the truth of facts—and indeed Freud writes, in a note accompanying the translation of Charcot: "If we could only know what exists"—but of the truth that determines motives, that defines what torments the subject. One may have underlined everywhere the lies, the hystrionics, the comedy of hysteria, and whatever is the justification of all this "at the factual level;" it is nonetheless true that she has a specific relation with the truth of the object, with the truth of what desire is. She can trifle with the level of facts, but never with the truth of the object.

Hysteria, which already displayed the structure of the symptom, thus becomes a teaching about the object and the fundamental fantasy. Not that she knows the truth in order to assume it. The truth is much too unconscious for that. The truth will appear in the hysteric's complaint and in her symptom, which are addressed to the Other, a complaint that means that she will become plaintive, a plaintiff. The ab-ject object is a nothing, a veil above the abyss, a curtain over the nothing, a semblance that maintains desire, due to the fact that desire can never be fully satisfied, but the object is also cause of eternal and indestructible desire. The object a, as pure obnubilation, however, falsely promises that a sexual rapport can exist, from which the subject gains the illusory certainty of having found the True, the Unique, until the approach of the object makes it fall back into the disappointing "That wasn't it."

It is this unconscious truth that appears through the complaint and the symptom of hysteria: the sexual for a human being is in principle without relation, which does not prevent him from dreaming of the contrary. Of this contrary, the hysteric dreams; she even clings to it, but this does not at all detract anything from the truth that she embodies— sharing between *sein und sollen*: there is no sexual relation, but there should be one. Where the phallus is the perfectly empty signifier, but also the only signifier to signify man as well as woman, not only does there arise a fundamental dissymmetry, an unavoidable absence of rapport in the sexual, but it also appears that any relation between man and woman is marked by the masquerade that tries to hide the want of being. It is this object as mirage that astonishes the hysteric: "How do they manage to be content with this, to resign themselves to this; how can this be enough for them? They pretend to ... " Translated, this means: the master does nothing to really reestablish the sexual rapport. He too keeps to the semblance and tinkers with it. The hysteric refuses, quite relentlessly, any complicity with the world of the seeming. On that point, no master can convert her to lies. She is ready to follow him in anything, possibly without limit, as long as she is allowed to dream about the existence of the sexual rapport, about equality with regard to the signifier of sexual identity.

It is precisely through this lack of bridges between these two large dimensions, between what the sexual rapport is for the other and what it should be for her, that the hysteric remains prisoner of her pathology. The truth of the object concerns the way the other approaches the sexual; the truth is not accepted.

Here is a short fragment in which a young woman reproaches her boyfriend: "I know, I am not smart enough to have conversations with you. I don't have enough taste to help you decorate your house, I am not good enough to be the mother of your children, I am not well educated enough to pass for your wife with your friends and colleagues, I don't cook well enough to be your housekeeper, I am not rich enough for your family. What use am I? What ... What am I for you? A ... " At the level of the signifiers "housekeeper-partner-wife," this young woman expresses her division, hoping to be reassured, assured of the contrary by the Other—which reassurance, moreover, she would immediately begin to question incessantly. At the level of the reproach, she describes the truth of the relationship: "I am nothing for you, whereas I would like to be everything for you, and you should also mean everything for me." The chimera of total reciprocity is posed in the future; the truth is not approached in order to be accepted, but is reproached. Unconsciously, she feels capable of this unpleasant truth, but her discourse will strongly denounce the other as the one guilty, responsible.

The pathological answer, which unceasingly repeats its own dead ends, cannot be overcome by forcing one or the other alternative, but is only guaranteed by the practice of the analytic treatment. As long as an analysand enters into the discourse of hysteria and submits to the ethics of free association, it will be impossible for him to sustain the undermining of the constitutive disjunctions and a revolution will take place between the discourses. Every change of discourse gives a moment of love. The essential thing is to recognize what is contingent in it, because what the hysteric imperatively demonstrates to everyone, she is not ready to assume.

The Pathological Hysteric

The other path of differentiation could be found in the different mathemes of fantasy, the fantasy that appears every time that "there is no sexual rapport" comes up, the fantasy that is used to mop up this inevitable. It always contains the $-\varphi$ as witness of the nonsatisfaction of desire, although there this imaginary castration is expressed in a different way.

The answer to the nonexistence of the sexual rapport is for man $\$\Diamond a$, and for the hysteric $\dfrac{a}{-\varphi}\Diamond A$. The hysteric, looking for an Other without lack, offers herself to him as phallicized object to make him complete, to install him as Other without flaw.

Should pathological hysteria be defined as a way to keep to such a form of fantasy, and to keep this fantasy separate from any movement that could lead it into dialectics? The inertia of the fantasy is targeted by the discourse of the analyst, but there are hysterics who prefer to give in to this inertia rather than risk crossing it. The position of master is as an accomplice to this refusal; the desire of the analyst forms the turning point from which one is entitled to expect a quarter-turn, a redefinition of the subject in relation to its fantasy.

Since, in treatment, every type of neurosis must go through the hysterical discourse, we are conscious of the risks involved in distinguishing pathological hysteria from the hysteria of all speaking beings [parlêtre] by bringing in the structure of the social bond. By neglecting the reference to analytic discourse, one runs the risk of being caught in the psychologism of intersubjectivity: the pathological hysteric would be more difficult to handle in treatment, would be a constant plague for the analyst; she would replace a fallen master with a new master rather than go through another kind of discourse.

—Translated by Françoise Massardier-Kenney

Notes

1. On Freud's different positions, see Sigmund Freud, "Hysterie," *Wiener klinische Rundschau,* vol. 9 (1895), 662–63, 679–80, 696–97; "The Aetiology of Hysteria," *S.E.,* vol. 3, 191–221; "Sexuality in the Aetiology of the Neuroses," *S.E.,* vol. 3, 263–85.
2. Elizabeth Zetzel, "The So-Called Good Hysteric," *International Journal of Psychoanalysis* 49 (1968): 256–60.
3. See Otto Kernberg, *Borderline Conditions and Pathological Narcissism* (New York: Aronson, 1975).
4. Sigmund Freud, *Studies in Hysteria, S.E.,* vol. 2, ed. James Strachey (London: Hogarth, 1955), 305.

7. Discourse Structure and Subject Structure in Neurosis

Alexandre Stevens and Christian Vereecken
with S. André, J. L De Coninck, Y. Depelsenaire,
A. Di Ciaccia, J. P. Dupont, R. Fajersztajn, P. Hellebois,
M. Krajzman, M. Kusnierek, M. Lambert, M. Liart,
A. Lysy, P. Malengreau, G. Michaux, and A. Zenoni

> Man does not think with his soul, as the Philosopher imagined. He thinks as a consequence of the fact that a structure, that of language—the word implies it— a structure carves up his body, a structure that has nothing to do with anatomy. Witness the hysteric. This shearing happens to the soul through the obsessional symptom: a thought that burdens the soul, that it doesn't know what to do with.
> —Jacques Lacan, "Television"

It is in the introduction to the case of the *Ratman* that we find the formulation that will guide us: "The means by which obsessional neurosis expresses its most secret thoughts, is, as it were, only a dialect of the language of hysteria."[1] Lacan goes so far as to see in this dependence of obsessional neurosis in relation to hysteria the very essence of the Freudian discovery.

It is necessary, however, to note from the start that Freud's sentence expresses a difficulty, for it continues, "But it is a dialect in which we ought to be able to find our way about more easily, since it is more nearly related to the forms of expression adopted by our conscious thought than is the language of hysteria."[2] In this idea that thought is more accessible to thought than are the mysteries of the body (that is, the leap from the psychic to the somatic, the hysterical conversion that defies the understanding called here to the rescue by Freud), don't we have a trace of the philosopher's prejudices, which is why this paradox— that obsessional neurosis is in fact much more difficult to understand than hysteria—Freud could not, at that time, explain, at the very moment when he was using all his talent to decipher the logographs of Doctor Lehrs?

We must point out now that, as early as in his article on the mirror stage, Lacan did not see a great mystery in hysterical conversion—understood as a particular manifestation of the fragmented body—and saw in "the schizoid and spasmodic symptoms of hysteria" the manifestation of "lines of fragilization that define the fantasmatic anatomy," the images of entrenched camp evoked by the very term of obsession in French being correlatively attributed to the opposite pole of the formation of the *I*.[3]

The mystery of conversion nonetheless takes us back to the first systematic presentation that Freud published on the two main neuroses, the 1894 article on "The Neuro-Psychoses of Defence,"[4] the subtitle of which should be recalled: "An Attempt at a Psychological Theory of *Acquired* Hysteria, of Many Phobias and Obsessions, and of Certain Hallucinatory Psychoses." This article aimed at extracting the common characteristic of these affectations, a common characteristic that resides in the appearance in the life of these subjects of an event giving rise to a representation intolerable for the ego, in that it cannot be integrated into the chain of its own representations. Freud noted three possible outcomes for this conflict, based on differentiated treatments of the "mnemic trace" and of the affect, both of which are indestructible: (1) a carryover of the "sum of excitation" into the corporeal realm (conversion), (2) detachment of the affect carrying over to anodine representations (false connection, which is at the origin of obsessive thoughts), and (3) rejection of the representation and the affect, which would be responsible for a state of hallucinatory confusion. (We won't insist on this early formulation of what Lacan later called foreclosure, a formulation that has not been much noticed by commentators.)

One can thus see that hysteria, obsession, and certain psychotic phenomena are being treated under the heading of a single language (that is, the treatment of a representation that cannot be integrated into the ego), leading to distinct phenomena. The inverse hypothesis (that is, the translation of similar phenomena into two or three different languages) was explicitly rejected by Freud in his 1913 article on "Disposition to Obsessional Neurosis."[5] This hypothesis was the one used in the psychiatric practice of Freud's time, a practice quite capable of noticing the link, quite obvious, between hysterical phenomena and obsessions and phobias, but placing them in the framework of "degeneration" and its stigmata. One can find this hypothesis when consulting Kraepelin, for instance. As for Pierre Janet, he resisted the promotion of obsessional neurosis by Freud through the invention of psychasthenia, the basis of which is to avoid making a distinction between obsessions and certain delirious ideas that are found, for instance, in attacks of depressive anxiety.

With this tripod, Freud had at his disposal a solid clinical grid, which, however, in its robust simplicity, is not quite without faults. That is why he returned, two years later, to the same problem in his article "Further Remarks on the Neuro-Psychoses of Defence."[6] This article contains a remark that is crucial for the subject under discussion, since the filiation of obsessional neurosis to hysteria is more clearly affirmed there than anywhere else:

Sexual experiences of early childhood have the same significance in the aetiology of obsessional neurosis as they have in that of hysteria. Here, however, it is no longer a question of sexual *passivity,* but of acts of aggression carried out with pleasure and of pleasurable participation in sexual acts—that is to say, of sexual activity. This difference in the aetiological circumstances is bound up with the fact that obsessional neurosis shows a visible preference for the male sex. In all my cases of obsessional neurosis, moreover, I have found a *substratum of hysterical symptoms* which could be traced back to a scene of sexual passivity that preceded the pleasurable action.[7]

In this text, two types of different oppositions are involved: the distinction paranoia/neurosis and that of hysteria/obsession:

Paranoia must, however, have a special method or mechanism of repression which is peculiar to it, in the same way as hysteria effects repression by the method of conversion into somatic innervation, and obsessional neurosis by the method of substitution (viz. by displacement along the lines of certain categories of associations).[8]

Lacan later developed this differentiation by decentering the question through advancing the concept of foreclosure. But, "A thing which is quite peculiar to paranoia and on which no further light can be shed by this comparison, is that the repressed self-reproaches return in the form of thoughts spoken aloud."[9] There is thus a relation of the subject to what comes to her from language that is quite particular. However, between hysteria and obsession the difference is a dialectal one within the same language.

One always find in obsessional neurosis a nucleus of hysterical symptoms, which can be brought back to what Freud defined at that moment as the etiology of this neurosis: a sexual trauma undergone (passively) in early childhood and accompanied by a real excitation of genital organs. However, in the case of obsessional neurosis, this hysterical nucleus is supplemented with an active sexual tendency that developed later. We see that, for Freud, hysteria and obsession cannot be opposed point by point, even according to this opposition passivity/activity that he also attempted to apply in the area of sexuation. Nor is hysteria transformed into obsessional neurosis according to certain conditions; rather, obsessional neurosis is, in some way, a hysteria complicated by the addition of new mechanisms becoming active at a later time.

This outline of the relations between obsessional neurosis and hysteria remained the same throughout Freud's work, however rich the detail through which the clinical picture of the two major neuroses was elaborated. If we look at *Inhibitions, Symptoms, and Anxiety,* for instance, we can observe that the major nuance is Freud's introduction of the role of the superego into obsessional formations.

As for Lacan, we must emphasize that most often he speaks of the two neuroses at the same time, expecting more from their comparison than from the exploration of the phenomenology of one or the other. He goes so far as to attempt to give the mathemes of the fantasy of one $\frac{(a)}{-\varphi}$ and of the other ($A \diamondsuit [a, a', a'' \ldots a^n]$) in his seminar *Formations of the Unconscious.* It is useful to go over these basic reference points because they are often misunderstood.

If we go back to a point much more recent in the psychoanalytic elaboration—that is, the putting into mathemes by Lacan of the discourse of the hysteric—we will see that these points are taken up again. That there is a discourse of the hysteric and not a discourse of the obsessional is a good indication—although discourse and language are obviously not the same thing—that Lacan takes up in his own way the Freudian metaphor of obsession as dialect of hysteria—that is to say, of a radically dissymmetrical opposition between these two terms. Of course, discourses are not clinical categories.

It is a common experience, for instance, that the obsessional finds a comfortable home within the university, whereas the hysteric finds it more difficult. This is no reason to make of scholarly discourse an obsessional formation. Rather, the issue is to realize that both hysteric and obsessional have a distinct relation to the primary discourse—that of the master, which is also that of the unconscious—and to those who embody that discourse. It is common knowledge that Lacan hammered out things in the form of aphorisms: the hysteric looks for a master in order to dominate him; the obsessional has found him and waits for his death in order to take his place, showing him in the meantime his goodwill at work.

Let us see how we can reproduce in terms of discourse the first Freudian discoveries about neuroses:

$$\frac{\$ \to S_1}{//\,S_2} \qquad \frac{S_1 \to S_2}{\$\,//\,a}$$

discourse of   discourse of

the hysteric   the master

That the hysteric places in the position of the agent of the discourse what could be called her symptom, her suffering, as well as her division as subject, was already apparent in two forms in the pre-Freudian practice. The division aspect was emphasized by Janet under the rubric of cleavage (but he saw there the effect of some organic breach), and the fading aspect—that is, the action of the bar—was emphasized by Breuer and his hypnoid states. Along came Freud, who claimed that the cleavage is the result of the hysteric's will, but that it is accompanied by an unconscious phenomenon, which is conversion: that is, the $\$$ in the place of the agent. On the second side—that is, where the master finds himself put in the place of the other—Freud did not give many explanations. This is, however, precisely where the trick is, the complication specific to the obsessional, since it is with this master, as dead, that he identifies, avoiding the Hegelian test that the hysteric does not flee. (One recalls that Lacan describes Hegel as a hysteric, which is why he could call the master a magnificent cuckold of history.)

From this angle, we could thus argue that, starting from the discourse of the hysteric, the obsessional performs a certain return to the discourse of the master, where, however, he figures only as dead or as a shadow, which amounts to the same thing: "making him be always somewhere else than where the risk is, and leaving there only a shadow of himself, because he annuls in advance the gain as well as the loss, by first abdicating the desire which is at stake."[10]

It is thus that Lacan opposes, in "Psychoanalysis and Its Teaching," the step from the hysteric to the obsessional strategy: "the hysteric experiences herself in the homage given to another woman and offers the woman in whom she adores her own mystery to the man whose role she plays without being able to enjoy it," [11] whereas for the obsessional, "the *jouissance* of which the subject is thus deprived is transferred to the imaginary other who assumes it as *jouissance* of a spectacle." [12]

Already in this 1957 text, and in a way that is thus quite consistent with the first Freudian texts, Lacan opposed hysteria and obsession, but in a dissymmetrical fashion, since both structures are placed under the sign of the hysteric: they are "contraries in many respects, but it must be noticed that the second does not exclude the first one, since, even elided, desire remains sexual." [13]

This is why, moreover, obsessional neurosis is complicated: it cannot easily be brought back to a structure of discourse. What the Freudian discovery indicates, in any case, is that it can be deciphered only by starting from the discourse of the hysteric, even if, at the level of phenomena, it is obvious that the hysteric likes to occupy the place of the rebel and the obsessional that of the overseer.

Thus, as Jacques-Alain Miller suggested in his paper during the Journées de Printemps in Bordeaux, there would be good grounds for extracting from this dissymmetry the formula of transformation.

—Translated by Françoise Massardier-Kenney

Notes

1. Sigmund Freud, *S.E.*, vol. 3, 156–57.
2. Ibid., 157.
3. Jacques Lacan, "The Mirror Stage as Formative of the Function of the I as Revealed in Psychoanalytic Experience," in *Ecrits: A Selection,* translated by Alan Sheridan (New York: Norton, 1977), 5.
4. Freud, *S.E.*, vol. 3, 45–61.
5. Freud, *S.E.*, vol. 12, 317–26.
6. *S.E.*, vol. 3, 162–85.
7. Ibid., 168.
8. Ibid., 175.
9. Ibid., 184–85.

10. Lacan, "La psychanalyse et son enseignement," in *Ecrits* (Paris: Seuil, 1966), 453.
11. Ibid., 452.
12. Ibid., 453.
13. Ibid.

8. The Other in Hysteria and Obsession

Alicia Arenas
with G. Brodsky, J. Delmont, E. Leon, L. Luongo,
and A. Waine de Tambascio

We propose to examine what characterizes the Other in hysteria and obsession; that is to say, we want to make more explicit a knowledge determined by analytic experience that could go beyond the meaning of the symptoms of a subject.

To say that this knowledge is determined by the discourse of the analyst implies that we will talk about what happens with hysterics and obsessionals in analysis. We will also deal with the passage through the discourse of hysteria, as the analytic arrangement introduces it in opening up the question of the desire of the Other. This does not eliminate clinical types but forces us to question their usefulness for directing the treatment.

It is interesting to observe that, in current psychiatry, the problem has been solved: hysteria and obsession no longer exist as autonomous nosographic entities. Hysteria is diluted between conversion and somatoform troubles; obsession shares with phobias and anxiety neurosis the whole of anxiety disorders. It is not difficult to explain this deletion. Psychiatric treatment puts together similar symptoms to form clinical types. As symptoms change—because the unconscious is sensitive to "hystory"—clinical types multiply to the point of filling up the five hundred pages of the "modern" *DSM III*.

Unlike psychiatry, Kleinian psychoanalysis does not consider symptoms: it privileges fantasy in its imaginary perspective—separate, as Freud notes, from the content of the neuroses—in such a way that the clinical structure is reduced to the modes of defense against psychotic anxieties.

With his graph, Lacan places both symptom and fantasy in relation to the enigma of the desire of the Other. Confronted with this enigma, the neurosis structures itself as a response when the psychic reality supported by the fantasy is troubled by the eruption of the discordant command, "Jouis." This triggering of the neurosis asserts desire as impossible or unsatisfied and establishes it as a defense against *jouissance*. If, at that moment, an appeal to the Other is produced, we should make no mistake: for the neurotic, there is no desire whatsoever to know. The speaking being *[parlêtre]* is condemned to exile from the Other sex. Between this knowledge, which mortifies the neurotic, and the passion for ignorance, which leads him to interpellate the Other of the signifier where he won't find any answer, the neurotic displays his trickiness.

It is to Freud's credit, as Lacan notes, that he realized that neurosis is not structurally obsessional, and that, in the end, it is hysterical. This is so because neurosis is tied to the fact that there is no sexual rapport. The absence of sexual rapport specifies the traumatic character of human sexuality and gives a new meaning to the "primary experience of displeasure" that Freud points out as a condition of hysteria but that he claims, from his early works on, to have found in all cases of obsessional neurosis. The displeasure is correlated with this absence, and the fantasy of passive seduction is but an attempt to fill with the phallus the gap of what never stops not being written. From this hysterical nucleus, we will be able to characterize the obsessional strategy as implying a double transformation of the sequence displeasure-repression that defines hysteria. First, the obsessional inserts between "the traumatic experience" and the defense a moment characterized by pleasure. Second, he replaces repression by its substitutes: undoing and isolation.

Before we come back to this point, we would like to distinguish this hysterical nucleus from what Lacan introduces as hysterization, as the subjective condition of the putting into action of the unconscious, according to the definition proposed by J. A. Miller. In this way, we see the coordination between hysterization and transference, an articulation that we will develop later. First, let us emphasize that, in our opinion, hysterization bears on the symptom. In order to become analyzable, hysterization must take a hysterical form. Since it is pure *jouissance* and does not call for interpretation, the stratagem of the analytic apparatus is necessary in order to produce the meeting between the symptom and the Other.

But what does it mean that the symptom must take a hysterical form?

Freud gives us an invaluable example with the case of the "Wolfman" when he analyzes the intestinal disorder that had affected the subject since his childhood. Freud writes:

Nothing changed, and there was no way of convincing him. At last I recognized the importance of the intestinal trouble for my purposes; it represented the small trait of hysteria which is regularly to be found at the root of an obsessional neurosis. I promised the patient complete recovery of his intestinal activity, and by means of this promise made his incredulity manifest. I then had the satisfaction of seeing his doubt dwindle away, as in the course of the work his bowel began, like a hysterically affected organ, to "join in the conversation," and in a few weeks' time recovered its normal functions after their long impairment.[1]

We have quoted Freud in full because his observation seems exemplary for the issue that concerns us; it demonstrates that the symptom is analyzable when it becomes hysterical because it "joins in the conversation." But to analyze it, Freud had to occupy its place, almost flirting with suggestion: he had to support, from his position as the Other A, that of subject presumed to know. To hysterization as subjective condition, the subject presumed to know responds as transphenomenal founding of the transference.

Moreover, the symptom takes a hysterical form when it is a compromise formation, and it participates as the return of the repressed within the framework of the mechanism of repression. But this is not the typical mode of the formation of the obsessional symptom. When Freud describes undoing and isolation as variations of repression, he is indicating the negation of the subject effect that obsessional neurosis entails.

Hysterizing the obsessional symptom means introducing it into the division by making it be represented in the face of another signifier, the place of which will be occupied by the analyst.

If hysteria is structural for all neuroses insofar as it results from the nonexistence of a sexual rapport, and if hysterization is the condition of analysis because it introduces the symptom into a social bond, differences in subjective position between hysteria and obsession are not for all that effaced. Contrary to what one might suppose, the point at which the hysteric is placed—on the level of the *semblant*—far from being the best one for understanding her discourse, constitutes its dead end.

The subjective configuration of the hysteric presents her as divided by the signifier. She founds an Other from which she subtracts the object, digging a hole that designates it in its true status: that of an alterity to interrogate. The hysteric lets the Other speak as locus of repressed knowledge, and, for this reason, the repressed—in Freudian terms—is in the power of the Other. This question is in fact deceiving and puts in a bad position those who position themselves as masters, since the hysteric has the answer on her side. This trap that she sets puts aside the element that is really repressed, that is, femininity—which is the lost signifier that occupies the place of the object in her fantasy. What she has under her feet and what supports her division as subject is only this point of nonknowledge of the unconscious. This is what hysterical amnesia is: the truth that she does not enunciate but that she possesses. The price of this truth that she makes the Other pay is the impotence of knowledge, which Freud bitterly acknowledges with Dora.

Would it be possible to show that by placing the Other in this position, the hysteric places the Other at the point of aporia that she promotes? This paradoxical position determines the vicissitudes and disadvantages of the hysteric's treatment, because, in the end, she prefers to support her desire as unsatisfied, leaving empty the place of *jouissance* that Freud persisted in filling with the penis. This substantialization of the phallus, within the limit of the signifying alienation to the Other, marks the place of the Freudian rock.

The hysteric is finally an implacable theoretician, since, opening between knowledge and *jouissance* a breach impossible to suture, she lends credibility to the infallible logic that she embodies most strikingly: there is some signifier, but this·signifier is not enough to name the Other sex.

After this point, which is a real "early trauma," the hysteric distinguishes herself from the obsessional. She positions herself as subject of the signifier and suffers in her own flesh the structure of language that tears her body up by mortifying it, and she makes herself, finally, the promoter of the subjective division. The passive position in the traumatic experience is nothing other than the very formula of the subject:

$$\frac{S_1}{\$} \rightarrow S_2.$$

In contrast, the active pleasure in trauma is the individual myth of the obsessional that Freud exposes in *Totem and Taboo.* The construction of a *jouissance* at the beginning, which Freudian observation places as a second moment in relation to displeasure, is the alibi with which the obsessional declares himself agent of the mortifying action of the signifier, by redoubling it. In "Subversion of the Subject," Lacan states, "*Jouissance* is forbidden to him who speaks as such, or rather it can only be said between the lines for whoever is subject of the Law, since the Law is grounded in this very prohibition."[2] The obsessional takes charge of this prohibition, pretending to be the master of the laws of language. What is paradoxical is that, in order to support this position of mastery, he lives condemned to carry on his back the weight of a guilt that is not his own, and to pay with forced labor a debt that is no one's.

But *he* would like to reabsorb the S_2 into the S_1, make the signifier into a sign, abolish the parasitism of the signifier in the subject. From this exhausting effort is deduced the phenomenology of obsession.

It is only outside of language that the obsessional can imagine himself as owning his being. By wanting to eliminate the "I am not" of the unconscious, which would make him subject of a knowledge that works without a master, he affirms a being that thinks, calculates, and judges: consciousness. This S_1 to which he is alienated occupies the place of the Other of the signifier, the alterity of which is put into question.

The "I don't think" forced upon him by his choice of the "I am" determines the specificity of the obsessional mode of thinking, which, dedicated to the impossible task of doing an accounting of *jouissance*—that is, of making it pass into the signifier—takes the form of a "compulsion toward concentration," the utmost manifestation of which is the erotization of his thought. But, in the end, all obsessional techniques miss the goal of avoiding the appearance of "the contradictory element," "the piece of malediction" that no incantation succeeds in suppressing and that is but the object *a* appearing in the breach in knowledge.

Obsession is this entire system put in place, which attempts "deliriously" to remove the gap of the cause by thus determining the impossibility of desire. By filling the signifying interval with the phallic signification, the obsessional does not want to put the real at stake. Psychoanalysis is a social bond, the instauration of which depends not only on the alterity of the other but also on the object *a,* a matheme that makes the tetrad of the four discourses possible.

The hysteric, who is already an analysand, keeps the object *a* as support of her discourse, placing it in the place of truth, thus displaying her own division of the subject. The obsessional, on the contrary, by hoping to flee *jouissance,* pays the price of the negation of the status of the subject. Analysis must lead him to the place of his subjective division with the introduction of this real that *jouissance* is. Only in this way, paradoxically, can a genuine alterity be constituted for him.

— Translated by Françoise Massardier-Kenney

Notes

1. Sigmund Freud, "From the History of an Infantile Neurosis," *S.E.,* vol. 17, 75–76.
2. Jacques Lacan, *Ecrits: A Selection,* translated by Alan Sheridan (New York: Norton, 1977), 319. Translation modified.

9. Con-jugating and Playing-with the Fantasy: The Utterances of the Analyst

Nestor A. Braunstein

Stranger perhaps than Pallas Athene's origin is that of the Moebius strip. The former admits having come, already formed, out of her father's head, whereas the latter was vainly running after his mother. This took place in Elea, in very distant times. He was running and getting tired, this light-footed father—as the utterance *[énoncé]* runs after the enunciation.

The object *a* is the Achilles heel of the utterance: because of it, the tortoise always arrives first. The foot will never step on the shell— another way of saying that the sexual relation does not exist.

The practice of psychoanalysis is supported by the analyst's speech even and particularly when the analyst is silent. Silence is only silence inasmuch as it is pregnant with the imminence of a possible speech that will precipitate its meaning. The saying *[dire]* of the analyst implies another saying, a saying in suspense, always present, which is that of interpretation.

There is interpretation in each of the four discourses. But the interpretation of the analyst is different. It is different because as agent of his discourse, in the place of the *semblant*, he does not express propositions that would have the pretention of speaking the truth. The analyst's interpretive utterance does not lend itself, or should not lend itself, to an analysis that would define it as true or false.

When is the speech spoken by the analyst an interpretation? To pose the question is already to recognize that not every saying of the analyst is an interpretation—that some of her utterances are interpretations and others are not. I think we can agree that there is an interpretation only when the analysand can use it as a lever to transform the meaning of his saying. Interpretation is not in what the analyst says, in A. It is in s(A), and it is through the retroaction of s(A) on A that it can be recognized.[a]

151

In any case, this is not where we find what is specific in the discourse of the analyst. The site where signification takes place is not different in regard to the three other discourses. In all discourses, signification takes place in s(A). What is characteristic of analysis is precisely that it "goes against signification."[1]

The discourses of the hysteric, of the master, and of the priest or the professor aim at transmitting a truth already constituted. In order to be able to be its agent, it is necessary to be able to believe in the subject supposed to know. The analyst's utterance, on the other hand, is founded on the destitution of the subject supposed to know. Its eminent function is not to speak the truth, but to make the truth work and produce in the other of his discourse: $\dfrac{a \to \mathcal{S}}{S_1}$.

The analyst knows that truth cannot be spoken because it is inherent to speech [parole] that what "is spoken [se dise] remains forgotten behind what is said [se dit] in what is heard."[2] Nonetheless something of the truth reaches the field of "what is listened to." Hence, crossing the conventional barrier of signification, of the distinction true-false, it is possible to reach the level of meaning, that is to say, of the unconscious as production.

The most widespread practice in psychoanalytic interpretation, the one to which Freud himself was no stranger since he was the one who discovered it, consists in the production of utterances that must be recognized as true or false in relation to a preexisting unconscious "content" that must be discovered and revealed. The Lacanian innovation consists in dissolving this idea of the unconscious as peopled with contents particular to each singular being in order to oppose to it the idea of the unconscious structured like a language, that is, of an infinite process of production. The principal tool of this mutation of psychoanalysis is the replacement of the Freudian *Vorstellung* by the signifier that is neither Augustinian nor Saussurian but Lacanian. This replacement includes a psychological emptying of subjectivity in order to replace it with a subject that is the effect of the signifier, the effect of the signifying couple, since the signifier has only one definition, that of being what represents the subject, and this vis-à-vis another (indispensable) signifier.

With this conception of the unconscious as process of production there is no longer any reason to dream of a real interpretation to be distinguished from another that would be false. Interpretation will be effective insofar as it makes the unconscious speak and thus retroactively constitutes the unconscious and the relation of the said with the truth.

If we accept this characterization, we consequently deduce from it that the utterances of the analyst cannot be propositions to be confirmed or refuted but must be prescriptions (injunctions) of an unuttered saying. This requirement is the result not of a technical rule but of the very condition of the existence of interpretation. The utterance, once said, will have been an interpretation or not depending on the capacity of the subject $ to create the S_1 that it is called on to produce. The analyst (the agent) pushes the barred subject (the other of his discourse) to the production of the master signifiers that constitute its unconscious.[3] Interpretation is then a push-to-say [*pousse-à-dire*], whereas the analytic act is a confrontation with the impossible of *jouissance,* which corresponds to the function of the superego as push-to-*jouissance* [*pousse-à-jouir*].

The saying of the analyst is recognized as ex-istent to the *dit-mension* [said-mention] of truth. It is not sufficient that it be a saying from which are erased the markers of the analyst's imaginary identifications (the "I" of the utterance); in addition, the marks of his subjective position—any shifter that would allow the linguistic subject of the enunciation to be recognized in him—must be absent.

"The essence of psychoanalytic theory is a discourse without speech."[4] This Lacanian motif of the 1968–69 seminar must be extended from theory to the psychoanalytic task in its entirety, beyond any debatable distinction between the theory and praxis of analysis. It is, in my opinion, the only way to understand Lacan's revolutionary proposal of a discourse that would be elaborated from the place of the object, of the *plus-de-jouir,* of the lack of signifier, S(A̶), which responds to the question of the subject (*che-me-vuoi*) and to the silence of the drive: ($ ◇ D). (This is the upper half of the graph of desire.)

How do we attain such a discourse? Is it possible to define some grammatical structure that comes close to the idea of an exterior discourse, without any imaginary identification? What types of utterances would be congruent with analytic discourse on the basis of its differentiation from the three other discourses?

A first position not at all absent from certain so-called analytic practices is that of an agent S_1 that is a hypnotizer or group leader who gives
directives, thus pretending, when they are followed, to obdurate his
division as subject, cause and truth of his saying *[dire]:* $\dfrac{S_1 \rightarrow S_2}{a}$.

Another position, which has often been that of Freud himself, consists
in making knowledge intervene as agent of the discourse that speaks in
the name of a preexisting truth, that of the psychological unconscious,
that of Freud, or that of science. This discourse of knowledge insists on
the fact that its propositions are "objective," foreign to any suspect
subjectivity. It is the (scientific) ideology of the foreclusion of the subject,
which presents itself as the contemporary form of a truth disavowed
(verleugnet) in manifest discourse. Whereas in the discourse of the master, subjectivity and its split were cause and truth of the saying, in the
discourse of the university they come to occupy the place of production;
subjectivity is thus the impurity of the other. Academics do not speak in
their own name but as civil servants of a transcendent truth, even when,
in these Popperian days, one insists with a false modesty on the fact that
this truth is only temporary and that it will be demonstrated—one day,
tomorrow, or the day after tomorrow—that it was false. The "analyst"
who places himself under the emblems of this discourse expresses himself through utterances in which he is linguistically effaced but that he
submits to the consideration of the other so that they are accepted
as real.

The third position, prevailing in Kleinian analysis, is that of an analyst who, under the pretext of transference and countertransference,
presents himself as subject of the utterance and of the enunciation in an
interpretive saying that the analysand, curiously positioned in the place
of the master signifier, will have to validate as the production of a
knowledge that confirms the adequation (in the Aristotelian sense of the
term) of the saying of his analyst *(intellectu)* to an ontological unconscious thus revealed *(res)*. The formula of these utterances is that of the
discourse of the hysteric: $\dfrac{\cancel{S} \rightarrow S_1}{S_2}$.

The Lacanian position with regard to interpretation is not normative;
that is to say, it does not distinguish between correct and false interpretations because it questions precisely the "Gloverian" terms of the prob-

lem.[5] It aims at speaking from the outside of any subjectivity, placing the object a as agent of discourse. It's difficult to think about this proposal because a is foreign to the signifier; it's the cause of desire, not a propositional function. From it can come no judgment of either attribution or existence, precisely because it is a condition of the possibility of judgment itself and of its modalities. There is nothing like $+a$ and $-a$, true a and false a, no quantifiable, relativisable, or falsifiable a.

The saying of the analyst must thus aim at this negative goal of not being a purveyor of propositional knowledge; it must also aim, in the positive, at his utterances being pushes-to-say *[pousse-à-dire]* that summon the unconscious to produce itself and to resignify, in the form of interpretation, what the analyst will have said.

How then could it be possible to say the interpretive saying, which Lacan teaches us is apophantic, meaning that it is not modal as the demand always is? This is a demand that, let us add, whatever it may be, accompanies any proposition of the subject, either explicitly or implicitly: a demand for recognition or acquiescence. Any saying could be closed by formulas such as "is it true?" "you see," or "you know?" as often happens in hysteria, and also in its obsessional dialect. Always the same—"do you accept me?"—the demand is for specular ratification of the ego image aiming at least at a nod by the other as a sign of agreement all the more necessary as the utterance is more dubious and subjected to the faithless side of hysteria.

The saying of the Lacanian analyst aims at having the other produce the signification, and for that, it must be in itself devoid of signification. What is such a saying? How is it formulated? It is the quotation that returns to the enunciator as a question regarding his enunciation; it is the enigmatic oracular voice that presents itself to the subject as objectivation of the x of the desire of the analyst and that forces him to make evident his subjective position as effect and as new response vis-à-vis this voice without subject. In other words, the subject is forced on his own to interpret the oracle and to thus produce the S_1, by grasping the unary trait *[trait unaire]* that unifies and gives consistency to the succession of his demands.

Thus, the proposition is a finished utterance; it is a production of the preconscious that obeys determined "purposive ideas" (*Zielvorstellungen*). The proposition is a proposal of acquiescence, and it is in opposition to the production of the unconscious as infinite process of enunciation.

Interpretation as formulation of propositions is characteristic of the three other discourses, other than the psychoanalytic, and its implied formula is, "I will tell you what your saying means" ["Je te dirai ce que ton dire veut dire"]. Its function is metaphorical, because it superimposes itself on the previous saying *[dire]* by substituting itself for that saying; this is why it has the structure of the symptom. In contrast, analytic interpretation does not enunciate a proposition, either real or falsifiable, creating another saying and consequently assimilable to metonymy and the structure of desire. Here we go back to Lacan when he argued in his 1958–59 seminar that desire is its interpretation.

To speak the truth? No, to provoke it so that it will speak, renouncing language acts that play the imposter and are a semblance of truth.

In order to do this, one must enter grammar, not the grammar taught in schools nor the grammar considered as a hereditary knowledge (Chomsky), but that of "L'étourdit," that which seconds interpretation, that tirelessly named by Freud, the grammar in which he had his subjects review their lesson, a grammar given to that *langue* that is the flesh of fantasy.

Lection of the analysand, diction of the analyst. The analyst must know what is going on with his own utterances so that they can be breaks and punctuations in the discourse of the analysand, and so that they escape the logic of propositions and open the field to apophany— closed breaks that, whatever they surround, make subject.

To enter into the grammar of the utterance implies that one also reviews the old lessons, the lesson of Aristotle in a treatise that is not accidentally translated as *On Interpretation,* in order to distinguish in the utterance what gives it the value of a proposition. It goes without saying that we are not speaking of placing in the Index utterances having the form of a proposition, and that nothing guarantees that the expressions not having the form of propositions are for all that apophantic. Let us quote the Stagarite:

Every sentence is not a proposition; only such are propositions as have in them either truth or falsity. . . . Every proposition must contain a verb or the tense of a verb. . . . Verbs in and by themselves are substantial and have significance, for he who uses such expressions arrests the hearer's mind, and fixes his attention; but they do not, as they stand, express any judgement, either positive or negative.

For neither are "to be" and "not to be" and the participle "being" significant of any fact, unless something is added; for they do not themselves indicate anything, but imply a copulation, of which we cannot form a conception apart from the things coupled. . . . A simple proposition is a statement, with meaning, as to the presence of something in a subject or its absence, in the present, past, or future, according to the divisions of time.[6]

When reviewing these old and extremely well-known lessons from the *Logic*, we can orient ourselves in the forest of utterances. The verb accomplishes its copulative function between the subject and the complement of the proposition, and it thus fills in for the absence of sexual relations. One acts as if truth had been spoken or could be spoken. Such suture, such copulative effect, does not happen, however, if the verb is left by itself, especially if it is not put in modal form by conjugation. The infinitive, the past participle, and the gerund are so many examples of this nonpropositional usage. By not con-jugating, one permits the free play of the verb; one leaves it as a joker opened to permutations: to see—to be seen—seeing—to make oneself seen. The pure grammar of the drives. Conjugation, on the other hand, modalizes the utterance and transforms it into a demand for acquiescence.

This restriction quite obviously disappears when one has recourse to quoting the saying of the analysand, because in this case, we do not ask him to sanction the saying of the analyst as true or false, but rather to respond to the subject of the conditions of his enunciation, which is independent of the grammatical structure of his discourse.

Nor is it possible to attribute full propositional value to the use of a proverb, even though the verbs appearing in the proverb seem to be conjugated. Take, for example, "God gives bread to those who are toothless." Such an utterance does not say anything in itself; it pushes-to-say, and this is why it can become apophantic and have the effect of an interpretation in the psychoanalytic sense.

It is helpful to relate the structure of propositions to that of fantasy: subject, verb, and complement, on the one hand, and $\$ \diamond a$, on the other. While the punch indicates the break, the impossible suture, the place of an impossible meeting, which is named unconscious, the verb proposes and imposes the copulative obduration of the gaping constitutive of being. The verb proposes the obduration as a knowledge that derives from the Other, and it imposes it by "corporalizing" the "sujet *supposé* savoir," which we prefer to translate as the "*supposed* knowledge subject" and not as the "subject who is *supposed* to know." As G. L. Garcia nicely puts it: "What we name as supposed knowledge subject, doesn't it transform all 'meaning' of the interpretation into an imperative? This is why it is fitting that the interpretation be enunciated in such a way as to have no other meaning than the one the listener can give it."[7] These words take on their full weight only when we remember that interpretation has no meaning, but that it "is meaning and it goes against signification."[8]

To be meaning by opposing signification: interpretation, the analyst's speech, oracular voice that summons to produce significations: "A child being beaten. . . . " "The taste of a madeleine. . . . " "So many rats, so many florins. . . . " "According to your wishes. . . . "

Interventions where there is no imposition of a preconstituted knowledge and where the Name-of-the-Father is not "imaginarized." Phrases said from A or *a,* phrases, not sentences, which are pushes-to-say: in the place of this absent cause of your desire, put a saying that would be your own, throw yourself this S_1 that organizes your re-petition and that is in disjunction with the S_2 that is the truth of my discourse as analyst. And when you will have enunciated your S_1, I will limit myself to sanction it with this minimal (and usually tacit) remark: "I am not making you say it."

The discourse of psychoanalysis and of the psychoanalyst: a discourse without words, which would be its very essence—that is, a discourse without propositions, a discourse that inherits more from Antisthenes[b] than from Aristotle, a discourse regulated by a truth that is "phasic," not "cataphasic."[9] Regulated, in other words, by the object *a* that, as lost, founds the judgment of attribution as much as its heir, the judgment of existence. Beyond the predicative truth of logic, beyond, also, revealed truth as *aletheia,* which we see appear at the beginning of the works of a Lacan fascinated by Heidegger, we find the essence of the discourse of the psychoanalyst—that is, of his ethics—in the act of nomination without signification.

This is the consequence—which we cannot give up—of the hypothesis of the unconscious: the subject of the enunciation and the subject of the utterance are incommensurable. Between two determinations, whatever they may be, there will always be a real difference, which is *a.* Such a difference will never be able to be reabsorbed into the utterance of the analyst. This impossibility would be, perhaps, the only universal utterance that we can perceive in terms of discourse.

Which makes of the analyst . . . a cynic.[10]

—Translated by Françoise Massardier-Kenney

Notes

1. Jacques Lacan, "L'étourdit," *Scilicet* 4 (1973): 37.
2. Ibid., 5.
3. Nestor A. Braunstein, "The Transference in the Four Discourses," *Prose Studies* 11 (1988): 50–60.
4. Jacques Lacan, *Le Séminaire, Livre XVI: D'un Autre à l'autre.* Course of 13 November 1968. Unpublished manuscript.
5. Edward Glover, "The Therapeutic Effect of Inexact Interpretation: A Contribution to the Theory of Suggestion," *International Journal of Psychoanalysis* 12 (1931): 399–411. Commented on by Lacan in "The Direction of the Treatment," *Ecrits: A Selection,* 226–80.
6. Aristotle, "On Interpretation," translated by E. M. Edghill, *Basic Works of Aristotle,* ed. Richard McKean (New York: Random House, 1941), 41–43.
7. German L. Garcia, *Psisoanalisi dicho de otra manera* (Valencia, Spain: Pretextos, 1983), 178.
8. Lacan, "L'étourdit," 37.
9. Antoine Compagnon, "Psychose et sophistique," *Folle vérité,* ed. Julia Kristeva (Paris: Seuil, 1979). "In Aristotle's terms the enunciative grasp of truth *(phasis)* was opposed to judgment *(kataphasis),* the truth of being was not opposed to falsehood or to mistake but to ignorance and blindness. This conception of truth was radically sustained for the early Cynics, especially by Antisthenes, founder of the school: he only admitted the identity judgment as manifestation of truth and rejected the judgments of existence and attribution as accidental."
10. Michel Onfay, *Cynismes* (Paris: Grasset, 1990).

Translator's Notes

a. The author is here referring to Lacan's graph of desire (see Lacan, *Ecrits* [Paris: Seuil, 1966], 806–8). His point is that whether an utterance is an interpretation or not depends not on the linguistic code, A, but on the meaning that the message s(A) assumes when received by the analysand.
b. Greek philosopher, founder of the Cynics.

Part III

Discourse and Society

10. Deference to the Great Other: The Discourse of Education

Renata Salecl

The leftist criticism of the education system usually gives the teacher the role of a Master who structures the field of the school discourse with his authority: the school is supposed to be the elementary model of the discourse of the Master. Lacanian theory, in contrast to this approach, insists on the structurally necessary borderline between the discourse of the Master and the social bond existing at school ("university discourse"). The easiest way to detect this borderline is by answering the question, which is the place wherefrom each of these two discourses enunciates itself? Which is their respective place of enunciation? The crucial point here is that the discourse of the Master does not speak from a position of presupposed knowledge: it just proclaims, affirms in an apodictic manner, the key elements (the founding words, what Lacan calls "master signifiers") on the basis of which a field of knowledge can articulate itself. Knowledge does not belong to the Master but to those who obey. The discourse of the Master is thus always characterized by a kind of fundamental ignorance with regard to its conditions; it proceeds in an unconditional manner and requires to be obeyed on the sole authority of its enunciation: law must be obeyed *because it is law* and not because there are good reasons to obey it. In the discourse of the University, on the contrary, utterances always refer to some field of knowledge; they purport to be justified by proofs and arguments. Apropos of a law, the attitude of the discourse of the University is, "Let us see how its authority can be justified: what purpose does it serve? how is it rounded in basic social norms?" etc. To exemplify this borderline, one needs only to compare educational discourse with legal discourse as the discourse of the Master par excellence.

The metanorm that constitutes law as such and establishes the subject's attitude toward all other norms is the famous statement, "Not knowing the law can be no excuse to violate it." If we violate a certain legal regulation, our not knowing the law cannot be an excuse for that. As Jacques-Alain Miller has pointed out in his seminar *Extimité* (1985–86), the law has the status of a certain knowledge that no one should ignore because and only because it is *written down*. Not knowing it cannot be an excuse because the law has been written down and is not just a word that we have perhaps heard or not heard. The law as Master discourse therefore implies that the subject *knows* the laws, in the meaning of the unconscious knowledge implied by the law itself, by the fact that the law is written down.

The attitude toward knowledge is just the opposite in educational discourse: the starting point of education is that the subject *does not know* and has only started to learn—the school provides knowledge for him. The school becomes the Master discourse when the subject's (pupil's) ignorance becomes his guilt, just as the subject of the law is guilty even though he does not know the law. The subject of the educational process, on the contrary, does not know even if he knows: *only his teacher tells him whether he really knows.* In the system of law, "the subject supposed to know" is literally the subject of the law; at school, he is the teacher, while the pupil is in the position of "the subject supposed not to know." In law nothing can justify our not knowing the laws, while at school we are supposed not to know. And exactly this different relationship toward knowledge proves that school is not a discourse of the Master but a discourse of the University.

The school as a discourse of the University is established by two modes of indirectness. First, analysis of indirect speech acts at school will show us that the school is actually a discourse of the University inasmuch as the teacher is bound to knowledge outside himself (in the Other). And second, analysis of education as a "state that is essentially a byproduct" will demonstrate why the educational aim has to be always unintended, conceived as an effect of the Other and not of our own intention.

Indirect Speech Acts in School

Aside from Foucault's theory, the authors of the latest works in the field of pedagogy also use speech-act theory to demonstrate how the educational process exerts discipline and control. McLaren's [1] opinion, for example, is that the performative dimension of speech acts at school is a new mechanism of control in the educational process. In this view, the pupil's hierarchic position would be created and confirmed by those performatives with which the teacher forms a moral order determined by the external social power. Bourdieu[2] also focuses on the external influence of institutions on speech acts, and like McLaren, he supports his theory of symbolic violence at school by the role of performative. It is his thesis that the functioning of the performative is exclusively dependent on an institution determining the conditions of a certain speech act. The institution confers authority on the speaker—mediates "the symbolic capital" to the teacher—who then exerts symbolic violence through communication. According to this view, the power proper to words thus intervenes in language from outside: it is supported by the institution that determines the speaker's authority.

Bourdieu[3] opposes his thesis to Austin's idea of illocutionary force, according to which speech acts possess their own force. Bourdieu's criticism of Austin refers to the forgotten source of power outside the language, and its influence on the speech act. Yet Bourdieu's criticism goes so far as to exclude the whole field of everyday speech acts and reduce language to the role of an intermediary between an institution and the hearer. The teacher, constituted by the institution (school) and made responsible through it to the ruling class and to the class-determined relations of power, is in the role of an intermediary who transfers this outer order to the pupils through his teaching, thus victimizing them with symbolic violence. Bourdieu constantly emphasizes that the school is not a simple copy of the outer social relationship but has its own structural functioning, that is, follows its own structural logic.

Yet precisely by conceiving performatives as transmitters, intermediaries of institutional symbolic violence, Bourdieu undermines his previous assertions about a specific logic of the school and renders it an instrument of power in a naive Marxist way. His analysis of school speech acts falls below the level of Austin's and Searle's speech-act theory because of this naive Marxist simplification. As the performative is always bound to authority, even according to Austin and Searle, the speech act exercises language power over other subjects, yet it is by no means exclusively bound to an external social institution. Even everyday speech acts have a performative power, not only the acts supported by the power of an institution.

If, according to Bourdieu and McLaren, performatives express a certain obvious dimension of power and constraint exercised by the authorities, then indirect speech acts, on the other hand, conceal and deny this dimension. Through his use of indirect speech acts, the teacher dissimulates the formalization and coercion openly expressed by the direct performatives. By saying, for example, "I can hear someone whispering," "There's somebody who's not listening," or "Could you keep quiet?" he conceals the real intention—the threat. This form of polite utterance thus prevents the disclosure of his authority: it masks the effective coercing function of the language and thus exerts an even greater violence by means of seemingly liberal speech.

Such conclusions, however, are theoretically weak, as we will see when we try to answer the question of why indirect speech acts are the usual manner of communication between teacher and pupil at school.

There are several types of utterances in which the intended meaning of the speaker's utterance and the literal sentence meanings differ: metaphor, irony, indirect speech acts, etc. Such utterances have two illocutionary forces, and the illocutionary force of a speech act of one kind can be used for accomplishing a speech act of another kind. Thus utterances having the appearances of *questions* (asking about the hearer's abilities) can effectively function as *requests*. Searle's example of such an act is the question, "Could you pass me the salt, please?" With this question, the speaker is literally asking about the hearer's capability of passing him the salt, but the meaning of the question is in fact a request.[4]

How is it possible that the listener understands a certain speech act as a request if this speech act is literally put as a question or a statement whose meaning is not a request? Concerning indirect speech acts at school, the question is how it is possible for a pupil to understand the teacher's question "Could you keep quiet?" as a request and not simply as a question about the pupil's ability to comply to the speaker's wish. Why does not the pupil simply answer, "I cannot do so at the moment, because I want to continue chattering with my schoolmate a little longer?"[5]

How can the hearer understand these speech acts (their indirect meaning) while he in fact cannot rely on a certain set of linguistic rules determining the deeper meaning of the utterance or on a set of conversational postulates and concealed imperative forces in the speech act? The hearer (1) has to be able to conclude that the real (primary) illocutionary point of the utterance is different from the literal, and (2) has to find out what the primary illocutionary point is.

It is thus essential for the indirect speech acts that they not have a definite illocutionary power as a part of their meaning. All questions beginning with "Could you" can by no means be reduced to indirect speech acts. It all depends on the context of the utterance. The essential condition for understanding indirect speech acts is the knowledge of general *principles of conversation* and *background information.* Essential background information, for example, is the knowledge of the hearer's ability to comply with the request. At the same time, the hearer has to find out from this background information whether the speaker's question is really only a question about some ability, or whether it is a request.

Searle's final answer to the question of why indirect speech acts are used at all when direct speech acts could be used—that is, why, for example, the teacher says "Could you keep quiet?" instead of commanding "Be quiet!"—is *for the sake of politeness:* there is a convention of politeness according to which the speaker usually uses indirect speech acts, and insofar as this convention is a part of the hearer's background information, he correctly understands the intention.

Yet the analysis of speech acts at school shows us that this answer of Searle's is insufficient. It could be said, of course, that politeness plays an essential communicative role between the teacher and the pupil at school, but everyone who has ever attended school will doubt that. The kind of indirect speech acts used at school justifies our doubt as to whether the school really is the most polite institution in society. The most basic experience tells us that the indirect form of speech acts only intensifies the aggressiveness and the relation of power. Saying "Shut the door!" is a direct order; through use of the polite form, "Could you, if you please and if it is not too difficult for you, close the door?" the same command obtains the dimension of a cynical irony to the subordinate subject-addressee.

But the insufficiency of Searle's theory of speech acts is demonstrated already at his starting point: in the analysis of the school situation, the question, "How is it possible for us to understand indirect speech acts?" should be turned around. The question is not why the teacher and the pupil *can* understand or use indirect speech acts, but *why they necessar-*

ily have to use them, why educational discourse has to develop through indirect speech acts and not through direct ones. The problem, then, is the radical unbearableness of the directives, that is, the fact that they cannot prevail in educational discourse.

It can be said, in the light of Lacanian theory, that the relationship between the teacher and the pupil is always based on a transference, that the teacher is "the subject supposed to know" for the pupil. Yet the teacher is by no means in the position of a Master: knowledge (S_2) and the Master (S_1) are mutually exclusive. The teacher doesn't occupy the position of a Master who commands or demands without further ceremony. He cannot say, "It is so *because I say so,*" but always has to give *sufficient reasons:* he always has to refer to knowledge that is *outside* him. Lacan's schema of university discourse, wherein the Master occupies the place of truth, determines knowledge as an agent starting up the entire discourse.[6] The teacher therefore cannot give commands; he can present himself as power executor only indirectly, by transmitting knowledge, by referring to knowledge and the law. The teacher is therefore polite in the relationship not to the pupil but to the knowledge of the Other, to which he is a responsible subject. The indirect statement "Could you please listen?" does not simply communicate in a polite form a simple demand: "Listen!" It also indirectly implies the reasons for doing it: "Because this is good for you," "Because the school authorities demand it," etc.; in short, "Because the Great Other wants it."

The teacher's speech is obligatory for the pupil insofar as it is bound to the teacher's position as an authority mediating knowledge. Yet it is obligatory not in the sense of the teacher being the Master whose word is directly legislative, but because the teacher appears as a representative of a *socially recognized* knowledge. The assertion that $5 \times 5 = 25$ is a statement that not only is factually true but also has its place in the socially recognized knowledge of the Great Other.

Searle, and also McLaren and Bourdieu, fail to take into account the same thing: the dimension of the Great Other, a symbolic structure into which the subject has always been clamped. This symbolic structure is close to what the late Karl Popper conceived as the "autonomy of world 3," the realm of the "objective knowledge" irreducible to the couple external reality/psychic interior.[7] It is not a positive social fact—that is, it is of a quasi-transcendental nature; it forms the very frame structuring our perception of reality. Its status is normative; it is a world of symbolic rules and codes. As such, it also does not belong to the psychic level: it is a radically external, nonpsychological universe of symbolic codes regulating our psychic self-experience. The respective mistakes of Searle and of McLaren and Bourdieu are thus complementary: Searle reduces the symbolic order to a psychological fact; for him, the philosophy of language is—as he puts it himself—part of the philosophy of mind. He remains entrapped in the psychological paradigms of language: what is determining, in his view, is intentionality (inner, imminent logic of meaning) on the one hand, and convention and background information on the other. In contrast, McLaren and Bourdieu directly externalize the Great Other: they reduce it to institutions in the social reality. And so all of them miss the same thing, namely, that language is *in itself* an institution to which the subject is submitted.

Here, a propos of the school prohibition that is always expressed politely, we can again draw a parallel with legal discourse. The judge, as well as the teacher, has to refer to knowledge—to the laws that are outside him. He is also deferential to the knowledge of the Great Other and expresses his submission by referring to legal regulations that constitute the legal Great Other. But in spite of this similarity of legal and school discourse, legal discourse is a discourse of the Master, in opposition to school discourse, which is, as said before, the discourse of the University. Who is then the Master in legal discourse? The position of the Master is not embodied by the judge; he only "establishes that the subject is found guilty" and determines the penalty according to his role as the bearer of knowledge. It is the jury that embodies the position of the Master: by a simple gesture, by the choice of "guilty" or "not guilty," it "guilts" the field of legal norms. The statement of the jury, a completely unprofessional finding of so-called common sense, is the gesture of the Master in its purest. As shown by Lacan, the essence of the Master is that he is an idiot, who with his mere presence and not with his cleverness enables the functioning of the social totality (a king, for example). Therefore the judge remains bound to the discourse of the University in the same manner as the teacher—by referring to legal knowledge. His knowing it confers on him the authority of arbiter who determines the degree of violation, the extent of the penalty, etc. Yet the position of the Master is taken by the jury as the extranormative, commonsensical element that fills up the empty place in the law.

Education as "the State That Is Essentially a Byproduct"

It has been shown in the previous section how, due to the teacher's responsibility to the knowledge of the Other, school discourse as the discourse of the University has to assume the form of indirect speech acts. We will now draw attention to another indirectness constitutive for the entire educational process. By means of the notion of "the state that is essentially a byproduct," developed by Jon Elster in his work *Sour Grapes,* we will try to show that another, even more fundamental indirectness conditions the entire educational effect. The states that are essentially byproducts are the states that we miss when we make them the direct goal of our activity: we can reach them only as a nonintentional byproduct of striving for some other goals. Typical examples of such states are love, respect, reputation, feelings, generosity, modesty, irony, etc. When we intentionally try to be generous, we will inevitably make ourselves ridiculous. The real effect can be attained only if we pursue some external goal (to help somebody, for example).

The following demands also have a different effect from the desired one: "Be spontaneous!" "Don't be so obedient." "Be independent." Spontaneity, independence, and similar states are typical examples of states that cannot be the consequence of a demand, an instruction, but can only be unintended byproducts of a certain action. It is similar when we wish to impress somebody or when we want to imitate a certain pose. The example of Bourdieu, quoted by Elster, is the middle-class imitation of the bourgeois way of life: intentional imitation of bourgeois nonchalance always turns into exaggeration, the effect of which is just the opposite—a parvenu behavior. In the words of Elster, "There is nothing so unimpressive as the behavior which tries to impress."[8] The lower middle class fails in its attempt to imitate upper-class habits because it shows too much out of fear of not showing enough.

To apply Elster's theory to the problems of education, we have to draw a distinction between two uses of the word "education." "Education I" is education conceived as *personality forming,* moral training, while "education II" is education conceived as instruction, acquiring *positive knowledge,* training of skills.

The aims of education in the theory of pedagogy constitute a certain ideological program, a binding element of the entire school system. These aims are supposed to connect the dominant social interest or purposes of the ruling ideology with the socially desired forming of personality. The aims of education should therefore represent a certain program planning the type of personality to be formed by the school, the kind of moral characteristics that should be acquired by the child in the educational process. These aims are, of course, ideologically various, so that certain theories of pedagogy swear to the education emerging exclusively from a "free development" of the child's nature (Rousseau), while other theories—Socialist pedagogy, for example—establish a complete program of an "all-round developed Socialist personality," planning precisely the results of such education.

Supporting a precisely determined educational result, that is, forming a determined type of personality—a motto of various educational theories—can be compared to Elster's analysis of the educational result of cooperation in a political system. It is a frequent thesis of the advocates of the democratic political system (J. S. Mill and Tocqueville, for example) that the only result of democracy is the education of people, as the democracy enables reformation and political awareness of people through cooperation in the political system; the labor zeal of people also increases in the democratic system, which contributes to greater production and better economic results. Elster's answer to this is that the educational effect of democracy can only be a state that is essentially a byproduct; it can only be a byproduct and not a consciously planned goal: the purpose has to be in democracy as such and not in the education of people or in economic prosperity. The existence of a certain external political goal is necessary to develop a certain type of character of citizens: people are educated by seriously trying to reach some external goals and not by cooperating in politics for the sake of their education.

Following the logic of Elster, we can say of school education that education I (education as personality forming) is "essentially a byproduct" that cannot be reduced to a consciously planned aim. The inconsistency of determining the aims of education exists already in confounding the two meanings of education (education I and II)—the purpose of education should be to produce desired results in the formation of personality by means of certain instruction techniques. But it is absurd to speak about education I as the goal of education: the goal of education can be only education II (instruction). The aims of education (education II) that are directly realized with the choice of the teaching subject, the manner of teaching, repetition, testing, and other disciplinary techniques bound to the educational process have education I only as their byproduct.

The way in which education I works essentially as a byproduct can be shown in the example of the ideology of permissive education. A number of permissive experiments were founded on a theory that it is necessary to abolish all school regulations and the coercion of education in order to release the child's own creativity and allow the child's nature to speak up by itself. The child's nature is essentially good: therefore it does not need the external constraint of education, but rather the right to autonomously decide, express the need for education, establish its own rules, and freely form its personality. But as Catherine Millot[9] has already pointed out by analyzing Neill's *Summerhill,* the fundamental illusion of permissive theory is that it does not realize the real mechanisms that operate in the educational process. Neill thinks that his experiment has succeeded due to the consistent consideration of the child's needs, the absolute freedom of education: he does not see that his success is only a consequence of a transference that he brought about by the power of his personality. The success has thus not been a consequence of a good theory but a consequence of an unconscious influence of the teacher upon the pupil. This proves that the educational result is essentially a byproduct. Realization of education I, namely, education, is not the consequence of certain theories but only a byproduct of identification with the educator. And as Millot says, "Neill does not know that the changes affecting the pupils are triggered by the power of the influence of his personality, and this proves that he need not know what he does to be a good teacher."[10] A good pedagogue is therefore an idiot who does not know why he succeeds—he succeeds simply because of his own personality, because of the transference that he triggers and not because of the ideology of good aims or the application of educational theories.

If, therefore, education I as an aim is not possible, we have to ask ourselves why Socialist pedagogy insists on it and directly binds education to the realization of Communist goals. The reasons why youth disapprove of or are indifferent to these goals are sought by Socialist pedagogy in faulty education. According to Elster, the Communist goals are always missed; pursuit of them is self-destructive. Consequently, it is not possible to realize the formation of the new type of man announced by the educational aims of Communist pedagogical ideology.

But is Elster's analysis of the Communist ideology and its self-destructiveness sufficient? What if the self-destructive character of the ideological goals is taken into account in advance? What if the fact that the set Communist goals bring about effects completely different from those demanded *is already part of the game?* What if the Communist power *knows* it and *wants* it?

Elster's mistake is that he does not see that in ideology, the aim is always realized in one way or another. There is no failure in ideology: an apparent failure is successful in the end. Let us take the Communist ideal type of personality: the authorities do not believe in it either; they don't really believe in forming some special Socialist personality, a man of a special mold. Yet the effect produced with the set goal—broken individuals, conformists devoted to the Socialist rituals—suits the authorities. The same holds true for the device of demanding respect for politics. In fact, the demanded respect produces irony, distance, mistrust, resignation. But all these are very useful to the authorities: irony and distance enable preservation of absolute power and prevent a real revolt.

We can by all means agree with Elster's theory according to which the states that are essentially byproducts escape if we try to make them a direct aim of action. Consequently, setting educational aims and planned forming of personality are absurd. Yet Elster's theory needs to be reversed if we want to grasp the functioning of the real-Socialist ideology: the impossibility of the realization of the set ideological goals is actually *a part of the functioning of this same ideology.* Proclaiming the goals to be impossible opens the field of ideological activity; a cynical distance from the Communist goals, which results from the ideological indoctrination, marks precisely the *success* of the same ideology.

The root of Elster's insufficiency is of course again the same as the one detected in theories of indirect speech acts: like them, Elster's analysis does not take into account the dimension of the Great Other. Let us take the example of the ideological ritual proper to real-socialism. Why this ritual, when it is self-destructive from the standpoint of its own efficiency, that is, when it does not convince anybody, since everybody maintains a cynical distance toward the ruling ideology? The answer is, of course, the Great Other. Even though everybody knows that "the emperor is naked," that nobody takes the ideological phrases seriously, it is necessary to maintain the appearance at any price: the fact that "the emperor is naked" has to be concealed *from the Great Other*. The cynical distance and irony can therefore consistently coexist with the naive belief in the Great Other in front of which it is necessary to maintain the appearance that the nation is unified and enthusiastically builds socialism.

After all, the Great Other is at work in the very heart of the "states that are essentially byproducts." Love, for example—it is not possible to fall in love according to plan. Love has to come "by itself": we cannot intentionally decide it. But what does this mean if not that *the Great Other has to decide instead of us?* The Lacanian Great Other is exactly that agency that decides about things for which any planned decision would be self-destructive: it decides that we fall in love, it decides that someone arouses our respect; in short, "states that are essentially byproducts" are simply *states that are essentially produced by the Other.*

Which is why we should not be surprised to find Elster linking "states that are essentially byproducts" to what Hegel called "cunning of reason": with our activity, we intend to achieve some definite aim, our activity fails, but this failure itself to achieve the intended aim brings about another, nonintended result that reveals itself to be the true aim of our activity. Let us refer to Hegel's own example: the murder of Julius Caesar. The conspirators against Caesar intended to reinstate the republic, but the final result of their act was exactly opposite to the intended one: involuntarily, they contributed to the institution of the empire. They were thus unconscious tools, means of historic Reason: the fact that their conspiracy brought forward the empire was an "essential byproduct" of their activity, that is, they obviously did not intend this outcome. The one, however, who *did* intend it and who used them as involuntary tools was the historical Reason, this Hegelian image of the Great Other, the symbolic order regulating our fate behind our backs. In other words, what was a nonintended "byproduct" of their activity was "essentially produced" by the Great Other who effectively pulls the strings of the theater called "History."

Notes

1. P. McLaren, *Schooling as a Ritual Performance* (London: Routledge & Kegan Paul, 1986), 105.
2. P. Bourdieu and J. C. Passeron, *Reproduction in Education, Society, and Culture* (London: Sage, 1977), 200.
3. P. Bourdieu, *Ce que parler veut dire: l'économie des échanges* (Paris: Fayard, 1981), 107–9.
4. J. Searle, *Expression and Meaning* (Cambridge: Cambridge University Press, 1985), 30–57.
5. Such acts at school run by no means only in the direction teacher-pupil but also vice versa. For example, a pupil might respond "We had a big game last night" to the teacher's question, "Have you done your homework?" The pupil is making a statement that, when literally understood, is not the answer to the question. But by means of this utterance, the pupil has indirectly communicated that he has not done his homework, even though he literally made only a statement that he had a big game.
6. J. Lacan, *Encore* (Paris: Seuil, 1975), 21.
7. K. Popper, *Unended Quest: An Intellectual Autobiography*. London: Fontana, 1982), 185.
8. J. Elster, *Sour Grapes: Studies in the Subversion of Rationality* (Cambridge: Cambridge University Press, 1983), 65.
9. C. Millot, *Freud anti-pedagogue* (Paris: La bibliotheque d'*Ornicar?*, 1979), 152–65.
10. Ibid., 158.

11. "I Don't Know What Happened": Political Oppression and Psychological Structure

Luz Casenave
with D. Allende, G. Bort, E. Cafferata, O. d'Angelo,
C. Massana, E. Perlino, N. Petricca, M. I. Porras, and
Charo Sanchez

> Do we have to extend the analytic intervention to the point of becoming one of those fundamental dialogues on justice and courage, in the great dialectical tradition?
>
> —Jacques Lacan, *Freud's Papers on Technique*

In hysteria, the symptom appears as an enigma to be deciphered. It is from this hidden and suffering place that truth exposes itself. The symptom speaks to the Other by looking for a signifier that would represent it.

The case that we are developing shows, almost paradigmatically, the way in which the drama narrated in analysis enables a symptom to be articulated, not only as the effect of a truth hidden in the female patient but even more as the effect of another truth, also hidden, but in a social reality: that of a country deep in terror and oppression.

This essay attempts to show how the signifiers of terror and death work on the subject through the discourse of the master. These signifiers articulate a hysterical symptom, amnesia, with the patient's history, with the irruption of the real, and, finally, with the social imaginary. This leads to the necessity of always keeping in mind, for the analytic act, the dialectic between the human being and his or her sociopolitical environment.

Milena came to her first session on November 3, 1983, a few days before the elections that were to decide the return of democracy in

Argentina. Milena named "several symptoms": neck pains, lack of interest, disquiet, weight gain. She spoke about them with ease and kept for last the enunciation of her "privileged symptom": amnesia. The articulation of this symptom functioned as the final point of punctuation of her entire discourse and thus gave meaning and signification to her presence and her request for an analysis.

Milena was thirty-six years old, the only child of a couple living in a small town in the provinces. Her mother was forty-eight years old and her father forty-nine when she was born. When she turned nineteen, she married a lawyer, fourteen years her elder, who was very involved politically and at the university. Her married life took place in a major province town where she enrolled at the university, became the mother of two daughters, and started her professional life teaching at the university.

In April 1976, a few days after the rise to power of the military dictators in Argentina, her husband was murdered in front of their house by an armed squad. The following week, Milena returned to her teaching, and at the moment when she began to lecture on the fundamental ideas underlying *The Trial* and *Metamorphosis* by Kafka, she suffered an amnesia attack that erased her literary knowledge and forced her to give up her class and her post at the university.

According to Albert Camus, "A symbol always transcends the one who makes use of it and makes him say in reality more than he is aware of expressing" (*The Myth of Sisyphus,* 124). About *The Trial* Camus writes, "People have spoken of an image of the human condition. . . . To a certain degree, he [Kafka] is the one who does the talking, even though it is me he confesses. He lives and he is condemned" (*Sisyphus,* 125–26). *Metamorphosis,* in turn, "certainly figures the horrible imagery of an ethic of lucidity" (*Sisyphus,* 126). "A symbol, indeed, presupposes two perspectives, two worlds of ideas and sensations, a dictionary of correspondence between one and the other. It is this lexicon that is the most difficult to establish" (*Sisyphus,* 126).[1]

Milena must keep silent, and she obeys the order of the master coming from the position of agent, $\frac{S_1 \rightarrow S_2}{S}$, but her amnesia reminds her that she knows: on the basis of what she does not have any longer, she can remember what she had. We could assume that by being based on the order not to think, imposed by the dictatorship, her amnesia served her as a support. The amnesia arose in front of an audience—in this case, her students, when she was commenting on two Kafka texts. Did the real of the fundamental fantasy crystallize at that moment? Milena only said, "I don't know what happened." In confronting herself with the lack, she does not find the signifier that represents her. This is a metaphorical *solicitation* condensing diverse scenes in which Milena does not find her place.

Freud notes:

Affective states have become incorporated in the mind as precipitates of primieval traumatic experiences, and when a similar situation occurs they are revived like mimetic symbols. . . . As I have shown elsewhere, most of the repressions with which we have to deal in our therapeutic work are cases of *after*-pressure. They presuppose an operation of earlier, *primal repressions* which exert an attraction on the more recent situation.[2]

For years, Milena justified herself in her own eyes by saying to herself that "she couldn't." In her discourse, one signifier was tirelessly repeated: "I don't know what happened." With the return of democracy, she lost her reasons for forgetting; nobody forced her any longer to keep quiet, and she wanted to get rid of her symptom. This is where the other drama started. The way she asked for an analysis leads one to think that she was looking for another commanding voice that approved of her or condemned her. Three quickly interrupted attempts at therapy during the years of military rule left her with the impression that her intellectual life was over.

Milena came to me because I offered her the guarantee of a safe place where she could speak: she knew that I had suffered from military repression. At first glance, she assumed that I knew what she was speaking about, that we shared an experience which allowed her to open up without danger.

What is a woman? What is a father? What is it to be alive or to be dead? What is a woman, a father, in Argentina, during the military regime? Milena came with imperious questions that she thought I would be able to answer: she deemed me the subject presumed to know on the basis of the political situation. She added: "I always go into therapy through the intermediary of a woman," alluding here to the person who gave her my name. This is women's business. Another woman who came into play and who guaranteed her security was my exiled daughter. It was this Other who gave her the guarantee that she could speak with me, because I knew. She invited me to take charge of her, and she knew that "I was dying to be with my daughter." I was, from the start, a desiring analyst who admitted the lack.

But her interpellation already ran up against a closing in the amnesia, since "the symptom is the answer that the subject gives to the question of knowing who he is for the Other. The share of the lack that is due to the subject is inscribed in the symptom s(A) in the form of a signification, a metaphor. I am such because the Other wants it this way."[3] After her husband Jose's murder, Milena left for Buenos Aires, where she took on odd jobs, outside of her profession, until 1982, when she settled in Mendoza. For her, as for thousands of Argentinians, these were difficult years. What was not said with words would appear in the real of a familiar neighbor or a friend who had disappeared, in forbidden songs, in those who left in order to be able to speak from another place, in books burned in the fireplace, in address books hurriedly destroyed, and in houses suddenly vacated. There was always an empty place occupied by the idea of death. The signifier "disappeared" always evoked a fantasy that had been inscribed in the social realm. Somebody who disappears can reappear. Where does he come from? From possible death, destruction, nothingness. The pure death drive becomes rooted in the social body. For survival, it was thus necessary to become the silent support of horror. What is the effect, on the psyche, of knowing that one was supporting the discourse of death?

Milena is an example of the way in which the individual inscribes itself in the transsubjective. Something that went beyond the family romance, beyond her imaginary, forced her to create a symptom in subordinating herself to the command of the dictatorship. This was the articulation of the individual imaginary to the social imaginary of these years. Milena was subjugated to a "schema of primordial domination."[4] She witnessed the agony of Jose, who bled for hours while she was prevented by the authorities from coming to his rescue. Similarly, thousands of Argentinians were powerless witnesses to the kidnapping, torture, and even assassination of the other, whether relative or friend, known or unknown.

We think that the scene of aggression and death actualized in Milena the oedipal fantasy of killing her mother. During a session, Milena said she remembered a scene in which her father, revolver in hand, threatened her mother, saying, "I am going to kill you." During another session, she recalled that one of her husband's assassins shouted, "We got you, son of a bitch!" after discharging his weapon on her husband.

The extreme violence of the murder precipitated old images that sent Milena into a panic, a panic that took her back to the real when the fantasmatic veil fell. By means of the amnesia condensed on the intellectual aspect—a negation of university discourse—Milena attempted to fill the lack. From the irruption of the real, Milena met the truth, a truth that always voids a knowledge. It is from this place that she had to lose her academic discourse.

But there was something else that structured her history: it was her rejection of a mother who had always persecuted her with the danger of death. The patient explained, "Do you know that I wasn't supposed to be born? For the family, if I were born, mother would die. My mother used to say, 'God, let me live until the kid graduates from high school, until she graduates from college, until she gets married!' But she was able to see me become a mother, a professor, a wife, a widow. That bothers me a lot. What else does she want to see? One or the other, fucking command!"

Beginning with her gestation, Milena offered her mother a new respite. It was at the limit of fertility that Milena appeared, allowing her mother to obtain a new signification regarding her femininity. She appeared in a challenge in which the life of one of them was at stake (one or the other). In her prehistory, Milena was a fibrome; the space she occupied was interpreted as a pathology and the absence of menstruation as the exhaustion of a function.

About her birth, she stated, "They pulled me out of the tree; suddenly I found myself detached. [This was her idea of a Caesarian.] For me, there was a time when there was no time. I feel as if I hadn't been born." Among others, we meet in Milena's history these images of the uncanny, which slip with metonymical signification and are condensed in Jose's assassination, to be precipitated a few days later in the symptom.

When referring to the disquieting scene, she said, "There is a piece that I am missing. I am not allowed to attain it. This middle between the very alive and the very dead—I am not allowed to arrive at it. This step between life and death, this tangible moment, I was left with the sensation of the very alive and a moment later, the very dead. They would not let me come near; the policeman was kicking him with his boot to see if he was still alive or already dead." As Freud observed, "An uncanny experience occurs either when infantile complexes which have been repressed are once more revived by some impression, or when primitive beliefs which have been surmounted seem once more to be confirmed." [5]

We posit the repercussion of the historical moment in the suffering of which Milena is speaking on the basis of the place that she herself assigned to it in her own discourse. She used it as backdrop to historicize her life, divided by the traumatic fact of Jose's assassination. A before and an after signal a moment that was structuring for the subject. When the analysand said, "I don't know what happened," she was referring to the amnesia and to the difficulties she had in understanding her own experience. We suppose that the experience of abandonment and complete impotence made her regress to originary situations. Suffering an aggression of extreme violence—the omnipotence of the Other (powerfulness in being)—puts Milena in an extreme situation of submission and impotence, which is homologous to the abandonment of the *infans*.

We consider that a new fact, such as the one suffered by Milena, left her without recourse to the referents that would have signified it for her. How many enigmatic infancy scenes became actualized when for hours she had to confront one already dead who moved or one still alive who was as if dead? We think that the amnesia functioned as a support, replacing the hole dug by the intolerable of the real, this impossible to bear. She thus clung to a symbolic element that allowed her to speak on the basis of the effacement, just as those who disappeared or were "sucked up"—that is, assassinated—spoke to the whole world as fantasmatic actors of a national tragedy.

The time that elapsed between the traumatic fact and the appearance of the symptom poses several questions. Milena remembered this lapse of time only tangentially. She put together assassination and amnesia without solution of continuity.

There is a fissure where two alternatives are in play: being crazy and denouncing what she saw, which was a "crazy thing" to do, or following common sense and keeping silent about what she knew—a terrible contradiction that would explain why, when her university discourse started up again, in the position of the agent, her memory faded and created large unknowns. Let's remember that Milena lost her memory in front of an audience that was willing to listen to her. She left them without her words, unsatisfied, in a spectacular actualization where she as well as the Other kept mum. What was the effect on Milena of putting herself in the place of knowledge, a place successfully occupied by Jose? Did she think that she had to speak of her trial—imaginary and possible—of Kafka's *Trial*, of the Kafkaesque military process? Was she to endure this metamorphosis so that common sense would prevail on the side of life? Was it about the metamorphosis of her husband being drained of his blood? Was it about this passage from the live to the dead that she was supposed to speak?

Faced with the question that she evoked in others—that is, "What happened to you?" (today, yesterday, a few days ago)—she would always reply, "I don't know what happened," an adequate answer to a police interrogation of the times. It was better not to know anything, because knowing entailed a danger.

With Milena, metonymic sliding and metaphorical production are very rich. Her ability to articulate lived scenes to fantasmatic scenes and to actual scenes permanently leads back to the desire that is suspended from and constantly attributed to the Other.

The nonsense of her symptom led her to say that her life had no meaning. She requested an analysis to recoup literature: literature—that through which she was able to think of herself as being somebody. Months after the beginning of treatment, she said, "It was so terrible that I can't understand why I did not lose consciousness."* But she did lose it a few days later. She had lost what she thought she could fill: her lack. This is why, for years, she lived with the impression of being half alive, with only part of her being.

Starting from the signifiers *The Trial* and *Metamorphosis,* she reformulated her identity: now she is an ex-professor. She speaks of herself by saying that she underwent a metamorphosis, that when she is about to reach the revelation of a truth, it vanishes.

At the present time, she has lifted the amnesia from a great part of her literary knowledge. Curiously enough, she regained memory of European literature. She remembers a little about Latin American writers, but when she manages to do so, she is incapable of specifying their country of origin. It would seem that what she lost with Kafka, she gets back with Kafka.

The "I don't know" slid to the innermost part of her being. She

---

* *"Perdre connaissance"* means "to faint" but literally it means "to lose knowledge, consciousness." —Trans.

started to wonder how many assertions, desires, and facts appear in her life only as negations. The "I don't know what happened" is expressed today in a heartbreaking questioning about the meaning of her existence.

If the symptom is an opening onto the real, would the amnesia lead us toward the real of the symbolic manifested by the fantasy? Is amnesia the real of the fantasy to which we gain access through its signifying articulation? These are questions to which we find no answers at the moment.

Milena tried "to kill death" with her silence. This attitude toward death had consequences on her life, which became impoverished when the great wager in the Argentina of the years 1976–82, the wager on life itself, could not be risked.

Within the context of World War II, Freud states, "We tried to kill life with silence." Such killing is the primitive omnipotence that the dictatorship recreated by taking human beings away from the question about their constitution as subjects ($). It is through such questioning that life handles its finitude, structuring itself on the basis of the originary wound, as punctuation of the drive derivatives toward thought and the search for symbolic realization.

Because of their constitution, humans are exposed to the totalitarian offer of responding to everything, of filling all spaces. For Milena, the constitutive command was precisely that of filling the lack—an offer of order and omnipotence resulting from the request for the absolute in which the subject constituted itself as ego in the other, subject of desire, subjugated in the plot of an imaginary hope of completeness. The discourse as well as the despotic action found an echo in her. Power always attempts to lean upon terror, but it also requires an acquiescence.

The danger to which Milena exposed herself was, consciously or unconsciously, to obey a proposition of order, the absolutism of which would be deadly for her.

—Translated by Françoise Massardier-Kenney

Notes

1. Albert Camus, "Hope and the Absurd in the Work of Franz Kafka," in *The Myth of Sisyphus and Other Essays,* translated by Justin O'Brien (New York: Knopf, 1955).

2. Sigmund Freud, *S.E.*, vol. 20, ed. James Strachey (London: Hogarth, 1959), 93–94.

3. G. Miller, et al., "Acerca de la clinica de la psicosis" (Concerning the psycho-analytic treatment of psychosis), in *La Practica analitica O: Como se analiza hoy?* (Buenos Aires: Fundacion del Campo Freudiano, 1984).

4. L. Torres, "If I Think about What I Have Been Capable of Doing, I Want to Die," paper presented at the Third International Meeting of the *Champ freudien*, Buenos Aires, 1984.

5. S. Freud, *S.E.*, vol. 17, 249.

12. On Blasphemy: Religion and Psychological Structure

Miguel Bassols and Germán L. Garcia
with E. Berenguer, R. M. Calvet i Romani, E. Guilana,
V. Palomera, and E. Paskuan

The contents of the hysterical deliria often turn out to be the very circle of ideas which the patient in his normal state has rejected, inhibited and suppressed with all his might. (For instance, blasphemies and erotic ideas occur in the hysterical deliria of nuns.)

—Sigmund Freud, "The Mechanism of Hysterical Phenomena"

And why not interpret one face of the Other, the face of God, as supported by feminine *jouissance?*

—Jacques Lacan, "God and the *Jouissance* of Woman"

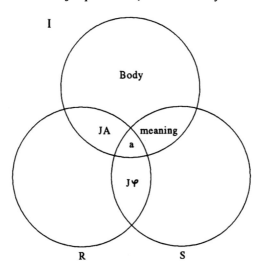

—Jacques Lacan, "La Troiesième"

Our interest in blasphemy arose out of the frequency with which it appears among the different clinical types, which brings into question the persisting opinion according to which it is supposed to be an exclusive trait of obsessional neurosis. The blasphemy that imposes itself in obsession, the blasphemy that is invoked in hysteria, and that which is revealed in psychosis are not articulated in the same way.

When working on this paper, we ran up against the complexity of the discourse on religion in Lacan's teaching and thus against the impossibility of answering the questions that arise as a result of referring to his pronouncements. It was necessary not to obscure these questions that thus mark out our path.

Freud speaks of blasphemy in "The Ratman" and "The Wolfman." These two references share an ellipsis—a term that derives from "lack"—and the attempt by the subject to construct a euphemism, to find the right tone. In these cases, blasphemy is imperative. Censorship introduces ellipsis, and euphemism is the place of return.

Emile Benveniste has noticed three euphemistic modes (as blasphemy concerning the name): substitution, mutilation of the name,[1] and creation of a nonsense—that is to say, metaphor, synecdoche, and the way Freud described the *jouissance* of words when they become freed from the imperative of signification.

Linguists only find there a few general operations. For instance, Benveniste solves the problem through a comparison with Freud's thesis on taboo: desire and obedience. "In the same way," Benveniste writes, "the interdiction of the name of God muzzles one of the most intense desires of men: that of desecrating the sacred. . . . Religious tradition wanted to keep only the divine and excluded the sacred curse. In its own way, blasphemy wants to reestablish this totality by desecrating the *name* of God, because the only thing of God that we have is his name."[2]

In this perspective, blasphemy is situated in the interdiction of a certain *jouissance,* at the limit of a *jouissance* of the Other that men can attribute to a woman and that a woman can infer—as phallic *jouissance*—in men. How could this *jouissance* outside sex *[hors-sexe]* exist outside of words? This *jouissance* of the Other outside of language and this phallic *jouissance* outside of the body are articulated in blasphemy and euphemism: what "cannot go through the mouth"—the *jouissance* of the Other—by means of the ellipsis of desire, returns as phallic *jouissance* (substitution, mutilation of the name, and creation of nonsense). Couldn't we read thus the "letter-litter" of the blasphemer James Joyce?

The effect of a real, the private religion called neurosis becomes the passion of an innocent desire to know (the sincere negation of the obsessional, the authentic hysterical desire that its law gives itself).

A formula of Jacques Lacan's (March 12, 1968) can situate the sincere "no" of religious vocation and the authenticity of revelation and/ or possession:

$$\mathcal{S} \ (s \bigvee SA \ )$$

sincere ↙   ↘ authentic

no   being

The disjunction between "sincere no" and "authentic being" is that existing between the one who announces himself as not being what he articulates and the one who forgets, not knowing that he forgets. In this formula, the signifying Other is the signifier Other (SA), which comes in the place of the repressed signifier—a substitution the effect of which is the divided subject, $\mathcal{S}$.

The request for a response addressed to the Other, according to Lacan (21 March 1963), leads to what, in Freud's terms, is called *Versagung:* retraction, misleading word, the breaking of a promise, curses.

And on this point, Lacan reminds us of the ambiguity that links, after certain transformations, blasphemy to blame (reprobation, censorship, vituperation, *Versagen,* to fail to keep a promise, not to keep one's word, blasphemy and blame).

Racine's *Athalie,* according to Roland Barthes, illustrates the language of blasphemy. It is a schism: a rupture of the alliance between God and his people, the Father and the Son. The cross, in this matter, is the restoration of the collective contract. There is in it a battle, a tussle, and blasphemy: "You win, you God of the Jews!"

In Barcelona, during the tragic week, convents are burned down and nuns are raped. Joan Maragall writes, "The revolutionary spirit is strong like wine, the filth of the city seems to be ordered by the thermometer, beggars swarm like flies, there is a lot of dust and noise, and if you look at it closely, bombs, blasphemy, and counterfeit money all have the same origin."[3] He also says that at that moment, Barcelona is like the "famous infamous" city.

We observe the break of the pact without any question about what it founds, because when you live according to daddy's ideals, things turn sour if daddy doesn't have any ideals.

Lacan, when speaking of the blasphemy of Judge Schreber (God is a w——), refers to *L'Expérience intérieure* and *Madame Edwarda* by George Bataille.

This is a theodicy where blasphemy is the "term where culminates the process through which the signifier became 'unchained' in the real, after bankruptcy was opened in the name of the Father—that is to say, to the signifier which, in the Other, as place of the signifier, is the signifier of the Other as place of the law." [4]

The Name-of-the-Father is the self-consistency of the Other as law; it is the signifier that makes the Other (A) consistent. Blasphemy responds to the lack (Ⱥ).

The theodicy of Schreber speaks of God according to another principle of reason, a principle that takes away from God attributes that are suitable and gives him other attributes that are not at all appropriate. Schreber's theodicy is based on an attributive assertion, whereas compulsive blasphemy is an exclamation that can be called a denial. In the fall of 1893, Schreber is taken over by an idea that he would have refused indignantly: to be a woman during coitus. Here starts the odyssey that will end in theodicy.

Let us recall a few points made by Lacan in "On a Question Preliminary to Any Possible Treatment of Psychosis." [5] In a first stage, the R-schema can be read in the following way:

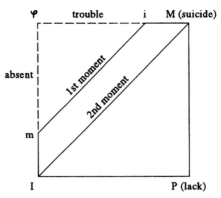

The feminine form that appears in m (at the level of primary narcissism) conflicts with the masculine self-love from which Schreber is indignant in I (secondary narcissism). For the feminine form to be bearable, it would be necessary that the alteration it proposes in i have a solution in the phallic image. But from the side of the phallus, nothing answers. If Schreber runs to take refuge at his mother's a few days after this fantasy, it is most certainly to find protection against the trouble he experienced. But he hardly finds a refuge there. So he decides that very night to take his own life, a first illustration of what is the leitmotif of his delirium: dropped from the hand of the creator. It is the Other who drops him. Thus, not being able to sustain himself in the phallic signification and condemned to disappear in M (the mother), Schreber tries to respond to the initial trouble in two ways: either he will feel the imminence of his own death, or he will develop in a *jouissance* not regulated by the reference to the phallus (*jouissance* of the Other).

On the imaginary side, Schreber's struggle is situated against nonphallic *jouissance*. The *jouissance* without law, which in schema I[6] presents itself to him in i, he recounts as transformations that go from the swelling of his breasts to the feminine softness that his skin takes on.

It is this *jouissance* without law that he names voluptuousness, opposed to what for him the legitimate *jouissance* of souls after death represents: blessedness. This polarity indicates the *jouissance* of the Other (outside the law and inside the body) and phallic *jouissance* (outside the body because reserved for souls).

But how to find the limit of the blessedness of souls vis-à-vis the voluptuousness of bodies? For Schreber, it is a matter of going from one opposition, where he is the object of God's *jouissance*, to another, where he will be able to benefit from the *jouissance* that the law of the order of the universe allows to souls.

In this imaginary struggle between two *jouissances*, the emasculation demanded by the voices is an outrage. It is presented as the condition for Schreber's transformation into a female whore handed over to men. On this point, the delirious construction will consist in an inversion of the meaning of emasculation: from outrage, it becomes, insofar as it is a necessary condition for the restoration of the order of the universe, a sacrifice accepted by Schreber. It is through this sacrifice that Schreber has access to the place that Lacan will later call (in relation to Joyce) the place of the redeemer, and that appears here as the place of the Virgin, the wife of God, mother of a regenerated human race—that is to say, nothing other than Woman, extreme of the delirious metaphor.

From this point of view, blasphemy is the culmination of the construction of delirium as revelation. It supposes this very passage where
the process of inversion of the meaning of emasculation ends, when
emasculation is articulated in the reference to phallic *jouissance*.

If we consider the Schreberian odyssey as a theodicy (that part of
theology that deals with proofs of the existence of God, of his wisdom
and of his justice, of his relation to the human soul), this restitution
could thus be localized:

$$\text{God is a w} \text{——} !$$
$$\text{Voluptuousness} \longrightarrow \text{Blessedness}$$
$$\text{JA} \qquad \textit{Blasphemy} \longrightarrow \text{J}\Phi$$

From God to Woman, blasphemy is the ultimate revelation of his
existence in "the blessedness which knows no bounds."

It would here be impossible to speak of the superego as we could in
relation to blasphemy in obsessional neurosis. In Schreber, nothing is
left of the sentence, "Let him who blasphemes the name of the Lord be
punished with Death." Nothing either of Jesus Christ, who was condemned to death for having called himself son of God.

Indeed, there is a history of the demand made to the Other to respond. The laws of King Saint Louis punished blasphemy with a "hole
in the tongue," which was to be made with a red-hot iron. Pius V
(1566) proposed a graduation of the punishment in cases where the
blasphemous act was repeated.

The instauration of Christianity broadens the meaning of blasphemy:
it is no longer a question of uttering a word that implies the *name* of
God, but of any affirmation that gives and/or takes away anything from
legitimate doctrine—that is, the name of God is immediately captured
by the discourse of its representatives. The Arians will be accused of
blasphemy for having said that God is a simple creature, the Manicheans
for saying that the good God finds himself obliged to allow evil, the
Pelagians for having given a metaphorical sense to redemption, etc.

"If he has faith, why dare he commit blasphemy? And why does he
blaspheme if he does not have faith? . . . It seems impossible that a
Catholic dare as much; it seems just as impossible that the atheist would
use words which mean nothing to him," states Father Ramon Font in a
small treatise in 1887.[7]

Blasphemy is an utterance that denies, subject of the impossible enunciation since there is no response to the master signifier. Excess and deficiency, blasphemy is an act of enunciation the utterance of which is meaningless. Ramon Font thinks that "its existence is inexplicable and its origin incomprehensible," that it is a matter of a useless and pernicious *jouissance,* that it does not propose anything to communicate.

Another priest, Father Carlo Salicru, in September 1929—in the newspaper *La Vanguardia*—launched a manifesto in favor of the legal repression of blasphemy in order to support the action of the Royal Association against Blasphemy.[8] He also supports the activities of the Works of the Good Word and of the Spiritual League against Evil Speech, societies founded at the end of the twenties, which received a broad diffusion and a lot of publicity.

A *jouissance* beyond *jouissance*—addressed to God, to woman— introduces the evil of substitution, mutilation, and nonsense. Language will not respond with a lesser profusion of euphemisms.

Lacan has emphasized that the path that leads from theology to atheism shows the Christian God as one and three to be a radical articulation of kinship: a symbolic kinship of the Father, the Son, and Love.

For religion asserts that God ex-sists, that he is repression personified. That is why religion is true. Ex-sistence, repression of phallic *jouissance,* religion as the ideal of neurosis—of ideal neurosis, which is obsessional—the ob-cession, gives in in several ways. Between the real and death, the symbolic *jouissance* of speech, and the imaginary of the body (RSI), love can be situated: divine love, symbolic mediation between the real of death and the imaginary of the body; courtly love, imaginary mediation between the real of death and the symbolic *jouissance* of speech (RIS); Christian love, mediation of the real of death between the symbolic and the imaginary (IRS) (this is thus what is called masochism).[9]

If theology consists in substituting the term "end" for the term "desire," Christian love transforms desire in the relation of the body to death. It is thus not a question of Schreber's theodicy, but of the practice of virtues of an ascetic theology (which can be compared to obsessional neurosis, just as mystic theology is hysterical in its search for perfection).

If ex-sistence is phallic *jouissance* and repression of this *jouissance* in the name of God, blasphemy aims at the Other *jouissance.*

Sartre writes, "God saw me, I felt His gaze inside my head and on my hands. I whirled about in the bathroom, horribly visible, a live target. Indignation saved me: I flew into a rage against so crude an indiscretion, I blasphemed, muttered like my grandfather: 'Sacré nom de Dieu de nom de Dieu!' [Sacred name of God of name of God!]. He does not watch me anymore."[10]

It is also Lacan's grandfather who reveals to him the dimension of blasphemy: "this horrible character thanks to whom I gained access, at an early age, to the fundamental function of cursing God."[11]

There is a lot to say about the grandfather and his relation to "the obscure authority of the Other" embodied by the parents, this obscurity that, for Sartre as for the Ratman, is a gaze that knows what the subject desires, because the subject has no other desire than that of this gaze.

But why is blasphemy a fundamental function? "In the place where the unspeakable object is rejected in the real, a word makes itself heard"[12]—a formula that situates blasphemy as what can be heard when the object is left without symbolic inscription (psychosis), or when the object comes to the limit of imaginary consistency of the ego-other dialectic, in neurosis.

This real at the limit of imaginary recognition defines the insult as what "reveals itself through the epos to be the first as well as the last word of the dialogue."[13] In this case, "to blaspheme" only retains an etymological relation with "to blame" (from *blastemare,* through dissimulation of the second labial). In certain languages, as is the case in Catalan, it mixes with the onomatopoeia *flist-flast* of fustigation and with the verb "to fustigate" itself. Would it be possible, from "A child Is Being Beaten," to situate blasphemy in perverse fantasy?

Madame Edwarda speaks of the desire to be vile, until reaching the certainty that she, the whore, is God, as the Lord *Sans-sens* (Without-sense) writes it at the limit of the already invisible, of the impossible reciprocity. The blasphemy ("God is a w——") reaches the object expurgated of some kind of knowledge about the torture of *jouissance.* Since "if God knew, he would be a pig."[14]

In the seminar on transference, Lacan, when referring to *The Hostage* by Paul Claudel, speaks of an image of desire reduced to the Sadean reference, a substitution of the image of woman for the Christian symbol of the cross, an opening beyond any value according to faith. Bernanos, says Lacan, avoided this work as if it were blasphemy.[15]

By the intermediary of Woman, the other side of God, let's return to

Schreber: "Indeed, for whoever knows how to listen, myths represent the greatest blasphemy of all: divine amazement which disguises itself as human virtue. . . . Being loved is to enter into the chain of the desirable, . . . because if God is desirable, he is more or less so, and what we desire in God is then what is desirable, and no longer God."[16] What makes God desirable, more or less, is blasphemy, inasmuch as it retracts and accords certain attributes to God.

Possessions, demonic or divine, pose for us, from a different angle, the question of the *jouissance* of woman and of her Other: God. Hysteria makes an invitation that ends up by demonstrating his impotence. If the devil figures a knowledge of *jouissance,* God, not knowing hate, seems rather not to know. It may be that it is only the case of the God full of morality produced by Christianity, and not that of the Old Testament, whose wrath was to be feared.

Testimonies about possessions indicate it: the inducement frequently takes the form of blasphemy, which goes up the ladder of church dignitaries and comes close to God himself: "Cure her! God is all powerful." But the convulsive woman imposes her law on God. Castration appears in the Other: the possessed body remains the object the inaccessibility of which is redoubled by its phallic character. Amazement of the observers: the evil attacks the most pious ones, and during sacramental rites! Hatred of God, impossibility of praying, necessity of blaspheming, of cursing one's neighbor, of screaming.

Here, blasphemy, like screams, takes place at the limit of speech, mimicking the radical exteriority of a *jouissance* outside language, which, on the flip side of the coin, is mimicked by euphemisms, the model of which, according to biblical testimonies, is silence (sometimes figured by an imperceptible whispering of the celestial voices in Yahweh's presence).

Those who have applied the rigor of phenomenological analysis to religious experience haven't been able to go beyond this observation: the multiple figures of the fear of God that characterize religious experience are reducible to an excess of signification that is superposed to what is "radically heterogeneous," radical exteriority, a figuration of the divine in relation to the "creature." This surplus, which Otto describes with a neologism, "the numinous," falls like a shadow on the subject of the experience, affected with a minus sign: this is "profanity." A taboo against the contact will thus increase the impossibility of a meeting between heterogeneous orders. Blasphemy projects this shadow again, like a boomerang, onto the field of the Other.

The fear of God is not born from experience; it is born from an a priori in the Kantian sense. Its most elementary manifestation lies in the feeling of the uncanny *(Unheimlich)*, which is distinguished from common fear by a somatic sensation: shaking.

Otto sees quite well what psychology stumbles against in order to describe this experience: "The division pleasure/displeasure still bothers us. It is not legitimate to differentiate pleasures by considering only the diverse gradations of the tension of a single sentiment."[17]

In the field of aesthetics, the correlate of the *named* experience is the sublime, the first and the most elementary insinuation of which is the feeling of repugnance, between the profane and the sacred. Bodies start becoming sacred when they decompose, and the shadow of the divine becomes evident in rot. Let's remember that Schreber's God is an expert only in corpses. Sin itself, for the being, must carry the shadow of the divine; it must carry a negative "numinous value" indicating a plus elsewhere. Let's think of *jouissance* as an aggravating circumstance to a superior degree of relentlessness, in legal discourse. The non-sense of an excess of *jouissance* beyond some presumed motivation is found here ordered by the discourse of the law, which advises to moderate the "numinous value" of *jouissance*.

Blasphemy is the purest expression of an operation the essence of which is discourse: this is the weakness of the phenomenological analysis of Otto, who posits it in terms of rational/irrational. Responding with blasphemy to the irruption of this order heteregeneous to language fills the mouth that otherwise can remain strangely empty, in what Otto calls "amazement": to gape, the common root of the Hebrew and Greek expressions that describe swooning in the presence of the divine as "that which comes out of the circle of the innermost." A conjuration, invocation, or an ejaculatory prayer of *jouissance,* blasphemy responds in discourse to the zone that is at the center of the psychic economy, which Freud called *Das Ding*—at the center but excluded. Lacan will make it into a neologism—"extimacy"—to account for its topology in connection with what is innermost in the subject.

A limit operator in each language, blasphemy allows the passage from a consistent Other, the impossible of *jouissance,* to a barred Other that reactivates desire:

blasphemy

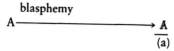

(a)

A narrative by Pierre Klossowski, *Vocation suspendue [Suspended Vocation]*,[18] shows us, in the unfolded form of paraphrase, the sliding toward blasphemy of this passage. Its title already indicates to us the point where that which invokes, once the subject of the intention is suspended, appears confronted with the object obscured by the intention. Where desire insists on supporting itself as impossible against an Other that makes *jouissance* be abandoned, blasphemy will play the role of hinge between two zones continuously evoked throughout the narrative "from one zone to the next": from God (or the church as his body) to woman (a woman whose name offers to the Spanish translation the chance of a wonderful ambiguity: Sister Theo (in Spanish, *Sor Theo = Sorteo*, "drawing lots"). Of the neighboring zones, which desire holds to be disjunct, the subject will cross the common border without knowing which step crossed it: from the obscure God whom he sees appear after an interminable inquisitorial plot line, to the woman who will embody, under the whiteness of the habit, the last question about his desire: "Double faced divinity: sometimes death, other times desire, other times impulse, other times inertia."[19]

The last step, of which Jérôme, the seminarian hero, compulsively delays the verification, will finally be invoked by the blasphemy that brings an end to the narrative. Thus, in between the lines, he offers us the operation of blasphemy as inverse of the operation of sublimation that a courtly love would have solved by elevating the object to the status of *Das Ding*.[20]

Klossowski gives the whole narrative a euphemistic tone. Always, something, the supposed nucleus of the subject of the enunciation, will be named through displacement onto another scene, under another name. In a style that Cervantes would have claimed as his own, the narrative alludes to another narrative, already written in another place and at another time, which, under the same title, would have recounted autobiographically a religious experience as apologia of the spirit of obedience, of the impossible escape from the obscene and ferocious insistence where we learn to recognize the imperative of the superego. Jérôme, an intrepid novice who is searching for the ultimate truth of his vocation, continues his pilgrimage from convent to convent, until he runs into the enigmatic company of the "Black Party," an inquisitorial sect that, near the end of the plot, will be substituted for by another order, about which it is said that the apparent tolerance will bring our seminarian to "suspend his vocation."

Between the submissive search for a good and ultimate order and the culpability of embodying he knows not which character in a suspicious scene, always for an unknown superior, Jérôme moves from one impossible—to know—to another—to say. The strange episode of an unfinished fresco that represents the vision of dogma prefigures for the seminarian the buffoonery of the sacrilegious scene in which he will end up participating in an imaginary play with his perverse double, the painter Malagrida. At the suggestion that he makes concerning the characters who should complete the fresco according to the right order, Malagrida and the Conners brothers will insult him with imprecations and blasphemies: "provoker . . . Jesus Mary . . . Son of a Jewess . . . from our Enemies, protect us, Mary . . . , from the plague, free us, Lord . . . Antichrist, nun's runt. . . . "

And here, the author will introduce for the first time a female character, Mother Angelica, who astounds Jérôme with her majestic beauty and the sweetness of her gaze. Veritable representative of Woman, she will be at the center of the plot and will soon become the accomplice of the seminarian's doubt in his labyrinth. It thus would seem, in the interminable plot, that Jérôme has succeeded in finding a consistent Other, on whom he will be able to lean his dislocated pedagogical order. But the introduction of such an angelic character goes hand in hand with that of another: an educator of youth, La Montagne, whose only aim will be to free, in Jérôme as well as in his perverse double, the most obscure object of their soul. To this trio—where the hero recognizes himself more alienated in his imaginary character the more he recognizes his implication in the schemes of the woman—will be added the eminent character of Father Persienne, whom the irony of the author will place at the rank of Father Therapist, and who will ask the seminarian how he managed to pass from "one zone to the other," from devotion to the most obscure profanation, from faith to radical doubt, from the sacred to the obscene, from grace to offense. But "that is exactly the question that Jérôme wanted to ask him." How can one find the guarantee of the Other beyond the inconsistency where his just order leads him?

From then on, the narrative unleashes the series of encounters of the protagonist with the imposters, each time more complex and redoubling one another, of each of his interlocutors. And this in as many forms as the subject is confronted with the question "What do you want?" that makes present the lack of/in the Other.

The subject thus remains in question, in suspense in relation to this Other, the obsessive form of which he had offered the fantasy of his mortification, in an exemplary description: "The man who had the pretentiousness to say, 'Where you live, I am dead, and where you are dead, I live,' must now admit that he was playing dead and that he lived much more where he reproached the others with living." The fact that the function of the Other is at ease with that of the dead implies that this dead is not experiencing *jouissance*. But also, the least sign of life that will make this Other move will return on the subject as a being of unbearable *jouissance*.

But what is going on in this other place discovered by his fantasy where the being is implicated up to the limit of the living of others? Every ritual set up to sustain this scene thus turns out to be in a false position in regard to the "Royal Presence" of the object (from God to Woman) that will hurl Jérôme into the horror of his own annihilation. Not only does he himself no longer believe in the innocence of his desire, but every new step he will take to put an end to what has become his own imposture will show him that he only takes it to satisfy a new strategy arising from the impostures of the others. It will be Mother Angelica who will introduce to him one of her young novices, Sister Theo, to create "love difficulties" for him, only for "experimental" reasons. Once again, Jérôme will follow the schemes of the obscure power of Mother Angelica, who, at that point in the narrative, has already shown herself to be a version of the Father, a euphemistic version who imposes and forbids simultaneously.

Didn't Freud state about the Ratman that it is as a euphemism that we must understand his "mental associations," associations through which the desire of the death of the father makes the path that conditions the access to the object?

If the hero Jérôme stops here—leaving in suspense the "vocation" in front of the "compact mass of words" in which he hopes to be able to modulate his imprecation to the Other—Klossowski's narrative will continue to reserve for itself an "ultimate demonstration" that in reality punctuates the conclusion of the narrative and hurls Jérôme to the limit of the sequence.

In the play of imaginary identifications, he will now try to replace his former double, Malagrida, and he will propose marriage to Sister Theo. In the play of mirrors, a time thus opens up, as aggressive tension, where the vacillation or the certainty of the other is what is decisive for the conclusion of the vocations and of their truth. "If she accepts, it will have been proven that she didn't have an authentic vocation either. If she hesitates, the priest will have to fuel her hesitation to the point of leading her to a refusal." But it is well known, in the logical circuit thus proposed, that the only possible conclusion is the identification with the other, if not the return to waiting for death.

One thing that Sister Theo considers when she hesitates indicates the routing of the object toward a different place, where sublimation would offer a release to *jouissance:* "It is better for him to worship the Lord in a form which does not offend his conscience." History teaches us that it is with this metaphor (woman in the place of God) that the modern concept of love took shape. That is the step that courtly love (RIS) takes, starting from divine love (RSI), when it elevates the object to the status of the Thing—the form in which Lacan showed the operation of sublimation.[21]

But the final, negative response of the novice, which refuses to Jérôme the possibility of a new love, leaves him facing the limit of his desire, already enmeshed in all the possible imaginary combinations. The turn taken seems to invert the path of sublimation toward an eschatology that is less divine. (In passing, let's remember Lacan's reference in 1961 to Arnaut Daniel's sextina, where the courtly love poet uses puns to put his "gentle lady" at the level of scoria.)[22] At this point when the discourse goes toward the encounter with the unutterable object, only one act remains for Jérôme: "He himself remains fascinated with the reprehensible aspect that he imprints on a situation which wasn't so in itself and which he wants at any cost: blasphemous."

A suspended vocation, blasphemy reduces invocation to its prime signifying dimension. It is not a matter of a sacrilegious utterance, but of the act of enunciation of a name, the name of God, on which the interdiction falls.

And it is with the ways in which blasphemy has come into common usage in every language that we can come to better understand the discontinuity that it establishes between the said and the saying, between the utterance and the enunciation. A jingle marking the holes in meaning in the discourse, a meaningless refrain at the end of every sentence, said in passing and without any communicative intent, it already belongs to this "common heritage" that the Other of language consists of. That it gained this place only at the cost of euphemism accounts for the fact that there is no cause introduced in the subject that isn't an effect of language. Deformations, aphaereses, displacements, and condensations give to its basic form—"Nom de Dieu!" ["God damn it"; literally, "Name of God"]—a series of variations with a very large rhetorical range. The variation that expands "Nom de Dieu" into "Vingt Dieux" ["Twenty Gods!"] appears to want to make countable a space that Achilles was never able to traverse. Another variation, perhaps: the one that operates, in several of our Romance languages, a sliding toward the feminine—the common Catalan of "emc——de Dieu," which produced that no-less-common "Me caso amb dena" [literally: "I marry *dena*," nonsignifying form of the feminine gender].

If theology substitutes for the term of desire that of the end, blasphemy makes a hole in the end in order to reassert desire.

—*Translated by Françoise Massardier-Kenney*

Notes

1. Emile Benveniste, "Le blasphème et l'euphémisme," *Problèmes de linguistique générale,* vol. 2 (Paris: Gallimard, 1975), 254–57.
2. Ibid., 255.
3. Joan Maragall, "Ah! Barcelona," *Elogi de la paraula i altres assaigs* (Barcelona: Editions 62, 1978).
4. Jacques Lacan, *Ecrits: A Selection,* translated by Alan Sheridan (New York: Norton, 1977), 221.
5. Ibid., 179–225.
6. Ibid., 212.
7. Ramon Font, *La Blasphemia* (Gerona: Tomos Carrera, 1887).
8. Carlos Salicru, "La represion legal de la blasfemia," *El desnudo de arte* (Barcelona: Hormiga de Ora, 1930).
9. Jacques Lacan, "R.S.I.," *Ornicar?* 2 (1975).

10. Jean-Paul Sartre, *The Words,* translated by Bernard Frechtman (New York: Braziller, 1964), 102. Translation modified.
11. Seminar of December 6, 1961.
12. *Ecrits: A Selection,* 183.
13. Lacan, "L'étourdit," *Scilicet* 4 (1973): 44.
14. Georges Bataille, *Madame Edwarda, Oeuvres Brèves* (Paris: Pauvert, 1981).
15. Jacques Lacan, *Le séminaire, livre VIII: Le transfert, 1960–61.* Text established by Jacques-Alain Miller (Paris: Seuil, 1991), 326–27.
16. Lacan, *Le Transfert.*
17. Rudolf Otto, *The Idea of the Holy* (New York: Oxford University Press, 1950).
18. Pierre Klossowski, *La Vocation suspendue* (Paris: Gallimard, 1950).
19. Ibid., 67.
20. Jacques Lacan, *The Seminar of Jacques Lacan, Book VII: The Ethics of Psychoanalysis, 1959–60,* ed. Jacques-Alain Miller, translated by Dennis Porter (New York: Norton, 1992).
21. Ibid., 85–164.
22. Ibid., 161–63.

13. The Discourse of Gangs in the Stake of Male Repression and Narcissism

Willy Apollon

Do gangs endorse the feminine? The least one can say about this subject is that more and more women—at least a few—do not recognize themselves in what gangs endorse of the feminine. The gang as institution is a social bond among men. Thus it maintains itself with a particular discourse, the basic articulations of which we will be attempting to pinpoint.

Every instauration or institution, as act, is an exclusion. It defines an "us" starting from a censorship. Here we want to make evident what of the discourse of gangs defines an "outside" and what institutes a social bond. But this operation among males, or, more exactly, in the discourse of gangs, aims first at the exclusion of female desire or at what in the female discourse links up with the troublesome familiarity of the unbearable. What is found censored here is a part of female sexuality, if not female desire as such. But this does not occur without the promotion of what the feminine is for the gang. Hence, at the same time there is an absolute transgression and a misunderstanding. And then what? A few schemata go with this argumentation, for information and discussion.

What Makes Men Run?

As backdrop of these theoretical reflections on sex in regard to gangs, we find a double preoccupation. On the one hand, we remain dependent on a certain approach and practice in relation to the notion of group that determines for us the very concept of group in relation to another concept, just as controversial, that a theorization of our practices allows us to evaluate better: the notion of institution. On the other hand, even if it does not pretend to reach it, this presentation is part of a longer effort aiming at theoretical precision concerning what our preoccupation

with psychotic men showed us to be the object of *an impossible demand.*
This notion we shall name here with a very vague term, unfortunately:
the term "masculine."

We owe the concept of gangs, as specific to the masculine, to Michèle
Montrelay. Like all the other concepts that guide us here, its interest is
linked for us to what it yields in terms of "knowledge," and thus of
structure concerning what we take for "our" experience. Thus it would
be better from the start to warn you that our theoretical practice, pure
game against death, has nothing in common with any hope or any truth.

Group-Institution

It would not be without interest here to oppose the notion of gang to
that of group and institution in order to capture some of its significant
aspects. The term "group" encompasses several meanings. What is under
discussion for us here is something at the same time rather simple and
rather specific: a global structure with an internal law of composition—
for instance, the law of inclusion or, if you will, of belonging. We have
here a boundary concept, some aspects of which we simply want to
work out as far as logic will allow us. Thus, the group would refer
neither to the sum of its members nor to their relations, but rather to
their positions in a global structure and to the mobility of its positions,
and to the relations of some of these positions to other positions, independently of the individuals who occupy them. In other words, beyond
unconscious, fantasmatic stakes, which are repeated for everyone in a
group situation, is there a structure that produces the group effect and
that everyone is at grips with, beyond the fact that there are other
partners in the group? For us, obviously, the answer is yes, since it is this
dimension that we refer to with the very concept of group.

Of course, this purely logical dimension—perhaps we should say this
logico-mathematical dimension—has no existence of its own. It can only
be symbolized and calculated. But nonetheless it rings true, impossible as
its existence may seem. Here we perhaps find the distracting dimension
of the group. It makes you nuts. This is also its interesting side, for
against that we have no real psychic defense mechanism. We only have
rhetoric. But should it be lacking—and that is the crux of the matter for
us—then the group must be imagined as an other or marked in a real

person, often in a boss, to whom is attributed this all-encompassing power that characterizes fantasmatic characters.

As for the institution, it is a discourse. It is a local discourse that produces a social bond. As with the group, we think that the examination of the concept of institution should not take individuals into great account. An example will allow us to clarify this concept and give us a glimpse of the problems with which it can confront us. Are physics, biology, and psychology sciences, or are they institutions? Without settling this question, which would be arbitrary and quite beyond our intention, we can propose certain theoretical questions—quite familiar, actually, at least to specialists—and very enlightening ones. A local scientific discourse—that of physics, for example (but it could be psychology as well)—first claims to have an object of study. It is even defined on the basis of the validity of this object. However, a very rigorous analysis of the facts never manages to evacuate the unavoidable: this discourse, the independence of which must be established at all costs, is the object of a passion (the word is not too strong).

First, this discourse and this passion that maintains its independent objectivity are the only links between practitioners. Also, for each of them, it seems to be their "life," all their life, to see the discourse and passion operate. It is this kind of local discourse that passion makes alive and detachable in a specific objectivity—let us call it emotional— that I am calling "Institution." It is the discourse of an Other, or it is the Other discourse. We are not about to confuse this discursive phenomenon with the unconscious, the discourse of the Other. Of course, this Other of the institution, as discourse, is not without being embodied. As with the group, its symbolic dimension, its being of pure language, is not bearable where metaphors are not currently used. Indeed, for the group as for the institution, it is a matter of being purely discursive; their consistency is only symbolic, as is their praxis. Moreover, when the dimension of the metaphor is lacking, they can only take an overly emotional delirious imaginary form.

There is an interesting illusion, for all it can still carry of belief (belief in a truth, for instance): it is the denial that as subject one is always, one might say, off center and in exteriority in relation to the group as well as to the institution. It is noticeable, by the way, that as long as it is a question of a hypothesis for action and a pure and simple illusion, its value lies entirely in its pure logical efficacy. This is hardly negligible when it works. Nothing goes amiss! But hypothesis is not law.

Thus we are going to use the concept of group as structure of equivalent positions implying interrelations between these positions. For us, the question of the origin of groups is without interest. As such, the group does not exist; it is a formal (logico-mathematical) necessity of which it is hardly necessary or useful to imagine more consistency than its symbolic efficacy in practice. What is interesting is knowing what it can allow as access to the real of gangs and sex. As for the institution, it is a discourse that creates a social bond, that is to say, a space for passion. You can also call it life if you will, or, like Freud, life or love drive—that is to say, this dream that is the only reality (that one is psychic) and from which we must not awaken someday. It would be death, finally—the real thing . . . or perhaps psychosis.

Gangs Are Not Groups; They Are Institutions

Let us start again from this rather blunt affirmation. It is less interesting to try to ground it than to make use of its openings. First, what is a gang? We are going to sketch what seems to us to be its structure, which is quite noticeable in every masculine stake, always somewhat on the verge of the tragic and the ridiculous. To say that gangs do not constitute groups implies a distinction to be made between the gang effect and what the group structure presupposes and/or imposes. We shall have to come back to this. Logically, it is necessary to analyze the gang effect in its specificity, above all. That the gang is an institution leads us to think that it is a discourse, or in any case, the effect of a discourse that would first institute not an object—other than the supposed objectivity of this discourse—but an emotional bond between those whose identification is sustained by such a discourse. Here, an example will provide some guidance.

Psychology as discourse does not produce a specific object—for instance, the parapsychological phenomenon or psychism, the reference to which or the consistency of which in an experimental field would determine the scientificity of psychological discourse. Rather, we must ascertain that such a discourse does not produce any other object than its own objectivity as discourse, inasmuch as this objectivity is a belief necessary to the psychologist. Indeed, it is psychology, as instituted discourse, that constitutes the link between psychologists. Moreover, this discourse institutes their social identity, instead and in place of a symbolic identity that would be sustained by the Names-of-the-Father. You are a psychologist or a doctor or a biochemist before being Mr. or Ms. So-and-so. The socioprofessional identification founded on an instituted discourse called "scientific" (but that is an ideological guarantee) functions as a substitute in regard to the relation that the subject has with the Names-of-the-Father.

On the other hand, psychology, or any other instituted discourse, presents itself in its supposed objectivity like the object of a passion, which links them, and it ensures their sociohistorical and professional identification. A similar passion for psychology as scientific object links them to one another and founds their professional incorporation. They form a body thanks to this object, the scientific objectivity of the discourse of psychology. The affection of everyone for this object is what motivates the institution to recognize it as "incorporated," a socioprofessional incorporation. But it is also what guarantees its relation and its communications to the *other parts of the body*.

When we say that the gang is an institution, this is precisely what we mean. It is a discourse that institutes the sociohistorical identification instead and in place of the symbolic identification or of the relation of the subject to the Names-of-the-Father, as signifier of its "being for death." And furthermore, the discourse of gangs ensures that everyone is recognized by the others.

The Form of the Discourse of Gangs Is Negative

The first difficulty that occurs when analyzing the gang as institution is that the fact that the gang is a discourse is not obvious and that, if this fact were granted, the problem of locating such a discourse would not necessarily be simplified. Thus, rather, we will start off from the hypothesis that the gang is *first an institutional discourse*. This hypothesis, like any other, is the fruit of a decision, a theoretical act of violence that is worth only what it allows of *mise en seme*[1] in the analysis of a certain amount of data. We must add that this *mise en seme* of given multiplicities, this knowledge, is meaningful only in the interventions it allows. The last reference is thus ethical and political.

The first question to be asked is that of the form of such a discourse if it exists. Our first apprehension of the discourse of gangs presents it in the negative form of insults. We have noted three insults that in what they bring to mind are not without differences, but that seem to center a hollowed-out life that is made to man, as an imposed ideal from a superego. These insults would be, it seems to us, the negative form of a positive discourse that up till now we have not succeeded in identifying in its positivity. What is interesting about these insults is that they haunt the masculine fear of rejection by the gang. It is not rare in the context of treatment that they appear as the signal announcing special sexual problems. These problems are special for us in their very name. They are referred to as being problems of sexual impotence. Their being labeled and put together under such an appellation points out to us the cluster where these insults focus something of the order of an impossibility.

These insults are insults said to a man by a man. Whereas when sexual impotence enters discourse in the insult mode, whoever the speaker may be, the place from where it is heard as insult supposes that it would be a woman's insult aimed at a man. This is a decisive difference.

We could also consider representing these insults when taking into consideration this fundamental difference. We would then have the *simplex* or the *cartel*[2] of figure 13.1, in which the three masculine insults imply the *non-dit* that can surface in the mode of an insult from woman to man. All in all, this structure puts in place what seems the most feared as devalorization and invalidation for the sociocultural identification of the male in the discourse of gangs.

This structure of insults as representation of invalidation metaphorizes the *non-dit* that grounds the discourse of gangs. It represents

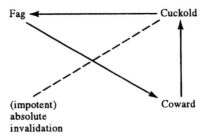

Figure 13.1

the negative form of the forbidden, the outer limit of meaning in the space of the gang. Indeed, it points out and at the same time grounds the conditions of invalidation and of loss of identification. This structure of positions to be avoided also determines an ensemble of combinations and logical implications, ruling from another place, a logical one, the discourses of exclusion and of invalidation with which we see the psychotic man struggling at the productive moment when his delirium is stirred up and takes its first logical forms.

Here, when we are examining the structure that accounts for the logical combinations of this negative form of the discourse of gangs, it is interesting to first point out the following. What forms the vortex, the empty and whirling center, in this structure is understood and apprehended as an insult coming from a woman and directed to a man. It is thus, even in the negative form of the discourse of gangs, a *non-dit*, in the logic of insults from man to man. There, it is a limit. There, invalidation is absolute. There we would thus have the supreme insult for masculine narcissism, the very preclusion of identification. The whole masculine self-image seems to be bound to collapse with the imaginary montages that invalidation by woman (this Other of the masculine) takes away.

As censored, in the very logic of the discourse of gangs, such an insult suggests to us, on the one hand, that the positive form of the discourse of gangs must logically be of the order of injunction and concerns a "must do"; and on the other hand, that woman, as other sex, logically must be in a position of exclusion in the discourse of gangs. This exclusion is logically necessary if one must rule out all risk that a discourse that is other, the discourse of contestation or of questioning as to the positivity of a "being man," ruptures the sense that the discourse of gangs founds socially and historically for the identification of the masculine being. Thus, the hysterical challenge, or simply feminine desire, or even its mere evocation, can tip the whole masculine montage into the realm of insanity.

In the same way, it is noticeable that the pattern of insults that men direct to one another in the gangs—"fag-cuckold-coward-fag" (figure 13.1)—presents itself as excluding the supreme invalidation insult, which is the insult that a man fears coming from a woman: impotent. Such an operation of logical exclusion should not escape our attention when we analyze what comes to us as the positive form of the discourse of gangs. Already we can hypothesize that such a discourse functions essentially to hide an impotence—that is, the specific impotence of masculine montages to efficiently repress the desire of the Other, which the feminine metaphorizes. Is it already for us a first indication that male conscience, or what is called the superego, or "the loud voice of conscience," cannot be conceived without hiding, denying, or repressing what Freud calls castration, and what Lacan defines as essentially a defect or a fundamental lack in the symbolic order? The sexual "no connection" posited by Lacan between these imaginary montages in which the masculine comforts itself and this wandering of desire of which woman provides a metaphor with her body appears all the clearer.

The Discourse of Gangs: Its Positive Version

One would expect that the discourse of gangs in its positive form would clearly define the "being man," that it would define an ego ideal of man. The discourse does not say what the being of man in fact is, but it nonetheless demands its actualization. One could say that, in its most apprehensible form, the discourse of gangs institutes the "being man" in the mode of an empty injunction. It would be, one might say, an imperative with a content that would be *non-dit;* perhaps this is a specific trait of the male superego.

Nonetheless, we still have traces of this empty discourse that is imposed as an imperative. Indeed, the discourse of gangs supports and directs a structure of sociocultural representations of masculinity. We are not speaking here of a definition, but rather of a certain number of demands that pose as code of honor and that define a field, set the limits of a sense and of a norm for masculinity. This structure of male representations conditions at least the sense of acceptable behaviors within the gang. Therefore, an outside—insane and an object of reprobation—is distinguishable from an inside, from the limits of a sense, from a masculine probability. This structure of representation could take the shape of a system of reference between positions as in the structure of insults. As a matter of fact, even if it is possible to point out a *cartel* of interesting positions logically corresponding with the positions of invalidation in the discourse, analysis reveals that these positions do not create a system of logical reference. One axis determines this structure of positions; that is the axis father-son. The structure revolves around this axis, which can regulate perhaps a kind of injunction or imperative that seems to overdetermine male conscience (the superego). This injunction could be formulated in the following way, if we attempt to grasp the stake of all the shapes it can take: "You must have at least one son." This formula is interesting for what it yields as analysis of everything that a man can feel as social expectations or demands on himself.

Thus, for the male, the formula seems to make of this demand to be a father a fundamental demand to be recognized as *a man*. It is the very sense of masculinity that is imposed on him with its closure. This "being a father" thus posed as an a priori condition of "being a man" is defined at the same time in the formula as something very specific. It involves being father of another man, of a son, not of a daughter. What this brings forward is the demand of the transmission of social and historical identification, through the names of the father, as ground of a sense to male existence. One may even say that having six daughters and no son is a tragedy for this male ideal, that it is almost a taint. It puts into question the "sexual potency" transmitted by the father; on a social and historical level, the name is not transmitted any longer. The name dies because no one can transmit it. This "cannot" or this "not" reappears as symptom in the structure of insults, in the central position of the assumed impotence. Indeed, the discourse of insults is the discourse of hypothesis. The insult is a supposition. If some event ever happens to slightly confirm the hypothesis, the effect is catastrophic. The stake of paternity for man is thus imaginarily trapped and compromised by the insane montages of a male ideal.

Another characteristic of paternity, which makes it a central element of the sociohistorical representation of the "being man," is its symbolic dimension. The paternal function has only a language consistency. And this being of pure language rests on a woman's utterance. Whatever the pretentions of the progenitor may be, the paternal function holds only when guaranteed by the law that defines it, and the paternal function is open to questioning by the words of the mother, in an almost absolute way, in our type of society. In other words, what a certain ideology, which is far from having been affected by legal changes, calls paternal power in fact hangs on the good faith of women's words. We can see here why we must hold to the hypothesis that the central insult is invalidation by women.

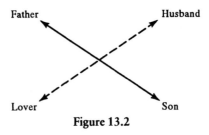

Figure 13.2

But it is now that we must point to the empty and catastrophic center of the gang as institution; the paternal function without its symbolic nature is unavoidably fragile. It is represented as threatened precisely where women's words can be freely uttered. Indeed, the very freedom of these words supposes that we cannot predict when, why, or how they express an invalidation. From this point, it is possible to predict what the whole institutional discourse of gangs denies in advance—that is, that the condition of the gang's possibility as discourse is a certain silence of women, a silence that can equally be required, imposed, or forced. Moreover, the only guarantee of this silence can only be conceived as being an exclusion. Perhaps here it would be better to speak of censorship and of denial of feminine desire. This stake necessary to the discourse of gangs, denial or censorship of femininity, is the fundamental condition of the production of a sense for basic masculinity. By this, of course, we mean a social and historical sense.

The second structural aspect of this axis of sociohistorical representation of masculinity is its son-father dimension (figure 13.2). It is the dimension of the deadly confrontation of the son with the father. If the paternal function grounds a social and historical articulation for the son, he intends death for the father while underlining his fragility in the symbolic. Transmission of identification through the name means first that the father is a being for death. He dies so that the name can be a name, a pure name. And in that way he shows to the son his own being for death. The name is not owned by the progenitor; it is transmitted as and with language. It is the mark simultaneously of history and of death on the subject. Moreover, it has a transmission value only insofar as a woman wants it. But this is a characteristic of the name that the discourse of gangs must hide at all costs. Assuredly, the name is a stake between father and son, but only if woman, who herself does not have a name, agrees to join the name to her desire rather than burn this name. For the feminine wounds the name and burns it. The feminine exposes the being to the vertigo of the unnamable, when the passion of the nothing of the other and of emptiness voids all signification.

Thus, between father and son the stake of the name joins the death of man to the desire of woman, hot spot of escape, of vertigo, of void and collapse of all identification, spot to erase at all costs, for the gang. This maelstrom that must absolutely be gotten around does not cease, however, to fascinate and to hurl masculinity to its threshold of shadow: emptiness, incongruity of the trait.

The relation husband-lover (figure 13.2) could be considered as the second axis of the structure. But this is not the case. In the discourse of gangs, the two positions are mutually exclusive through what they bring into play. First, the function of husband refers to a social and legal instance of economical responsibility. In the discourse of invalidation, it would refer to the coward, the one who does not fulfill his responsibilities and who goes from failure to failure socially, professionally, and economically. Invalidation presupposes indeed a masculine weakness that would create the failure to face up to socioeconomical family responsibilities. The wife and/or the mother usually does not hesitate to point out this fact. Indeed, the discourse of gangs, even if it fundamentally excludes women, is nonetheless a discourse spoken as much from the space of femininity, especially in regard to men.

On the other hand the position of lover in the discourse of gangs introduces the woman-Other. This position perhaps would support a division that is essential and protective of the gang. This division makes a distinction between the wife, through whom man faces social injunctions, and the female lover who, released from such injunctions, allows the stake of desire. This division that negotiates an aesthetic space of play, for desire against a space of norms, is a symptom of a division essential to masculinity. The repression of the relation to death and to the symbolic in the organization of the sexual machine—a subject that we shall deal with later—projects the whole field of desire into the feminine. Indeed, in the position of male lover what is at stake with the woman-Other is the search for a space beyond the sexuality of the gang that only knows whores. The female lover reintroduces into the gang what will have been excluded and censored beforehand: other sexualities and desires, in a word, a femininity, the unknown[3] of a fundamental trouble that undermines the scaffolding of masculinity until it collapses.

It is worth noting that in the discourse of gangs the position of son remains privileged compared to that of husband and even compared to that of male lover, which is an illusory and comical repetition of it. Indeed, in the discourse of gangs, nothing is greater or stronger than the love of the mother for the son. The discourse of gangs is the bond that ties the relation mother-son. Never will the son get from another woman what the mother gives him right away: an illusion regarding the certainty of never being invalidated whatever may happen.

Here, we have an unparalleled protection and a defense against everything that can be organized in the gang as discourse and as condition of invalidation. Thus the hypothesis of a structural link from the position of son to that of lover must be put forward. Indeed, in the position of lover, what is at stake is an initiation to an excess, to what concerns desire, and inasmuch as the gang conditions desire to be the desire for recognition, identification, and validation, then the female lover replaces the mother for the son. Thus is created this space of buffoonery where most male recognition shines.

The Object of the Discourse of Gangs: Women

Every discourse produces an object from what it excludes or discards. The institution produces an object of passion but not without defining an outside, an internal exteriority, trash or rot that, by its very exclusion and the censorship that it is struck with, grounds and justifies passion for the object set in place and instead of the absolute. Thus, as institution, the discourse of gangs produces, on the one hand, a structure of sociohistorical representation of femininity and, on the other hand, what we are going to call here a sexual machine. The structure of representation must be the operation of exclusion of the *desire of woman* or of the *being woman,* and the sexual machine is the operation of production of *the* woman and of the *body-of-woman,* as fantasm that protects against the return of what has been excluded. Thus we can temporarily, as a working hypothesis, see in this double movement the dynamic structure of the operation of inhibition in the discourse of gangs. Later, we will raise the question of what is intended by such a mechanism. At first sight, at least, it is only the operation of exclusion or of foreclusion of the feminine that is at issue. But for the moment the question remains of that which with this exclusion must be the object of a fundamental omission.

Censorship

The mechanism of censorship is the stake of a system of sociohistorical representation of femininity in the discourse of gangs. In this regard, it would be interesting to attempt to verify at the sociological level whether the discourse of gangs is dominant in regard to the sociohistorical representation of femininity, including the discourse of women themselves.

We attempted to investigate this question of the representation of femininity. This involved bringing a group of young women, twenty-four to thirty years old, to research the representations of femininity that their mothers were faced with at the same age, and to compare these representations with those that the same social formation could offer them twenty-five years later. The result, as a psychoanalyst could predict, is always the same. In spite of social transformations and enormous changes in conditions of life and education, the same operation of exclusion of femininity is upheld in forms quite diverse but all the more effective because their logical subtlety is less noticeable.

For the main part, three positions refer back to one another in a play of positions, and the dynamic structure of these is motivated by the exclusion of one of them (figure 13.3).

The sociohistorical representation of femininity seems to be grounded in the discourse of gangs on a censorship that bears on an important part of female sexuality insofar as the relation of desire to *jouissance* is

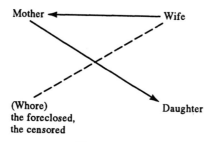

Figure 13.3

involved, and also the structure of this representation is borne by the axis of the mother-daughter relation (figure 13.3). What we mean here by mother-daughter relations refers to the notion that maternity as a function of production or reproduction is the dominant pole and that, in the discourse of gangs, the mother-daughter relation must determine first of all the transmission from mother to daughter of the knowledge and censorship that constitute this function.

The dynamics that govern the representation of femininity do not replace, of course, femininity itself. Woman or the feminine, as locus of desires, dreams, plans, multiple sexualities, is not represented as such. It is symbolized only in relation to the father, husband, and son. Where it could have been conceived of as a space, we find it as a position that is ideologically elaborated as a position of downfall, aiming at every sexuality but the sexuality that is at stake in the relations with the father, husband, and son. Indeed, the whore is not the female equivalent of the male lover (figure 13.2). This position is mainly a position of foreclusion. It refers to what the son cannot stand in his mother. Indeed, if the mother is a whore, according to this representation of the gang, the son cannot trust her word to economize the foreclusion of the Names-of-the-Father that is the stake of psychosis. The fear of insanity reinforces in him the exclusion in the gang of the representation of feminine sexualities. In the same way, the husband cannot bear it when his wife is a whore because of what this implies for him as position in the negative discourse of invalidation in the gang. There he would face a complete invalidation: impotence. Last, the father, for whom the daughter refers, in the inverted Oedipus, to the position of his own mother, would surely not get used to the idea that his daughter is a whore. Curiously then, indeed, father and son would be confronted in different structures with a similar fundamental problem, quite identical: *emptiness,* with which psychosis confronts masculine beings.

When looking at the matter closely, we would have to conclude that this dimension of the partial censorship of female sexualities, especially insofar as it must fundamentally valorize the axis mother-daughter, is not without having a close tie to these two other aspects of the discourse of gangs: the injunction to be a father and the barrier of invalidation that reinforces the injunction. What is excluded and censored in femininity is precisely what, returning in the realm of experience of daily life, triggers invalidation for men. The freedom of practice for women, in matters of sexualities and desires that they experience, seems to be bound to make men face the impossibility of satisfying the injunction, and in this very way to expose them to the risk of invalidation. Every feminine request where the indestructible part of desire in its relation to *jouissance* and to death would allow to surface something other than what is activated by a representation of femininity where the wife is the place of conjunction of mother and daughter cannot but hurl the gang into the field of invalidation. What would follow in terms of anguish toward a void so opened would signal the inevitable collapse of the imaginary constructions that buttress the male ideal.

The Production of Woman

However, this censorship of femininity is not enough. What is foreclosed can come back in the real, and this insanity must be avoided at all costs. The best defense against this return of the foreclosed would be, for gangs, the establishment of what could be called the sexual machine. It specifically involves a machine reproducing imaginarily Woman, in the place left empty by the exclusion of the feminine. This production obviously aims at ensuring the occultation of the censored by a fantasmatic ideal. Thus what is at stake is of course the organization of oblivion. What must absolutely be forgotten is what the feminine demand can take away insofar as the phallus, the sexual, joins *jouissance* to death. Such a conjunction is the point of insanity, a vortex where the masculine can hurl itself, taken in its own loss.

The fantasmatic mise-en-scène of what gangs term "Woman" defines a space in a system of positions. It is a place for a fantasmatic object, an ensemble of holes, bumps, roundness, skin textures, perfumes, curves, silences, and undefinable things. But it is also a place where, entranced by the voice, there is always at least one who can risk herself, offering herself as the one who would actualize the fantasm. It is a risky game, out of which she can only come hurt, if not destroyed. The fantasmatic structure of gang sexuality is truly in this sense the tomb of femininity.

The fantasm sustains the erection of the gaze. What is its object? The impossible real where what has been lost can be found again and of which the fantasm is the nostalgia. The "at least one" cannot, whatever the aesthetic value of her evocation may be, deceive the impossible that curses the desire that lives in the gaze. Total failure cannot be avoided.

There are no sexual relations. The gaze, fed by the drive, is eaten up from within by the nothing that worries it. And what presents itself to dress this wound reopens the wound opened onto the void where death meets *jouissance*.

Is this impossible object of the gaze that the fantasm deceives what sustains the discourse that is expressed in the very stead of this gaze? Sweet talker? Perhaps! Or must this discourse be understood as the fruitless, useless, but quite necessary effort to find a consistency of language in this fantasmatic being "Woman" who, at the same time, sustains this immoderate desire and guides it toward its own failure? Strike one in vain!

What feeds the erection of the gaze, to which the fantasm gives its shape, is the *drive,* insofar as it detaches the penis, like a political stake, where the organ gives in to the symbol of mastery. A whole set of gestures rushing the male into appropriation, power, and act of submission is motivated by this political illusion. The mastery of what is given in the real as realization of the fantasm builds up masculine defense par excellence against the demand of the Other and the categorical imperative.

Indeed, what confronts man the most with invalidation, castration, and death is this demand from the Other, metaphorized by the feminine, where man must face what always seems to him to be an impossible demand sustained by a categorical imperative. The impossible requirement to be a father, thus to have a son—ideal that is doomed to fail from the start by the structural invalidation, because paternity is only founded on a woman's words—this immoderate, crazy requirement, takes the dimension of a cancer that attacks any demand in order to compromise it from the start. The production of woman, as object fantasmatically possessed, would then offer an illusory defense, but imaginarily always guaranteed against this return of the forgotten. The object of the discourse of gangs, this imaginary feminine, would thus maintain in oblivion the female exclusion of women's desire, and, with it, the danger represented by this desire whose rise confronts man once more with a demand impossible to satisfy and thus against phallic invalidation. Thus the discourse of gangs, by protecting man against an immoderate feminine desire, would guarantee for him the bar of repression that hits his own desire, if it is true that man's desire is the desire of the desire of the Other (thus, of woman!). In this way, the discourse of gangs would organize the repression of desire and would constitute the masculine as closure of the unconscious. The feminine as produced by the discourse of gangs would thus keep man oblivious of his own desire, as desire of the desire of woman, thus of passion, or even of the immoderate and the unbounded in which his life, in the end, would be consumed to no purpose.

Neither Woman nor Group, but Production of a Bond of Passion

Far from having to or being able to sustain the feminine, the gang as institution is the very organization of the censorship of the feminine, and the instauration of a fantasm that provides a substitution for this censored. The function of such an operation is the setting and the consolidation of masculine repression. The phallus as signifier of the desire of the Other, signifier in excess, carrying the immoderate female desire in the midst of the narcissistic reassurances of masculinity, can only be perceived among gangs as absolute danger. Hate of the phallus as signifier of lack and of desire will thus be fueled in and through the cult of the penis. The phallus puts into question the bond of passion that holds men as brothers, enemies but united among themselves within the gang against outside danger, against the devastating return of the foreclosed that drives you crazy. Female passion reminds every *One* in the gang of the structural relation that links *jouissance* and death. Struggling with the demand to produce the signifier of his lack, as desire of the desire of woman, man cannot economize the question of knowing up to what point satisfying the Other brings into play his own demise. For, to desire female immoderateness, this excess of the Other—is it not to give up all guarantee regarding what is for him the limits of the bearable, his narcissistic indulgences, his imaginary statue?

And why then would the gang fear the group as much as it fears female desire? The group indeed is a structure of equivalent positions that refer back to each other. As for the gang, it is constituted as a structure oriented and founded on the exclusion of one position and on the substitution of another. In what the discourse of gangs institutes, the paternal function is central insofar as it must represent for everyone the categorical imperative to have to show a "something more." But at the same time, this priority given to the proof of validation by the gang is founded on the exclusion of that without which, in fact, at the symbolic level, paternity loses all meaning: female desire founded in a credible speech. Thus the very operation that propels the discourse of gangs makes it assuredly a bond of passion between males, but excludes the possibility of appearing as a group structure. The group does not refer like the gang to a body or even to the mass of others where some functions are emphasized while others are excluded. The group refers to the rules that govern relations between positions that everyone can occupy rather than referring everyone to the mass of others as invalidating or as support of identification. In its structuration, the gang emphasizes content—for instance, female desire—rather than form, and therefore rather than the system of relations between positions that can equally be occupied by men or women.

Thus, it seems to us that all attempt to introduce rules that would modify the structure of gangs toward a group dynamic would be bound to fail. Indeed, right away, the dangerous game of rules and of systems of positions is denied and turned around in a relation of chiefdom and mastery where competition and invalidation make impossible and crazy the equivalence of positions and the rules of circulation between these positions. The very formalism of the group game does not make sense in gang practices and is perceived there as something unbearable, as the intrusion of an outside through which the biggest invalidation and the vertigo of the void can suddenly appear. For nothing is more castrating in the stakes of the gang than this logical formalism that invalidates every illusion sustaining competition in gangs, and the struggle to death of pure prestige where narcissism attempts to save its foundations.

Thus, whatever appearances may be and whatever may be said about it, only gangs can make men run. They have toward women only the most motivated disinterest, hidden by a feigned indifference, where cajoling and seducing say that the hate of the Other is the most assured limit of the masculine ideal. Indeed, sex, women, groups can tip men over in the excess of lack of meaning. This confrontation with the limitless of which the phallus increases the passion is the breaking point where masculinity moves from a precarious sense to the fascination of a self-loss where death and non-sense consecrate the vanity of all identification.

—Translated by Françoise Massardier-Kenney

Translator's Notes

1. In French, *"mise en sens."* This expression (literally, "putting into meaning") parallels the cinematic *"mise-en-scène."*
2. A concept specific to Lacanian discourse, where it refers to a small group.
3. In French, *"insu,"* for example, what is outside the known, but to be confronted.

Contributors

Marshall W. Alcorn, Jr., is associate professor of English at George Washington University.

Serge André is an analyst practicing in Brussels and a professor of psychoanalysis at the University of Brussels.

Willy Apollon is a professor of philosophy at Laval University, director of the Freudian Interdisciplinary Group for Clinical Research and Interventions (GIFRIC), and an analyst practicing in Quebec City.

Alicia Arenas is an analyst practicing in Caracas.

Miguel Bassols is an analyst practicing in Barcelona.

Mark Bracher is associate professor of English and associate director of the Center for Literature and Psychoanalysis at Kent State University.

Nestor A. Braunstein is an analyst practicing in Mexico City.

Luz Casenave is an analyst practicing in Mendoza, Argentina.

Ronald J. Corthell is associate professor of English at Kent State University and the editor of *Prose Studies*.

Germán L. Garcia is an analyst practicing in Buenos Aires.

Aida Der Hovanessian is an economist in New York City.

Françoise Massardier-Kenney is associate professor of French at Kent State University.

220

Jacques-Alain Miller is director of the department of psychoanalysis at the University of Paris VIII, editor of Lacan's *Seminar,* and an analyst practicing in Paris.

Julien Quackelbeen is professor of psychoanalysis at the University of Ghent and an analyst practicing in Ghent.

Renata Salecl is on the law faculty at the University of Ljubljana, Slovenia.

Alexandre Stevens is an analyst practicing in Brussels.

Christian Vereecken is an analyst practicing in Brussels.

Slavoj Žižek is senior researcher at the Institute for Social Sciences, University of Ljubljana, Slovenia.

Index

Lightning Source UK Ltd.
Milton Keynes UK
UKOW04f0934211115

263219UK00003B/41/P